IN & AROUND
ALBANY
SCHENECTADY
AND TROY

Books Published and Available from Washington Park Press Ltd.

O'Albany! Improbable City of Political Wizards, Fearless Ethnics, Spectacular Aristocrats, Splendid Nobodies, and Underrated Scoundrels
William Kennedy, Viking Penguin Inc. and Washington Park Press Ltd.

Flashback: A Fresh Look at Albany's Past
C. R. Roseberry, edited by Susanne Dumbleton.

Provisions: 109 Great Places to Shop for Food in the Capital District
Peter Zaas, Sue Jones, Gary Jones, Lindy Guttman.

Saving Union Station: An Inside Look at Historic Preservation
Thomas Finnegan.

An Albany Girlhood
Huybertie Pruyn Hamlin, edited by Alice P. Kenney.

Also Published by Washington Park Press Ltd.

In and Around Albany: A Guide for Residents, Students and Visitors
Anne Older and Susanne Dumbleton. 1980

In and Around Albany 1983 Calendar and Chronicle of Past Events

In and Around Albany, Schenectady & Troy
Susanne Dumbleton and Anne Older. 1985

IN & AROUND
ALBANY
SCHENECTADY
AND TROY

By
Anne Older, Peggy DiConza and
Susanne Dumbleton

Washington Park Press Ltd.
7 Englewood Place, Albany, New York

Washington Park Press
7 Englewood Place
Albany, NY 12203
(518) 465-0169
(518) 438-5391

We are again indebted to:

The many individuals and groups in the community who responded promptly and fully to our requests for information.

Families and friends who provided enthusiasm and encouragement throughout the undertaking.

The feature writers of the region's newspapers, who continually kept us alert to the changing scene.

TABLE OF CONTENTS

INTRODUCTION

The Capital District is an exciting place to visit and a wonderful place in which to live. There are interesting sites to tour and entertaining things to do throughout the year. The arts flourish, and sports thrive.

In addition, magnificent natural settings and premier cultural attractions lie within range. Mountains, lakes—even the ocean—form the environment residents consider their ordinary frame of reference. Three major cities—Boston, New York, and Montreal—are within easy driving distance.

It is not always simple, however, to discover the assets of the region. No literature discusses the advantages of the area as a whole. Although specialized works describe the architecture or survey the restaurants or narrate the history, none portray the wide spectrum of opportunity open to the visitor or resident.

Since 1980, we have published two editions of this guide, starting first with the focus only on Albany and the Capital District. The second edition expanded to include Schenectady and Troy along with Albany.

This book—the third edition—updates and expands on the two previous volumes. It is a composite depiction of the history and the people, a compendium of information about schools, hospitals, transportation, and reference sources, a comprehensive guide to drama, music, art, dance, restaurants, stores, and hotels. It also includes information on surrounding areas, suggested day trips, and favorite places to visit in Boston and New York City. In a single volume this book aims to provide a valuable and useful source of information that everyone in the area— for a few hours, a few days, a few years, or a lifetime—might look for.

New York State Capitol

THE CAPITAL DISTRICT

Guidebooks: *New York State Operated Parks: Historic Sites and Programs*, compiled by the NYS Office of Parks and Recreation, lists the events and activities available at New York State parks. It may be obtained from the NYS Office of Parks and Recreation, Agency Building 1, Empire State Plaza, Albany 12238, 474-0456.

Exploring New York's Past, compiled by the New York State Office of Parks and Recreation, Agency Building 1, Empire State Plaza, Albany 12238, 474-0456, describes sites of historic significance in New York State.

Albany

Albany, All America City 1991. Albany was designated by the National Civic League as one of ten cities in the United States to be honored for excellence in community problem solving and community initiative. Albany was chosen for its plans to fight drug abuse, its affordable housing initiatives and the many arts enhancement programs available to its citizens.

Albany Urban Cultural Park is one of the fourteen urban cultural parks located throughout New York State. The cultural park comprises all of the downtown areas including commercial and office areas, museums and historic sites, the governmental complex, and adjacent parks and neighborhoods.

The Albany Visitors Center, 25 Quackenbush Square (corner of Clinton and Broadway), 434-5132, orients visitors to the historical and cultural heritage of Albany. Along with exhibits and an orientation show, the center has a "Building

434-0405 NumBeR cHANGe 7/99

MAJOR DOWNTOWN ALBANY STREETS

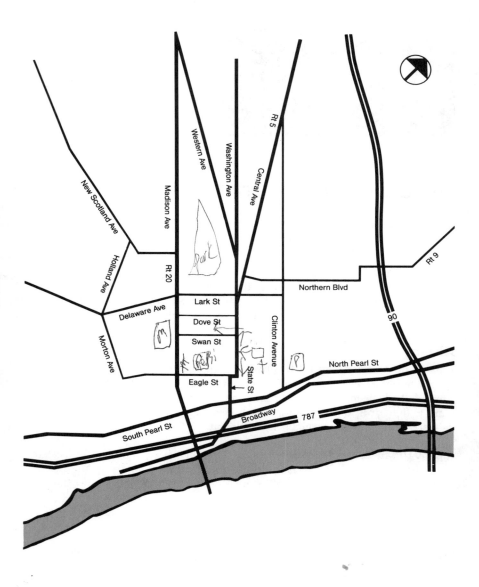

Blocks of the City" room where children and families can explore Albany's architecture. Group tours by appointment as well as self-guided walking and driving tours are offered. Trolley Tours operate during the summer. The Henry Hudson Planetarium schedules shows throughout the week.

Albany City Trolley Co., sponsored by the City of Albany and the Capital District Transportation Authority, provides lunchtime transportation, from 11:45-1:45, making round trips from Quackenbush Square through downtown, up State St and Washington Ave, along Lark St and down to the Empire State Plaza. On Thursday from 2-4 it provides a step-on/step-off tour of Albany landmarks. On Friday from 2-3:30 a tour explores historical landmarks of Albany from the comfort of the trolley. On Saturday from 10-12 in June and July, the trolley provides an educational tour of downtown Albany. The trolley is available for rental for private parties or special events. For information on the tours, which can change weekly, call ~~434-5132~~. For rentals call 465-3632.
434-0405

Guidebooks: *Albany Architects: The Present Looks at the Past*, a booklet prepared by Historic Albany Foundation, 44 Central Ave, Albany 12206, describes and comments on interesting buildings in the city. It is available through Historic Albany Foundation.

Albany County Travel Guide is available from the Albany County Convention and Visitors Bureau, 52 S Pearl St 12207. Call 434-1217.

Downtown Albany

Four bronze tablets are appropriately placed in the downtown area to identify structures and significant buildings from that vantage point. These helpful and attractive markers, produced locally, may be found at City Hall on Eagle St, State University of New York Plaza on Broadway, NYS Education Building at Swan St and Washington Ave, and at the Albany Cultural Park Visitors Center at Quackenbush Square.

We suggest you start your tour at the Visitors Center, 25 Quackenbush Square (corner of Clinton and Broadway).

First Church in Albany, North Pearl St at Clinton Ave established in 1642, is the oldest "religious community" in upstate New York. It was originally housed in the "block church" often represented in old prints of the city. Although the handsome church building itself is of more recent vintage, the pulpit dates from 1656 and the weathervane is a reproduction of the original which is on display at the Albany Institute. The church retains an active community of worship and works to meet the social needs of the people who live in its sphere.

ALBANY POINTS OF INTEREST

Ten Broeck Mansion is described in the chapter on museums.

St. Mary's on Capitol Hill, built in 1798, occupies the site on which Isaac Jogues hid from the Indians who later executed him. The church is of interest too for the angel which graces its top, a departure from the cross traditional to a Roman Catholic Church. The recently refurbished church serves one of the most active congregations in the city.

St. Peter's Church, State St, was established soon after the English took over the settlement from the Dutch because England's monarch at that time, Queen Anne, was particularly interested in sponsoring missions among the Indians. Relics of the early days of the church remain. The bell, struck in 1751, is still used. The silver communion set, on display at the rear of the church, was a gift from Queen Anne to Thomas Barclay, founder of St. Peter's parish in Albany in 1712.

City Hall, Eagle St between Pine and Lodge, a fine example of the unique architectural style of H.H. Richardson, was erected in 1882. The building houses the offices of the mayor and other city officials, three courtrooms, and the Common Council Chamber. Documents and paintings line corridor walls. A special feature of City Hall is the sixty bell carillon which sounds over the city each week day at noon. Visitors may tour the building guided by a fine self-tour booklet. Free. It is also interesting to sit in on the public sessions of the various courts; there are three in this building—city courts I and II and traffic court.

The Court of Appeals, Eagle St at Pine, a beautiful structure both inside and out, is the oldest state office building in the city. The highest court in the state convenes here in a handsome oak courtroom lined with portraits of robed justices. Visitors are welcome to sit in on the hearings each afternoon or simply walk around the handsome rotunda and halls.

The New York State Bar Center, 1 Elk St, stands opposite Academy Park and the Joseph Henry Memorial. In the late 60's the New York State Bar Association purchased the three 19th century townhouses on the corner of Elk St opposite the Supreme Court and the Court of Appeals. The Association's announced plans to demolish the buildings and construct a modern complex on the site roused the local citizenry to furious protest. The Bar Association responded, and the two groups reached a compromise that attracted national attention and has served ever since as a model of what can be done to retain the old while adding the new.

The Joseph Henry Memorial opposite City Hall was designed by Philip Hooker in 1815 as The Albany Academy, a private school for boys. When the academy outgrew this building, it was renamed the Joseph Henry Memorial in honor of Joseph Henry, who in 1830 discovered the properties of magnetic induction

Court of Appeals

within its walls. The building today belongs to the city and houses the offices of the Board of Education. While the building is not open to the public for tours, groups make use of the auditorium upstairs on occasion.

The Vietnam Veterans Memorial, a joint project of the City and Tri- County Council of Vietnam Era Veterans is in Lafayette Park. Suggested by Mayor Whalen and designed by Merlin Szosz, the memorial's half million dollar cost was funded by the city, county, and state grants; by contributions from the towns of Bethlehem, Colonie, and Guilderland; and by private donations. The memorial is made of sixty tons of pink granite mined in Brazil and cut in Portugal. It includes two six-foot bronze tablets. One tablet lists the names of the sixty-six killed and the four missing-in-action from Albany County in the Vietnam War. The other tablet depicts a soldier assisting a wounded buddy in the vegetation indigenous to Vietnam. The memorial was dedicated in May, 1992.

State Education Building is the colossal structure on Washington Ave to the north of the Capitol modeled on the Greek temple, the Parthenon. It repays close study, for many little touches of sculpture—such as the teacher and child on the lamps at the entry—should not be overlooked, though they are overwhelmed by the building's massiveness. The building houses many of the offices of the State Education Department.

Cathedral of All Saints, Elk and Swan Sts, is the seat of the Episcopal Diocese of Albany. The exterior is impressive in its intent. The style of the interior, with its stonework and banners, lends grace and grandeur to religious ceremonies. Also worthy of note is the Gothic front of the episcopal offices opposite the Cathedral's entrance. The Cathedral serves an active congregation and contributes to cultural life in the city by sponsoring concerts and events throughout the year.

Albany Institute of History and Art, 125 Washington Ave, is described in the chapter on museums.

The Alfred E. Smith Building, Swan St between State and Washington, is a state office building named after the man who served as governor of the state until his fateful run for the Presidency in 1928. On the facade of the building are inscribed the names of the counties of New York State. A tunnel runs beneath the building joining it to the Capitol.

Capitol Park, located at the front and back of the Capitol, is a favorite spot for people who work downtown. During the lunch hour street vendors sell their wares while workers and local residents enjoy the formal gardens, the fountains, and the handsome statue of General Philip Sheridan.

The Capitol Building, an ornate structure composed of many different architectural styles, took over thirty years to complete. Within its walls many major decisions were made and many careers were forged. The chambers of the legislature, the offices of the executive, the lobbies and the hallways—all of which are open to the public—serve as the forum for lawmaking in New York State. Visitors may see these rooms as well as the million dollar staircase or watch the legislature in session (usually January-May). The handsome Senate Chamber and Gallery were restored with meticulous attention to authenticity and beauty in 1979. Six years later the Executive Chamber was restored and reopened, now as

Million Dollar Staircase, New York State Capitol

a ceremonial room designated for public bill signings and other grand occasions. The history, artistry and current function of these chambers are interestingly presented by Capitol Guides. Also of interest is the flag room housing flags flown by New York State units in wars in which the United States fought. Tours leave from Capitol Guide Center in the building, weekdays 9 am-4 pm on the hour; Sat, Sun and holidays 9, 10, 11 am, 1, 2, 3, 4 pm. The tour takes about 45 minutes. Further information is available at 474-2418. Free.

The Nelson A. Rockefeller Empire State Plaza is described in detail at the end of the section Downtown Albany.

Cathedral of the Immaculate Conception, Eagle St at Madison Ave, is the seat of the Roman Catholic Diocese of Albany. Made of dark brownstone in the mid 1800's, it now sits in rather somber splendor beside its neighbors, the ornate Governor's Mansion and the ultramodern Nelson A. Rockefeller Empire State Plaza. This setting obscures the fact that it is Albany's largest church.

The Executive Mansion, 138 Eagle St, is the official residence of the governor of the State of New York. It was built by the Olcotts in 1850 as a private home and was subsequently rented and then purchased by the State. In 1961 the Mansion was severely damaged by fire but has since been completely restored and fireproofed. The art collection in the house represents many periods, from the Revolution to the present. Public tours require two weeks notice with advanced reservations, Thurs afternoon only, at 1, 2, and 3 pm. For information call 463-2295.

Schuyler Mansion is described in the chapter on museums.

Cherry Hill is described in the chapter on museums.

State University of New York Plaza is the elegant grey Gothic structure at the foot of State St on Broadway. Designed in 1918 by the prominent Albany architect Marcus T. Reynolds, it reflects the style of the Belgian Guild Hall. The six foot weathervane atop the building represents the Half Moon, the ship in which Henry Hudson sailed up the Hudson River in 1609. Formerly the offices of the Delaware and Hudson Railroad (hence its nickname among long time residents—"The D & H") and the *Albany Evening Journal,* the building has been renovated in recent years to house the central offices of the State University of New York and the apartments of the Chancellor of the University. Extensive preservation has restored the facade.

The public is welcome to stroll through the arcade, which runs the length of the building, and browse in the park in front. Scattered throughout are plaques marking historical events, such as the landing of the Half Moon, the drafting of the Articles of Confederation and the launch of the Clermont, all of which occurred near that spot.

Peter D. Kiernan Plaza, on the east side of Broadway two blocks north of State St, is now headquarters for Fleet Financial Group's New York operations. The building, first opened in 1900, was the Union Station of the New York Central and Hudson River Railroad until it closed in 1968 and fell into disrepair. In April 1984 it was acquired by Norstar Bancorp, Fleet's New York predecessor. As part of a twenty million dollar project it was rehabilitated for the corporate headquarters, reopening in September 1986 as Norstar Plaza. In September 1989 it was rededicated as Peter D. Kiernan Plaza. The lobby is opened to the public during business hours, and brochures on the restoration are available. Directly across Broadway from Kiernan Plaza is **The Tri-Centennial Park of Albany,** which was dedicated in 1986. Albany cartoonist Hy Rosen designed the statue.

Quackenbush Square, corner of Clinton Ave and Broadway, is a restored area nestled inconspicuously amidst the waterfront arterial, the Federal office building and the Palace Theater. The city undertook this project in 1976 as part of the bicentennial effort. Quackenbush House, built in 1730, is one of the oldest houses in the city and serves as a restaurant. The Albany Urban Cultural Park and Visitors Center is located on this site.

Empire State Plaza

The Nelson A. Rockefeller Empire State Plaza, generally referred to as The Plaza, dominates the southeast center of downtown Albany. This modern complex for state government houses state office buildings (with 10,000 employees), the Empire Center at the Egg (a performing arts center), and the Cultural Education Center.

The idea for the marble complex decorated by major works of contemporary artists was conceived by Nelson A. Rockefeller in 1962 during his term as governor. Designed by Harrison and Abramowitz (architects of Rockefeller Center in New York City) to be completed in the late 60's at an estimated cost of $350 million, the structure was caught in labor disputes (inevitable perhaps when 2500 workers are under dozens of contracts at one time) and, as a result, the project was in fact completed in 1978 at an actual cost in excess of $2 billion.

The Plaza is not a static location to be toured once and then forgotten; rather it is a vital center of activity. The Office of General Services coordinates a year-round schedule of activities which use all parts of the Plaza. They range from car shows to fireworks displays, from ethnic celebrations to the arts. Also, the Plaza offers a natural playground for unorganized activities—picnics, strolls, rollerskating, shopping. The visitor can do some things all year:

a. Visit the museum and library
b. Inspect the architecture
c. Tour the Plaza level and enjoy the sculptured pieces
d. View the contemporary art on the concourse level
e. Observe the city and surroundings from Corning Tower
f. Enjoy restaurants

Parking: It is advisable to use one of the four visitor parking lots connected to The Plaza because finding a place to park on the street is very difficult, especially on weekdays.

Albany City Trolley

Two lots are located outside, on either side of the entrance to the Cultural Education Building. The other two lots are located inside The Plaza. The entrances are off Swan St for those driving toward the river and off the arterials for those driving away from the river. Access to both of these lots is clearly marked.

Private parking lots are scattered about the area just below The Plaza.

Tours: Tours are conducted weekdays at 11AM, and 1PM; they take 45 minutes. Information is available at information booths along the concourse and at Room 106 on the Concourse, the Office of Visitors' Assistance, 474-2418.

Information: Information is available from four sources:

1. Information Booths at two positions on the concourse level of The Plaza.

2. *Events at the Empire State Plaza,* a biweekly calendar of events, distributed free at information booths in the complex. Call 473-0559 to be placed on the mailing list.

3. *Up and Coming at the New York State Museum,* a news-sheet, published periodically and sent to a mailing list. For information call 474-5877 or write:

   The State Education Department
   New York State Museum
   Cultural Education Center
   Albany, New York 12230

4. Telephone numbers for information or assistance as listed below.

Promotions & Public Affairs 473-0559
*Capitol Tours 474-2418
Information on use of Convention Center 474-4759
Empire Center at the Egg 473-1845
New York State Museum 474-5877

*Assistance to Handicapped Provided

"Triangles and Arches" by Alexander Calder, Empire State Plaza

The Platform: All of the buildings except the Cultural Education Center sit on or at the edge of the main platform structure. It is difficult to think of this structure as a building because only its roof (the plaza) is visible from street level. In fact, however, it descends six floors below the ground and has a square footage of 3,807,000—nearly twice the floor space of the Empire State Building. Four of the levels provide for parking, special laboratories, delivery facilities, and service areas (mailroom, duplicating machine rooms, maintenance equipment storage for example). Above these are the concourse and the plaza.

Albany Skyline

The Concourse Level: Just below the plaza level, accessible by elevators or stairways inside any of the buildings, runs a mammoth hallway called The Concourse. Leading to and from this Concourse is a network of hallways connecting all parts of the complex and the State Capitol on the other side of State St. The visitor will be interested in the following features:

The Nelson A. Rockefeller Empire State Plaza Art Collection: Displayed throughout the complex, is a collection of art of the New York School of Art from the 1960's and 1970's which is owned by the citizens of New York. The pamphlet *The Empire State Plaza Art Collection* is available free of charge at the information booths or the Office of Visitors' Assistance on the concourse level. For further information, call 473-7521.

The Convention Hall is a 28,000 square foot multi-tiered room with a stage and dance floor. It is capable of functioning as a theater, a ballroom, an exhibition hall, an auditorium or a large forum. The room, the only one of its kind in the area, may be reserved for use through the Office of General Services, 474-4759.

General Facilities: The Concourse also contains cafeterias, rest rooms, a post office, information booths, shops, banks, ticket offices and other services for the 10,000 persons who work in the complex and the thousands who visit. The information service posts up-to-date notices on the many bulletin boards on the concourse level.

The width of The Concourse makes it an appropriate scene for major commercial displays such as boat shows, auto/truck shows, and regional craft shows. Such events are advertised in advance in the local newspapers.

The Plaza Level: The description which follows will proceed along a path defined on the map below. The starting point is on Madison Ave, the south end of the Plaza. (The visitor should be aware of the fact that the length of the Plaza from one end to the other is 1/4 mile. A complete tour will therefore demand a walk of more than 1/2 mile. At all points on the complex provision has been made for the handicapped visitor).

EMPIRE STATE PLAZA

A Reflecting Pool, with steel sculpture by Alexander Calder entitled "Triangles and Arches," extends from the Cultural Education Center.

Labyrinth, a teakwood sculpture by Francoise Stahly, incorporates visual design with areas for play and sitting.

The Corning Tower Building, a forty-four story structure of Vermont pearl marble, houses the State Health Department as well as other government agencies. Visitors are invited to view the city from the observation deck on the top floor of this building from 9 to 4. On weekends the visitor must enter the tower from the concourse level. The focal point of the Nelson Rockefeller Empire State Plaza Art Collection is on the concourse (painting) and plaza (sculpture) levels.

The Plaza Restaurant, The Sign of the Tree, offers a splendid view of the complex. For further description see the chapter on restaurants.

Empire Center at the Egg houses two handsome auditoriums, one seating 950, the other seating 450. The Empire Center sponsors top performing groups which highlight the best and brightest of New York State artists. There is a designated parking area under the Plaza. For rental information call 473-1061.

The Justice Building is a beautifully simple building which contains many of the offices and courtrooms for the State system of courts. The Vietnam Memorial on the first floor displays changing exhibits by New York State veterans of that conflict.

New York State Vietnam Memorial established by the state legislature in 1981 and dedicated by Governor Cuomo in 1984, consists of a memorial courtyard, a peaceful garden set aside for rest and reflection, and bronze tablets bearing the names of the state's 4,194 dead and missing in the Vietnam War. A resource center features a collection of materials and the memorial gallery presents art and photographs on the war by Vietnam veterans.

The Legislative Building houses the offices of 210 members of the State Legislature.

"Two Lines Oblique," a stainless steel kinetic sculpture by George Rickey, moves its 54 foot needles gracefully and elegantly, propelled by changes in the wind.

The Agency Buildings, four identical pillar-like buildings of Vermont pearl marble, as their names suggest, provide office space for various government agencies.

The Swan Street Building, the low-rise, Georgian Cherokee white marble structure which extends the entire length of the west side of The Plaza, houses the Department of Motor Vehicles.

The Playground, near the Swan St entrance at Hamilton St, is challenging and amusing for children of various ages. Comfortable seating for adults makes it a pleasant place for families.

Cultural Education Center houses the New York State Library, The New York State Archives, The New York State Museum, and part of the State Education Department. The museum is described in the chapter on Museums, the library and archives in the chapter on Libraries.

The Korean War Memorial is located just west of the Cultural Education Center. Situated in a park-like setting, it features the flags of the nations who fought in this conflict.

Other Points of Interest Around Albany

Albany Rural Cemetery, Menands, holds some interesting individual graves—those of President Chester A. Arthur and the Schuyler family, for example. There is also some fine sculpture such as statues by Erastus Dow Palmer. One corner of the cemetery contains original stones moved from the early cemetery which was on State St in what is now Washington Park. Also within its walls are graves of servicemen killed in every war fought by America.

First Lutheran Church, 181 Western Ave, though housed in a new building, is an historic congregation. Founded in 1649 in Albany, it is the oldest congregation of the Lutheran Church in America. *Swan of Albany,* a book length history of the congregation, is available at the church office or at the public library.

Port of Albany receives over 10 million tons of cargo each year, molasses, bananas, cars and gypsum being the principal shipments. A grain elevator with a 13,500,000 bushel capacity stores wheat to be exported to England, India and Russia. A continuing program for development and improvement insures a healthy future for the port.

The port occasionally hosts a visiting mercantile vessel, sailing ship or military craft open for inspection by the public.

Pruyn House Cultural Center, Old Niskayuna Rd Loudonville, was the country home of Casparus Pruyn, land and business agent to Stephen Van Rensselaer III. The house, now owned by the Town of Colonie, was opened in 1985 for public tours and for use as meeting space. It houses the Colonie Historical Society and a museum which exhibits works from the Colonie Art Guild and others. For information call Pruyn House, 783-1435.

Sensory Garden, Lincoln Park west of the James Hall Sunshine School, designed and made by the City's Beautification Committee and the Parks Department, contains thirty varieties of plants that can be recognized for their smell, texture, taste, and visual beauty. Five large wooden planters—at waist level so that they are convenient for viewing while standing or while sitting in a wheel chair—are arranged in a semi-circle around a nine thousand pound 1882 bell which had been used in the carillon in City Hall until 1986, when it was replaced. The Northeastern Association for the Blind provided Braille labels for the planters.

Shaker Settlement, adjacent to Albany Airport, is the first site in the United States where the Shakers owned property. It was here that they began to define their ideas about community living. The meeting house stands on the Northeast Corner of Albany Shaker Rd and Rte 155. The cemetery, a major Shaker burial ground, lies on the Northwest side. Those interested in preservation of Shaker heritage have established an interpretive center in the 1848 Shaker Meeting House to provide visitors with an introduction to the Shaker world. There are eight remaining Shaker buildings on site. Tours Mon-Fri 9-3 and by appointment on weekends. There is a gift shop. For information call or write Shaker Heritage Society, 1848 Shaker Meeting House, Albany-Shaker Rd, Albany, 12211, 456-7890.

University at Albany (SUNY), 1400 Washington Ave, although described in the chapter on education, requires comment as an architectural entity.

The buildings rest on a flat surface carved from the once-rolling hills of the Albany Country Club golf course. Totally geometric in design, the campus has a rectangle of academic buildings at its center. At each corner, a short distance from the rectangle, is a square of residential buildings from which rises a square twenty-two story tower, also for housing. In the middle of the academic complex is a perfectly proportioned rectangular pool with a splendid fountain and a tall, slender carillon tower. Also on the campus are an observatory, a weather station, a greenhouse, a gallery, a gymnasium, an infirmary, a commissary and a meeting hall with solar heating. All the buildings except the last were designed by Edward Durrell Stone in 1964 to blend into a single pattern and theme and provide a homogeneous setting for the rapidly expanding University. Visitors are welcome to roam the grounds of the campus.

The buildings of the old campus, the red brick structures between Washington and Western Aves, Partridge and Robin Sts, continue to serve as classrooms and dormitories. The University provides shuttle service between the two.

Washington Park, see chapter on Sports and Recreation.

Port of Albany

Schenectady

Schenectady Urban Cultural Park, one of 14 such Urban Cultural Parks located throughout New York State, comprises the Stockade, downtown Schenectady, Union College, Vail Park, Union St Historic District and the GE Realty Plot. The theme of the park is Labor and Industry.

The Urban Cultural Park Visitors Center, located at the Schenectady Museum and Planetarium, Nott Terrace Heights 382-7890 is marked by a Schenectady built Alco locomotive at its entrance. The Visitors Center provides orientation materials and brochures of the park and has exhibits tracing the 300 plus years of Schenectady history. Directions: Take Rte 5 State St to Schenectady, turn right onto Nott Terrace, then right onto Nott Terrace Heights by the locomotive.

Downtown

Canal Square is a triumph of civic pride, optimism and planning. This commercial shopping and office area situated in the center of the city rose up from the shell of abandoned or neglected buildings typical of downtown areas in small cities across the country in the 1960s. Residents of Schenectady determined to infuse renewed vigor into this area and set about doing it with a combination of private and government funds. What has come into being incorporates restoration with contemporary construction.

The old canal system has been filled in and converted to an outdoor plaza for shops and for dining.

Adjacent to Canal Square is a parking garage for the convenience of customers (two hour free parking). For information call 393-4735.

Center City, 433 State St, was completed in 1979. Government funding was used to restore the Wallace building and to add new construction. The building provides office space, stores and an indoor skating rink.

City Hall, 105 Jay St, is a handsome Georgian Revival structure constructed in 1930 according to the designs of McKim, Mead and White. Built at a cost of one million dollars, it is listed on the National Register of Historic Places for its federal design. The gold-leaf dome is a visable landmark throughout the downtown area. City Hall houses the offices of Schenectady City government.

General Electric was born in Schenectady in 1892 when the Edison General Electric Company merged with the Thomson-Houston Company. Today the weathered plant occupies many city blocks and operates the world's largest turbine and generator facility. As the principal employer in the city, GE infuses the commercial lifeblood of Schenectady. The importance of this industrial giant to the community cannot be over-estimated.

Proctor's Theatre, 432 State St, an elegantly restored former Vaudeville House, features the best in Broadway, dance, music, "name" entertainers and classic films on a regular basis. Built in 1926, this 2,700 seat theater is now a nationally recognized non-profit performing arts center.

Proctor's Gift Centre with items of theater memorabilia is located in Proctor's Arcade, a 1926 precursor of the present-day shopping mall. For information on shows and free public tours, call 382-1083. To purchase tickets, call the box office at 346-6204.

Schenectady County Historical Society, 32 Washington Ave, is described in the chapter on Museums.

The Stockade, a residential district of several hundred homes in the downtown area of the city, stands on the site of the original Dutch settlement. Although the

Schenectady Stockade

SCHENECTADY POINTS OF INTEREST

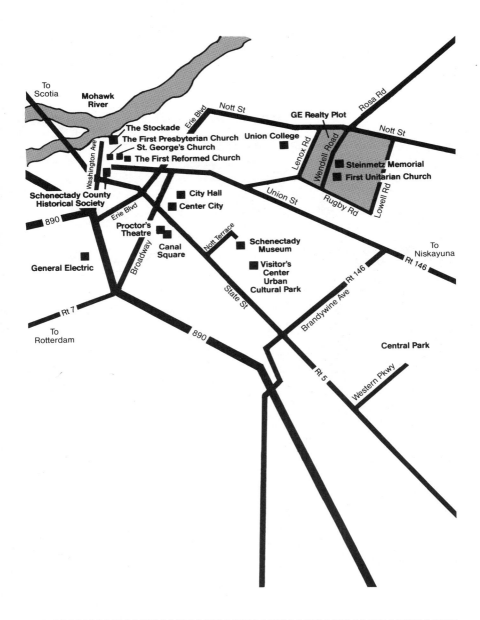

original homes were all destroyed by the French and Indian attack in 1690 and many of their replacements were demolished by a catastrophic fire in 1819, more than a dozen homes there predate the Revolution, and scores of homes have stood since the early 1800's. Because of this and because building in the area continued well into the 19th century, the Stockade harbors an interesting blend of architectural styles. Moreover, all of the houses function today as private homes and thus exhibit signs of life, individuality and sense of purpose often missing in "monuments" or areas designated as Historic Sites.

There are three historical churches within this area. **St. George's,** North Ferry St, was founded in 1735 and **The First Presbyterian Church,** Union St, was founded in 1809. These two churches are right beside each other and both have old cemeteries within their church yards. **The First Reformed Church,** at the corner of Union and Church Sts, was organized some time before 1674 and was the first church in the Mohawk Valley. From its Church Academy of 1785 grew Union College in 1795.

A well-written, helpfully illustrated map of the area is available at the **Schenectady County Historical Society,** 32 Washington Ave, 374-0263. Open: daily 1-5.

The Historical Society cooperates with the Stockade Association to sponsor a walkabout every September. This is described in the chapter on Other Things to Do.

Other Points of Interest Around Schenectady

Central Park is a lovely area of rolling hills and little lakes. A well- maintained, adventurously planned playground, shelters for ducks, swans and more exotic fowl, and a train ride make this park particularly attractive to families. Also, the gentle slopes are perfect for tobagganing and cross-country skiing when snow covers the grass. In June the rose gardens (entrance off Central Parkway) burst into a dizzy array of color. In spring and summer there are marathon routes and many ball fields available. In summer, there is a swimming pool; highly competitive tennis tournaments are arranged. On the second or third Tuesday of August, "Tuesday in the Park" is celebrated, with games and activities for all. Also available in the park is a music haven for those interested in performing in public free of charge. Permits for the haven are required and may be obtained from the Park Office. For information about any of the programs, call 382-5152.

Directions: Take Fehr Ave off State St.

The First Unitarian Society, 1221 Wendell Ave, 374-4446, was built in 1961 according to designs of Edward Durrell Stone, the architect responsible for the University at Albany SUNY campus. The exterior is constructed of customized cement blocks which form interlocking circles. The walls and fountains are lighted at night to dramatic effect. Inside, the Great Hall is an amphitheater with 300

Union College

seats on circular benches beneath a 60 foot wide dome. This gives "a sense of enclosure without constraint, unity without construction." The Hall serves as religious center, dramatic stage, recital hall, dance platform, and lecture rostrum. Also of interest are the gardens and sculpture.

General Electric Realty Plot, bounded by Lowell Rd, Nott St, Lenox Rd, and Rugby Rd, was developed in 1899 for scientists and executives of the company. Charles Steinmetz, the eminent scientist; Ernest Alexanderson, the television pioneer; and Irving Langmuir, a Nobel prize winner, had homes in the plot. The book, *Enclave of Elegance,* chronicles the evolution of this area, describes its homes, and narrates the fascinating lives that were lived within its boundaries.

Glen-Sanders Mansion, 1 Glen Ave, Scotia, 374-7262, is a colonial home built in 1658 along the north bank of the Mohawk River. It remained as the family home for 303 years. Soon after it was sold, the original furnishings, silver, and artwork were acquired for Colonial Williamsburg restoration. In 1974, the house was purchased and restored for Eblings Associates. In 1988 the house was purchased by new owners. While maintaining the original floors and artifacts, they added a 5000 square-foot restaurant and banquet facility.

Directions: Thruway to Exit 26; Rte 890 to Washington Ave Exit. Alternate directions: Rte 5 over Mohawk River Bridge; first building on left.

Green Corners School, a representative red-brick, one-room school house set in a rural setting of open farms and stone fences, is open for visits. The school is located in the Town of Glenville, on Potter Rd near the intersection with Wolf Hollow Rd Extension. Call 372-6314 for schedule of visiting times.

Jackson's Gardens, on the Union College Campus, are beautifully planned, well-maintained formal gardens. The plantings, begun in the early 1800's by Isaac Jackson, professor of Mathematics, have been continued since then by the college gardeners. Open to the public. Parking is available in the parking lots at Nott St and Seward Pl.

The Knolls Atomic Power Lab, River Rd in Niskayuna, is a branch of General Electric devoted to theoretical and laboratory research into uses of atomic energy. It is located next to the **Research and Development Center,** another branch of General Electric. Both of these centers attract major figures in the scientific community and both have won worldwide recognition for their contributions to the pure and applied sciences. The Knolls Lab is often the site of protest by opponents of Atomic Energy.

Schenectady Museum and Planetarium, Nott Terrace Heights, is described in the chapter on museums.

Steinmetz Memorial, Wendell Ave, marks the site where Charles Proteus Steinmetz, a pioneer in electrical engineering, lived from 1903 to 1923 while he worked for the General Electric Company and served as Professor of Engineering at Union College.

Union College Campus, between Union and Nott Sts, presents an interesting assemblage of architectural styles. It was planned in 1813 as a wheel design with a 16 sided domed structure at its center. Expansion of the facilities to meet the needs of a growing student body have noticeably altered the original plan, violating its symmetry, but the campus has nevertheless retained a handsome sense of continuity and integrity. The curriculum and student body are described in the chapter on Education.

Troy

Hudson-Mohawk Urban Cultural Park—Riverspark, one of fourteen state-designated urban cultural parks in New York, traces—with tours, printed material, and educational programs—the historic role of the rivers in shaping the life of the

Captain JP Cruise Line

TROY POINTS OF INTEREST

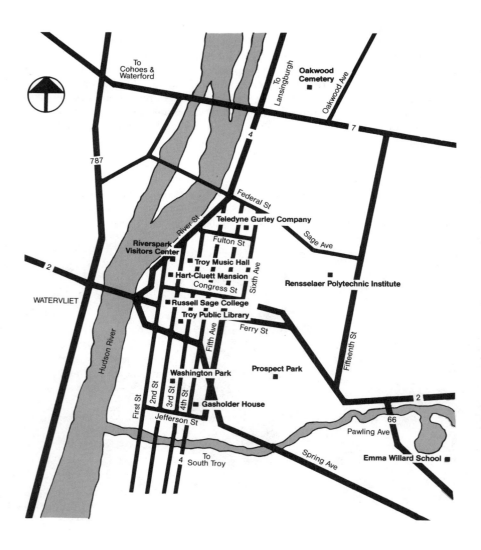

communities of Troy, Cohoes, Green Island, Waterford, and Watervliet. Riversp-ark Visitors Center, one door north of the Troy City Hall at 251 River St, includes a variety of exhibits and dioramas presenting the history and significance of the area and introducing the park's attractions. For information, call 270-8667.

Tours: The Rensselaer County Historical Society, (described in the chapter on Museums) 57-59 Second St, 272-7232, sponsors self-guided tours. Walking tours for school groups, called *"Architectural Scavenger Hunt,"* can be arranged by appointment only.

Guide Booklet: *Historic Troy: A Downtown Tour* is the title of a brochure pro-duced by Rensselaer County Historical Society, Hudson-Mohawk Industrial Gateway, and Russell Sage College. It provides a map and information about Russell Sage College, historic churches and homes, civic buildings, and the parks and squares in the downtown area. The booklet is available at the Rensselaer County Historical Society, 57-59 Second St, 272-7232.

Hudson Mohawk Industrial Gateway, Foot of Polk St, Troy 12180, 254-5267, is a non-profit educational corporation charted by the Regents of the State of New York concerned with nineteenth century industries and architecture in Troy, Albany, Schenectady, Waterford, Cohoes, Green Island, and Watervliet. The Gateway provides guided tours and cruises which interpret local industrial and architectural history and the past life of the communities at the confluence of the Hudson and Mohawk Rivers.

The Story of Uncle Sam is well told in the book *"Uncle Sam: The Man and the Legend"* by Alton Ketchum, available at area libraries.

It is a fascinating tale of a legend seeded by chance and fertilized by the human imagination in quest of a symbol. Sam Wilson, a meat packer whose business was centered in Troy, was congenially dubbed Uncle Sam by the men who worked for him. When the War of 1812 broke out, the firm was contracted to send meat to the troops. The barrels for shipment to the military were marked U.S. for United States, but dockworkers joked that it meant Uncle Sam. When they were subsequently inducted into the army, they told the joke to soldiers from other parts of the country. Soon the words Uncle Sam and United States became synonymous. The cartoon figure, another concoction of many minds, appeared first in 1830, dressed in stars and stripes at mid-century, and given a beard at the time of the Civil War.

Sam Wilson, the "source" of the legend, meanwhile lived simply, peacefully in Troy for 88 years. His obituary in 1854 described him as a "prominent businessman, involved in slooping, brickmaking, farming, slaughtering and distilling, and very active in local politics."

Near the River in Troy

Burden Building, at the foot of Polk St in South Troy, was the office for the Burden Iron Company. It is now owned by the Hudson Mohawk Industrial Gateway which spearheaded the restoration of this building.

Emma Willard, Russell Sage College, Troy

Hart-Cluett Mansion, 59 Second St Troy, is described in the section on Historic House Museums in the chapter on Museums. Open Tues-Sat 10-4.

Rensselaer County Vietnam Veterans Memorial in Riverfront Park, lists the names of forty-two veterans and one civilian photographer killed or missing in the war. A statue in the center depicts three Vietnam veterans facing the memorial wall. Funds for the memorial were raised from contributions throughout Rensselaer county.

Russell Sage College, between First and Second Sts and Congress and Ferry Sts, is housed in a variety of buildings, many of which face onto Sage Park, a lovely square maintained by the college. The college has also acquired many of the handsome buildings around the square. Once private homes or offices, they now serve as classrooms, academic offices and residence halls. Vail House, an 1818 Federal style townhouse, is used by the president for entertaining. Julia Howard Bush Memorial Center, formerly the First Presbyterian Church, is a lecture and concert hall (available for community use). Sage Hall, Vanderheyden, Wool House, Gurley Hall, and Anna Plum Memorial are also buildings of note. Some of them formed the original nucleus of Emma Willard School prior to its move to Pawling Ave in the early 1900's.

The Troy Gas Light Company Gasholder House, Jefferson St and 5th Ave, is an unusual landmark. In 1872 this "eight-sided" circular building was constructed to shelter the gas holder, the tank used to store gas until it was needed by residents in the city. The grace and beauty of its brick and iron architecture was unusual for a gasholder house, and it stands as solid testimony to the opulence of the times.

Troy Savings Bank Music Hall, 32 Second St (corner of State St) over the Troy Savings Bank, is renowned for its superior acoustics and its magnificent nineteenth century concert organ. Listed in the National Register of Historic Places and one of the finest nineteenth century auditorium structures in the United States, the hall is sometimes used for recordings by such artists as Issac Stern, Yo Yo Ma, and Immanuel Ax because of its superior acoustics. The Troy Savings Bank Music Hall Corporation, a non-profit organization, formed in 1979 manages and promotes the Music Hall as a performing arts facility. Membership, with special benefits, is available. The group sponsors Music at the Hall Series, and a Music at Noon Series; both are described in the Music section of the Arts chapter in this book. Information is available at 273-0038.

The Troy Public Library, on the corner of South Ferry and Second Sts, 274-7071, is a beautiful building. Erected in 1897 as a gift to the city by Mary E. Hart, the building is constructed of white Vermont marble in the Italian Renaissance style.

The exterior is decorated with carved arched windows, a rich modillion and denticulated cornice, and a full balustrade. The interior features marble walls, gold leaf highlights, wainscoting, a coffered ceiling, and many other handsome touches. Of particular note is the Tiffany glass window in which is written, "Study as if you were to live forever and live as if you were to die tomorrow." Information about the library and the window are available at the library.

Teledyne Gurley Co., Fulton St and 5th Ave, Troy 272-6300, contains a museum of surveying instruments as well as other engineering tools made by Gurley Company and other firms in the 19th century. The building itself is handsome and has been designated a National Historic Landmark.

Washington Park, beginning at 189 Second St, is a lovely little ornamental green surrounded by beautiful row houses dating to the 19th century and is one of the few private parks in the country with access available only to residents surrounding the park. Occasionally tours of the homes are arranged through cultural or historical groups. The residents maintain the park through a monthly tax, a system still in service in London, England.

Historic Churches

Churches in Troy have interesting pasts. Some were erected as splendid houses of worship for the affluent families who directed the industry. Others were to serve the laborers who came to the city to work in the factories. Because many of these laborers came to Troy as first or second generation immigrants, their churches often assumed an ethnic identity which shaped design and decoration. Because the times were marked by such prosperity, many of the churches were embellished by beautiful works of art.

St. Joseph's Church, 416 Third St, is said to have the largest number of Tiffany windows of any parish in America. Tiffany windows may also be seen in **St. Paul's Church,** 58 Third St, in **St. John's Church,** 146 First St, and in **The First Presbyterian Church,** which is now the Julia Howard Bush Center at Russell Sage College.

Up the Hill in Troy

Emma Willard School, 285 Pawling Ave, occupies a 55 acre campus on the East Side of Troy. The grey Gothic style buildings were designed to look very much like an English college. They house classrooms, offices, and dormitories. A modern library, arts, and music building echoes the colors and architectural lines of the original buildings. Most of the students are boarders, and many of the faculty and administrators reside on the campus of this school known throughout the nation for its versatility and rigor.

Oakwood Cemetery, Oakwood Ave, is a lovely cemetery with attractive landscaping, impressive monuments, and a fine view of the Hudson Mohawk area. It is the site of Uncle Sam's grave.

The Rensselaer Polytechnic Institute Campus, perched atop the slope rising from the river, is recognizable to those approaching Troy from the south by the predominance of three-story brick buildings topped by copper roofs. In addition, the campus holds some noteworthy buildings of contemporary architecture— a student union, a library and a center of engineering—as well as some lovely conventional homes which serve as fraternity houses. The college is particularly proud of the **Rensselaer Design Research Center** (formerly known as the Center for Interactive Computer Graphics). The building is an interesting modern adaption of architecture. Using a Gothic church located on campus, architects erected a building within a building, thus conserving energy and providing handsome vistas and commodius, varied work space. Visitors are welcome to tour the building.

The Visitors Information Center is an experiment in design for energy conservation. It features a passive solar collector, configurative placement of the building to make maximum use of the sun, an earth berme and a sunspace for insulation, and mirroring of light to minimize need for artifically generated power. The building uses about 1/3 the energy required by a conventional building, even though it is open 24 hours a day.

The George M. Low Center for Industrial Innovation is housed in a building constructed with a $30,000,000 loan from New York State. The center is used by industries and academic institutions throughout the country to solve problems in American industry and to provide opportunities for continuing education for industry.

Rensselaer Technology Park is both a place and a concept. In 1981, RPI announced that it would commit $3 million for the development of a 1,200 acre site in North Greenbush as a base for high technology enterprises. The college and community offer expertise and service to industries, and in return, the industries offer opportunities for experience and employment. Rensselaer established guidelines and restrictions so that the development would "insure an environment of the highest quality." The park is one of the nation's oldest, most reknown, and most successful university-based technology parks. It currently has sixteen buildings totaling 500,000 square feet.

Rensselaer Newman Foundation Chapel and Cultural Center, 2125 Burdett Ave at Sherry Rd, 274-7793, is a multipurpose building associated with Rensselaer Polytechnic Institute which provides a center for worship and meditation, a focus for cultural activities, and a meeting place for campus and townspeople, especially for educational and social events.

Lansingburg

Lansingburg, the northern section of Troy, was one of the early river-oriented communities along the Hudson River; its main focus was boat building. The Lansingburg Historical Society, located at 2 114th St, is housed in a former home of the American writer Herman Melville—author of *Moby Dick*—and his family, who lived there from 1838 to 1847. The small park across the street from the house was a boat building area when the Melvilles lived there. Melville himself learned about boat building there and wrote his first two novels while living in the house, which now houses a small museum of local history and some Melville memorabilia. The house is open May-Oct on Sundays, 1-3, and Nov-April by appointment. For information, call Mrs. Bernard Finnegan, 235-3266.

Cohoes, Waterford & Watervliet

Cohoes

Cohoes was a major center for the manufacture of woven and knit cotton in the mid 19th century. The Mohawk River and the Cohoes Falls produced the water power necessary to run the textile mills. The complex of mills and housing built by the dominant Harmony Manufacturing Company are still in existence. The city is part of the Hudson-Mohawk Urban Cultural Park.

A Lock on the Mohawk River

Waterford

Waterford is the oldest incorporated village in the United States. It sits like a pen dipped into a well made by the Mohawk River on one side and the Hudson on the other. It is of interest to the visitor because of the unique style of some of the older residential buildings, the visible remains of its formidable industrial past, the operational system of canals, and the collection of materials in the village museum.

Peebles Island, an undeveloped state park in the Hudson River near Waterford, holds the building which once functioned as the bleachery for Cluett Peabody, the Troy-based manufacturer of fine men's shirts. Here the process of sanforization of cotton (named for Sanford Cluett) was developed. The building, which now serves as the administrative headquarters of the Bureau of Historic Sites, is open once a year in May during National Preservation Week. Information is available through the Department of Parks, Recreation and Historic Preservation, Bureau of Historic Sites, Peebles Island, Waterford, 12188, 237-8643.

The Waterford Flight is a set of "lift locks" that raises boats from the Hudson River to the Mohawk River to circumvent the Cohoes Falls. Each of the five locks lifts the craft 33 to 34.5 feet. Each boat is thereby raised a total of 168.8 feet. The trail is well marked, and facilities are provided for visitors by the Department of Parks and Recreation. A brochure with more information is available through the Waterford Historical Museum (open Saturday and Sunday afternoons) or the New York State Department of Transportation, 457-4407.

Watervliet

Watervliet Arsenal, Broadway Watervliet, 266-5111, is a major U.S. Army Defense Plant which has been engaged in the manufacture of heavy artillery since the War of 1812. On the grounds are points of interest—the museum, the cast-iron storehouse and old residences including the home of poet Stephen Vincent Benet. Tours of the facility are arranged throughout the year by the Hudson-Mohawk Industrial Gateway.

Coulson's News Center, Albany

SOURCES OF INFORMATION

NEWSPAPERS

Four major daily papers and numerous weekly papers cover the area.

Dailies

The Saratogian, 20 Lake Ave, Saratoga Springs 12866, 584-4242, is published daily.

Schenectady Gazette, 2345 Maxon Rd, Schenectady 12308, 374-4141, a family-owned local newspaper now in its second generation, is published daily. Its staff writes news, features, and editorials, and the paper carries nationally syndicated columns and features. The magazine section on Saturday has book, movie, art, music and restaurant reviews. A TV Plus guide is an inset on Sunday.

The Record, 501 Broadway, Troy 12181, 272-2000, is published in Troy each evening. It covers major international and national news and stresses local news. The Sunday paper has multiple sections; the Thursday issue contains *Stepping Out,* an arts and leisure section; the Saturday issue contains a TV guide section. The Record has been serving its community for over 90 years.

Times Union, Box 15000, Albany 12212, 454-5694 is the daily with the largest circulation in the area. It appears each morning—including Sunday when it has many sections including the comics, *at Home* and *On TV,* a weekly magazine. The Thursday edition includes *Preview,* a weekly digest of the arts performances in the area and *Automotive Weekly,* a digest on automotive care with tips on purchasing and maintenance of new and used vehicles. The *T.U.*, as it is called, is a publication of Capital Newspapers, a link in the Hearst chain. It contains nationally syndicated columns and features as well as local news, editorials, features, and arts. The real estate and classified sections are very thorough.

Suburban Papers

Name	Address	Area Served	Schedule
Altamont Enterprise	123 Maple Ave Altamont 12009 861-6641	Albany County	Weekly
Ballston Journal	72 West High St Ballston Spa 12020 885-4341	Ballston Spa	Weekly
Chatham Courier	P.O. Box 355 Chatham, 12037 392-4141	Columbia and Rensselaer Co.	Weekly
Community News	Clifton Corporate Park Bldg. 400 Suite 429 Clifton Park, 12065 371-7108		Bi-Weekly
East Glenville Weekly	443 Saratoga Rd Scotia, NY 12302 399-9133	East Glenville, Burnt Hills, Ballston Spa, Ballston Lake, Clifton Park Saratoga	Weekly
Greenbush Area News	P.O. Box 340 East Greenbush 12061 286-6600	S. Rens. Co.	Weekly
The Spotlight	125 Adams St Delmar 12054 439-4949	Delmar	Weekly

Special Interest Papers

Capital District Business Review, 2 Computer Drive West, Albany 12212, 437-9855, provides news and information about business and the business community in northeastern New York.

The Evangelist, 46 North Main St, Albany 12203, 453-6688, carries news and features concerning the Roman Catholic Diocese of Albany which includes Albany and 14 surrounding counties, as well as national and international Catholic news.

Groundswell, a twice-a-year publicaton of the Hudson Valley Writers Guild, features the best of regional and national writers. It also includes interviews with prominent poets and fiction writers. Information is available through the Guild Press P.O. Box 13013, Albany 12212, or call 449-8069.

Jewish World, 1104 Central Ave, Albany 12205, 459-8455, is published weekly and covers news and features of interest to the Jewish Community of the region. Subscriptions are available, or the publication is available at some newsstands.

Metroland, 4 Central Ave, Albany 12206, 463-2500, carries in-depth coverage of the arts, media and entertainment in the Capital District. Can be found free of charges at newsstands, popular restaurants, and hotels.

Of Interest to Children

Kids Time Out, published by the Time Out Publishing Co., Rte. 203, North Chatham, 766-9553, is an annual guide full of ideas for family activities. It is distributed through schools, stores and health care offices.

REGIONAL MAGAZINES

Adirondack Life is a stunning magazine about the natural beauty, the arts, crafts, recreation, history and conservation of the area.

The Conservationist is a beautiful and interesting magazine published bi-monthly by the New York State Department of Environmental Conservation. It treats topics of interest to those concerned with wildlife, waterways, land and buildings. For information or subscription forms, write The Conservationist, P.O. Box 1500 Latham NY 12110.

Hudson Valley, 4 Central Ave, Albany 12210, (800) 274-7844, carries articles on the culture, lifestyle, and activities of the lower and mid Hudson river region and the Capital District.

New York Alive, 152 Washington Ave, Albany (800) 662-5483, is a bimonthly magazine sponsored by the Business Council of New York State. It is a general interest periodical with articles on business, education, recreation, sports, and rural, urban, and suburban life in New York State. It also features pieces on personalities, history, travel, and restaurants.

Upper Hudson Quarterly, 275 Hudson Ave, Albany 12210, is a quarterly magazine with poetry, short fiction, and visual art. The magazine welcomes submissions, which are not returned.

Want Ad Digest, 870 Hoosick Rd, Troy 12180, 279-1181, is a classified ad magazine with over 8000 ads and ideas. Published weekly and distributed throughout New York, Vermont and Western Massachusetts it can be found in most retail, convenience and magazine stores. Cost to advertisers if item is sold.

THE MEDIA

Television
Five local stations are available to all homes:

Channel 6, WRGB, an affiliate of CBS.
Channel 10, WTEN, an affiliate of ABC.
Channel 13, WNYT, an affiliate of NBC.
Channel 17, WMHT, an affiliate of PBS.
Channel 23, WXXA, an affiliate of Fox network.

Programming is announced in the local papers.

Capital Cablevision brings additional stations as well as 24 hour Cable News Network, Wall Street prices, weather, off track betting and T.V. programming for a monthly fee. For an additional fee the subscriber may add other specialty channels, such as HBO, Disney, and MSG. There is an installation charge. For information call 869-5500.

TCI of New York Inc/Schenectady is the local operator for cable in the Schenectady County area offering several additional channels not available to other regions. For information call 370-2525.

Troy New Channels is the local operator for cable in the Rensselaer County area offering several additional channels not available to other regions. For information call 237-3740.

Radio
This region has access to excellent radio programming. The stations are many in number and varied in their offerings. Schedules are not published in the newspapers, but Capital Newspapers periodically publishes an area Radio Log of the AM and FM stations.

WMHT and WAMC, both listener-supported stations, send monthly programs to subscribers. These are described in the music section of the chapter on the Arts.

WMHT-Rise is a radio reading information service for the print handicapped and visually impaired. The special receivers needed may be obtained by calling WMHT at 356-1700.

MAPS

A good map of the tri-city area is available at Albany-Colonie Regional Chamber of Commerce, 540 Broadway, Albany, 434-1214.

A good touring map of Rensselaer County is available at the Riverspark Visitor Center or the Rensselaer County Regional Chamber of Commerce, 251 River St, Troy, 274-7020.

JIMAPCO, 2095 Route 9, Round Lake, NY 12151, 899-5091, produces—for both retail and wholesale—clear, complete maps of forty counties from Canada to the District of Columbia, including maps for hiking, biking, and waterways, as well as topographical maps .

Many bookstores and newstands have a good selection of regional maps.

CALENDARS OF EVENTS

The Albany-Schenectady League Of The Arts Calendar, a bi-monthly listing of cultural events for the Capital District, is available through membership or at 19 Clinton Ave, Albany, 449-5380. Those scheduling a public event may call the above number to avoid conflict with other groups.

Troy Events Calendar lists the schedule of events pertaining to the arts, education, heritage, economics, and lifestyles in the city. It is produced by the Downtown Council of Troy in association with the RCCA: The Arts Center. It is available throughout downtown Troy and at selected sites in Albany, or call 272-8308.

273-9012

MAILING LISTS

Mailing lists are used by many area groups to keep their supporters informed of upcoming events. Colleges, museums, galleries, theater companies, dance troups, professional societies, neighborhood groups, libraries, musical societies and area night spots periodically send out notices to those they know are interested. Addresses of such groups appear throughout the book.

TELEPHONE NUMBERS

General Information

Federal Tax Assistance .... (800) 424-1040
State Income Tax Assistance .... (800) 225-5829
Weather and Time 476-1111

Senior Citizen Information

New York State Office for the Aging Hotline: 1-800-342-9871
Social Security: 1-800-234-5772
Medicare Information: 1-800-234-5772
Claims for Medicare: 1-800-252-6550
Albany County Department for the Aging: 447-7177
Rensselaer County Department for the Aging: 270-2730
Schenectady County Department for the Aging: 382-8481
CDTA Half Fare or Mobility Disabled Card: 482-7286

COMMUNITY DEVELOPMENT ORGANIZATIONS

The following is a group of organizations which promote and enhance the Capital District as an attractive place for living and working. Combined, they assist area residents who wish to play a part in the preservation and maintenance of the cities as well as advising business and industry of the advantages that the area has to offer.

The **Albany Beautification Program** is managed by a group of volunteers with a goal of enhancing and beautifying the streets and parks of the city with plantings of flowers, bushes, and trees. With limited funds and much hard work the group has been successful in transforming Albany into a more attractive city.

Albany County Convention and Visitors Bureau, 52 S. Pearl St, Albany, 434-1217, has as its main objective the promotion of the area. It makes available the *Albany County Travel Guide,* and it serves to assist in the smooth functioning of events scheduled in the city, performing such services as providing typewriters, brochures and badges, and co-ordinating the needs of groups with facilities at meeting sites and hotels.

Albany Colonie Regional Chamber of Commerce, 540 Broadway, Albany, 434-1214.

Albany County Historical Association, 9 Ten Broeck Pl, Albany, 436-9826, is the parent organization of the Ten Broeck Mansion; its main goal is to further restoration and visitation of the mansion. The association is described in the chapter on Museums.

Better Neighborhoods Inc., 968 Albany St, Schenectady, 372-6469, was established in 1967 as a non-profit organization. **Better Neighborhoods** uses state and federal funds to buy and rehabilitate houses for resale to low and middle income residents. The members offer home-buyer counseling, financial planning, and rehabilitation assistance.

Center for Economic Growth, 1 Key Corp Plaza, Albany 12207, 465-8975 or 800-626-0265, Fax (518) 465-6681, is a private business sponsored economic development organization promoting the eight county Capital Region for new business attraction and business expansion.

Council of Albany Neighborhood Associations (CANA) and **The Neighborhood Resource Center**. Citizens who live within the boundries of the city have organized into neighborhood associations some of which, over the years, have become strong

NEW YORK'S CAPITAL REGION

ENVISION THE FUTURE

Imagine the ideal place to
relocate or expand your business
◆ A region offering a **highly educated**
and **productive workforce** ◆ Quick
access to markets and materials
◆ **Transportation links** via air,
interstate, rail or water ◆ And an
unequaled quality of life
◆ A region with **room to grow** at a
cost to keep you **competitive**

YOU CAN REALIZE THIS VISION IN
NEW YORK'S CAPITAL REGION

for more information about New York's Capital Region
call the **Center for Economic Growth**
1 (800) 626-0265 or 1(518) 465-8975

political and social forces. In 1975 **Neighborhood Resource Center** was formed to stimulate neighborhood cooperation and to help new groups succeed.

One of the results of the Center's formation was the subsequent creation in 1976 of the **Council of Albany Neighborhood Association (CANA),** a volunteer committee drawn from representatives of active neighborhood associations. Three Delegates from each member organization discuss issues, strategies, positions, and other matters of mutual concern. The Council then serves as advocate on city-wide issues of neighborhood interest. Information is available through the Center, 462-5636.

Downtown Council of Troy, 251 River St, Troy, 272-8308, is a non-profit partnership of civic, government and business leaders which works to further the downtown revitalization and economic development of Troy.

Environmental Clearing House of Schenectady, 2858 Aqueduct Rd, Niskayuna, 370-4125, is a non-profit member supported volunteer organization providing education and information about environmental issues. The group offers school programs, nature walks, publications, a newsletter and guided cross country ski trips.

Historic Albany Foundation, 44 Central Ave Albany, 463-0622 is a non-profit organization of area residents interested in historic preservation of neighborhoods and commercial districts, offering technical assistance and educational programs. The foundation operates a parts warehouse at 399 South Pearl St.

Hudson-Mohawk Industrial Gateway, Foot of Polk St, Troy, 254-5267, is a non-profit educational corporation concerned with ninteenth century industries and architecture in Troy, Albany, Schenectady, Waterford, Cohoes, Green Island and Watervliet. The **Gateway** provides guided tours and cruises which interpret local industrial and architectural history and the past life of the communities at the confluence of the Hudson and Mohawk Rivers.

I Love N.Y., 1 Commerce Plaza, Albany 12245, is a venture of the NYS Department of Commerce designed to promote the products and tourist attractions of the state. Information is available by mail or at the office. Information toll free from anywhere in the USA at (800) CALL NYS. During the fall season there is a weekly foliage report: during the winter there are reports on ski conditions for NY state ski centers.

The International Center Inc., 8 Russell Rd, Albany, 459-8812, provides service and advice for the foreign visitor and temporary resident. It also gives members of the community the opportunity to offer hospitality to visitors who come to the Albany area from various countries around the world.

The Mayor's Office of Special Events, (Albany), 60 Orange St, 434-2032, can provide up-to-date information on the numerous events in the city throughout the year.

New York State Legislative Forum is a non-partisan, non-profit group designed to stimulate active interest in New York State legislation by providing information on current issues. The **Forum** meets twice a month on Tuesdays during the legislative session for ten meetings to report on bills before the legislature and to discuss current issues with state leaders. The meetings which are open to the public, are held at the Albany Public Library, 161 Washington Ave, from 10 am to noon, beginning the first Tuesday in February. A report is available on bills that were discussed by writing to the New York State Legislative Forum, PO Box 7152, Capitol Station, Albany 12222.

Preservation League of New York State, located at 44 Central Ave, in Albany, was founded in 1974 as a not-for-profit membership organization dedicated to preserving New York State's irreplaceable historic buildings and landscapes. The **League** provides technical and legal expertise, produces valuable and informative publications, serves as a resource center, sponsors conferences, and represents the cause of historic preservation in the halls of the State Capitol. Information about the specific activities is available at 462-5658.

Rensselaer County Regional Chamber of Commerce, 251 River St, Troy, 274-7020.

Schenectady Chamber of Commerce, 240 Canal Square, 372-5656.

Schenectady County Historical Society, 32 Washington Ave, 374-0263.

TAP, 406 Fulton St, Troy, 274-3050, is a non-profit corporation involved with community development in low income areas. It is supported by fees and grants solicited for specific services, and also receives funds from the New York State Council for the Arts and from the Division of Housing and Community Renewal. Licensed architects help low income owners with their house maintenance needs. They also advise other non-profit groups. Examples of some of the larger projects of this organization are the buildings of the Rensselaer County Junior Museum, the RCCA: The Arts Center, and the Legal Aid Society.

TRIP (Troy Rehabilitation and Improvement Program), 5 Broadway, Troy, 272-8289, is a private non-profit corporation founded in 1968 to provide housing rehabilitation, with an emphasis on home ownership for families. It helps people with low and middle incomes find housing suitable for purchase and also provides help in finding acceptable low income rental housing.

United Tenants of Albany, part of the New York State Tenant and Neighborhood Coalition, is an advocacy group working to protect the rights of tenants and landlords. It staffs a hotline to respond to complaints, attempts to educate people about their rights, and works to improve the quality of code enforcement. Information is available at the office at 33 Clinton Ave, Albany, 436-8997.

Washington Park Conservancy developed from a group of citizens concerned about preserving, protecting, and promoting this downtown park which was so beautifully planned at its origin. It saw as its primary task the formulation of a comprehensive master plan to serve as a guarantor of the park's future for generations to come. For information, write to Washington Park Conservancy, P.O. Box 1145, Albany 12201.

New York State Education Building

TRANSPORTATION & RELATED SERVICES

AIRLINES

Albany County Airport, the first municipal airport in the United States, is located off the Northway at Exit 4. It is served by American (463-5551), **Business Express** (1-800-345-3400), **Continental** (1-800-525-0280), **Delta** (463-2181), **Northwest** (869-1776), **United** (462-4494), **US Air** (462-5881), **US Air Express** (462-5881). Most other major airlines have offices in the area or have toll-free numbers listed in the telephone directory.

Airport Parking

Short and long term parking is available at the airport and at several lots close by which have valet service to the airport. Rates vary. For information, call:

Parking at the Airport, 869-0096
Airport Valet Parking, 11 Airline Dr, 869-1202
Park and Fly, 264 Wolf Rd, 869-8200
Airport Rapid Park, 698 Albany Shaker Rd, 464-4444

Ground Transportation

Airport Limousine Service, 869-2258, offers transportation between Albany County Airport and downtown Albany. Taxi service is also available. Many hotels provide van service to their facility.

There is no public van service providing direct transportation to New York City airports. Limousine services listed in the telephone directory will make individual arrangements.

Car Service

Advantage Car Service, 464-6464, offers an alternative in everyday business and personal needs. Luxury cars with uniformed drivers are available twenty four hours daily for a variety of assignments including meetings, airport and rail pickup, trips, outings, and errands.

SLS is a door-to-door transportation service, certified by the NYS Department of Transportation and a member of the local Chamber of Commerce, which transports customers to cultural and sporting events, ballgames, concerts, and points of interest between Lake George and New York City. It services rail stations, Port Authority Bldg. in New York City, the airports of metropolitan New York City, and the Albany Airport. Call 792-8931 or (800) 322-2757.

Visconti Limousines, 17-23 Dixon St., Newburg, 1-800-252-3022, offers transportation to major airports in New York and New Jersey from the Capital District.

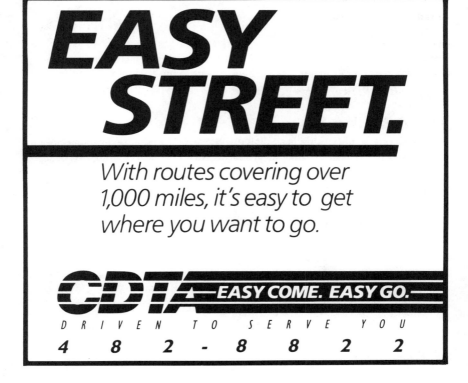

TRAINS

Amtrak has two passenger stations; one serves Albany and Troy and is located in Rensselaer at East and Herrick Sts, 462-5763. The other serves Schenectady and is located at Liberty and Erie Blvd, 346-8651. Overnight parking free of charge. Local bus service is available from the stations. Schedules are posted. In New York City, Amtrak disembarks at Penn Station at 34th street. Call ahead, as reservations may be required for some trips.

BUSES

Local Buses

The Capital District Transportation Authority (CDTA) runs buses frequently and on schedule. Routes follow the main arteries and make special concessions to major residential complexes. Exact fare is required, with free transfers provided for those who must travel on more than one route. Commuter passes and tokens are available at local banks. Senior citizens and the disabled ride for 1/2 fare with appropriate CDTA identification. Children under 5 ride for free if accompanied by a fare-paying adult. (Limit of 3 children to an adult.) Bus passes and tokens are available to school children for use to and from school.

During July and August CDTA runs buses from Albany to John Boyd Thatcher State Park, and from Troy to Grafton Lakes State Park. Most city parks are on the CDTA bus routes.

Schedules are available at banks, office buildings, and visitor information centers throughout the tri-city area. CDTA information numbers are 482-8822 for Albany, Saratoga and Troy area, 393-2101 for the Schenectady area. Information on other CDTA services is available at 482-3371.

Regional Transportation

Hendrick Hudson Bus Lines provides service from Hudson to Albany via Valatie and I-90 to the Albany bus terminal and to Empire State Plaza. Call 828-6868.

Upstate Transit provides morning and late afternoon service between Saratoga and Albany's designated Park and Ride lots. Call 584-5252.

Yankee Trails provides service between Hoosick Falls, Troy, and Albany. Several round-trips daily. Call 286-2400.

Charter Buses—Reliable charter service is offered by Yankee Trails 286-2400 and Wade Tours 355-4500 to functions in the surrounding area. Yankee Trails also offers direct service from Albany to New York City.

Albany City Trolley Co., sponsored by the city of Albany and the Capital District Transportation Authority provides "lunch time service," making round trips from Quackenbush Square through downtown to the Empire State Plaza. It also provides tours of Albany landmarks and tours focusing on the interests of children. The trolley is available for rental for private parties or special events. For tour information call 434-5132. For rental call 465-3632.

University at Albany runs a shuttle bus between the new campus and the old campus and also to the corner of State and Eagle Sts. The buses intended for use of students, faculty and staff only, keep a tight schedule.

Inter-City and Inter-State Buses

Adirondack Trailways, 360 Broadway, Albany, 436-9651, and 22 State St, Schenectady, 346-3415, services many small localities in New York State and offers connecting routes to many major cities from New York City. It also offers direct service from Albany to New York City. The line has commuter services to Albany from as far west as Gloversville and in summer runs routes north to popular vacation sites. Schedules are available at the terminals.

Greyhound Bus Lines, which has terminals at 34 Hamilton St (near Madison and Broadway) in Albany, 434-8461, 22 State St, Schenectady, 346-6113, and 84 Ferry St, Troy, 274-4351, provides direct service to major American cities. Into its terminal come buses of other lines to provide connections to other states. Local bus service is available from bus terminals. Schedules are posted in the terminals.

Both Adirondack Trailways and Greyhound offer excellent package express service to regions they serve.

Peripheral Parking with Bus Service

Peripheral parking with charter bus service to downtown Albany is available for state employees at three locations: the Washington Ave lot, opposite the University at Albany campus, the McCarty Ave lot, adjacent to Exit 23 of the New York State Thruway, and the Broadway lot in Menands, off I-787. Buses run every five minutes at peak commuting hours and make six stops downtown. Between peak hours a shuttle service operates from each of these lots every 45 minutes, weaving among other state office buildings. Schedules for this service are available from the Bureau of Parking Services, 474-8118. This service is also put into effect on weekends when there are special events at the Empire State Plaza.

Special Transportation for Handicapped Senior Citizens

Capital District

STAR, Special Transit Available by Request, is a CDTA service for Capital District Residents who are disabled. Transportation for shopping, visiting, appointments or work is provided for a reasonable cost. A **STAR** users card is required through physician referral. CDTA requests that reservations be made 48 hours in advance, at 482-2022.

Albany

Transportation Service, 25 Delaware Ave, Albany, will transport any resident over 60 years old to any of the Senior Service Centers or to a physician's office with 24 hour notice. Transportation for the handicapped is also available. Small fee. 434-4219.

Shopping Assistance and/or Transportation is available to the handicapped and to the homebound handicapped on Tuesday, Wednesday and Thursday. Handicapped-equipped vehicles and group contracts are also available for transportation outside the city of Albany. There is a fee. 434-4219.

Schenectady

American Red Cross provides free transportation for handicapped persons and anyone over 60 years of age to any destination within Schenectady County. Reservations are required in advance at 374-9180.

Troy

The Rensselaer County Department for the Aging, 270-2734, provides transportation for senior citizens to Senior Citizen Centers, to health and social service appointments, and for shopping. Appointments may be made by calling 270-2734 between 8:30 am and noon daily on a first-come, first-served basis. Suggested contribution.

Senior Care Connection, 2200 Burdett Ave, 272-1777, assists the elderly and their families. The elderly may enroll as members to take advantage of the many health and social services available in the Capital region. Persons with disabilities, regardless of age, may also become members. It is a not-for-profit organization and is a member of the Eddy Family of Services.

Handicapped Parking

Handicapped Parking is available at all public areas, shopping malls, parks, as legislated by the State of New York and enforced by local police departments. To obtain a handicapped permit or license plate, call your local police department for an application form. Follow proceedure outlined on the form, including getting physician's approval.

TAXIS

Taxis can be found at stands at the railroad station, at the airport and at the bus terminals, or may be called. A full listing of city and suburban taxis is found in the yellow pages of the telephone directory. They operate on a fee schedule determined by zones and are shared by passengers headed in a common direction, all of whom pay the set fee.

CAR POOLS

Car pools are not coordinated by any central office. Bulletin boards in office buildings sometimes display requests for rides or riders. City and business leaders are cooperating to make these arrangements more attractive. There are no "car-pool lanes" on freeways in the Capital District.

CAPITAL DISTRICT MAP

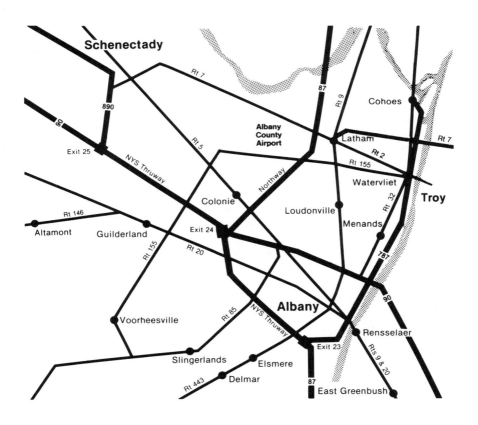

ROAD NAMES AND NUMBERS

Sometimes the interchange of names and numbers of routes confuses the new-comer. The following is a list of various names for the same roads.

Adirondack Northway I-87
Albany to Binghamton exit 25a NYS Thruway (free) I-88
Albany to Boston (toll) I-90
Central Ave (Albany)—State St (Schenectady) .... Rte 5
Delaware Ave and Loudonville Rd .... Rte 9
East-West Arterial joining the Northway,
    Exit 24 of the NYS Thruway and the Massachusetts Turnpike I-90
Latham Circle East to Troy .... Rte 2
Latham Circle West to Schenectady .... Rte 7
NYS Thruway (toll)
    Albany to Buffalo I-90
    Albany to New York City I-87
Riverfront Arterial .... Rte 787
Slingerlands By-pass .... Rte 85
Troy-Schenectady Rd .... Rte 7
Western Ave .... Rte 20

Hudson River

Mansion Hill Inn, Albany

LODGING

A number of factors have combined to make the Capital District a convention center and a place for visitors. As a result there are many good hotels and motels in and around the cities on all of the major roads. Because it would serve little purpose to describe all possible places to stay, we have chosen to give an overview, presenting information on elegant retreats, distinctive hotels, Bed and Breakfasts, and a listing of other good choices throughout the area.

ELEGANT RETREATS

Blantyre, Rte 20, Lenox, Massachusetts, (413) 637-3556, is a comfortably gracious, but opulent country house located on eighty-five acres just outside of the charming town of Lenox. Noted for its exceptional cuisine, service and ambiance it is rated as one of the best in the United States. The twenty-three guest rooms are tastefully decorated and there are ample recreational facilities offered.

Shelburne House, Shelburne Farms, Shelburne, Vermont, (802) 985-8498, situated on the shores of Lake Champlain surrounded by beautiful gardens and 1000 acres of serene countryside, was built in Queen Anne Revival style by William Seward and Lila Vanderbilt Webb in 1899 and maintained by the family as a private residence until 1976. There are twenty four bedrooms and spacious public rooms, all with original furnishings and decor. Fine food and warm hospitality are hallmarks of this distinguished hostelery.

DISTINCTIVE HOTELS

Albany Omni Hotel, downtown Albany at State and Lodge Sts, 462-6611, with 387 guest rooms, is a full service hotel with space for meetings and celebrations. Several restaurants, courtesy transportation to airport.

Albany Marriott Hotel, airport area at 189 Wolf Rd, 458-8444, with 360 guest rooms and a number of meeting rooms, is a contemporary, full service hotel tastefully decorated. Several restaurants, adjacent to major shopping centers.

Desmond, in the airport area at 660 Albany-Shaker Rd (exit 4 I87), 869-8100, has 322 guest rooms, attractive Colonial decor, several restaurants, interesting architecture, banquet and recreational facilities.

Equinox, a hotel resort and spa, operates year round in a beautifully restored old hotel, in Manchester Village Vermont, 1-800-362-4747. It offers 174 guest rooms, meeting rooms, sports facilities including a golf course, and fine dining in a country setting.

Gideon Putnam Hotel, a full service hotel within Saratoga Spa State Park Saratoga Springs, 584-3000, has 132 guest rooms, and a conference center. It is a year round resort, requiring early booking for the racing season in August. It serves a legendary Sunday brunch in its handsomely decorated facilities.

Mohonk Mountain House, Lake Mohonk, New Paltz, (914) 255-1000, is an impressive year round resort hotel of Victorian design with an imaginative optional activities program which includes bird watching and treasure hunts in acres of natural and beautifully landscaped surroundings.

Otesaga Hotel on Lake St, Cooperstown, (607) 547-9931, is a large and comfortable summer resort hotel convenient to the Baseball Hall of Fame, Farmers Museum and Fenimore House. Open May 1 to Mid October.

Queensbury Hotel, downtown Glens Falls at 88 Ridge St, 792-1121, is a full service hotel with 143 guest rooms, large formal dining room, and two informal dining areas.

Ramada Renaissance Hotel, downtown Saratoga at 534 Broadway, Saratoga Springs, 584-4000, is a full service hotel adjacent to the City Center Convention Center. Its Sandalwood restaurant is very popular.

CARING FOR GUESTS BECOMES SECOND NATURE WHEN YOU'VE HAD 223 YEARS OF PRACTICE.

At The Equinox, we've been welcoming
guests since 1769. And we've
learned a thing or two along the way.
Now completely restored, our historic resort
in Vermont's beautiful Green Mountains offers
163 guest rooms and suites,
meeting facilities, championship golf on the
Gleneagles Golf Course, redesigned by Rees Jones.
Plus tennis, swimming, outlet shopping, fine dining
and much more. So come experience The Equinox.
And find out how practice makes perfect.

For reservations or to receive our rate
and package brochure, call The Equinox
today at 1-800-362-4747; in Vermont,
802-362-4700, or contact your travel agent.

THE

EST. 1769
Historic Route 7A, Manchester Village, Vermont 05254

Red Lion Inn, Main St, Stockbridge, Massachusetts, (413) 298-5545, a charming 1773 inn with 100 guest rooms, is furnished in 18th century decor throughout and provides several excellent dining facilities. Norman Rockwell paintings have enhanced its renown.

Residence Inn by Marriott, 1 Residence Inn Drive, Latham, 783-0600, with 112 guest rooms is convenient to the airport and welcomes guests for a single night or extended stays in either studio or fully equipped suites. Continental breakfast is served but there are no restaurant or health facilities on the premises.

Sagamore, Bolton Landing, Lake George, 644-9400, is a year round luxury resort tastefully restored in 1985 from its original 1882 design. Comfort and style are notable in both guest rooms and dining areas.

BED AND BREAKFAST AND SMALL INNS

American Country Collection of Bed and Breakfast, 4 Greenwood Ln, Delmar, 439-7001, is a reservation service for Bed and Breakfast establishments in private homes and country inns in Eastern New York State, Western Massachusetts, Vermont, and New Hampshire.

Bed and Breakfast Association of Saratoga, Lake George and Gore Mountain, P.O. Box 99, Lake Luzerne, 696-9912, provides updated information on approximately twenty-five facilities in its Adirondack area and offers an attractive information packet.

Appel Inn, Rte 146, Altamont, 861-6557, is a circa 1765 historic home on the National Register. The first bed and breakfast in the Capital District it has four guest rooms with fireplaces and private porches.

Candlelight Inn, 53 Walker St, Lenox, Massachusetts, (413) 637-1555, is a full service air conditioned, year-round inn with four dining rooms and eight guest rooms with private baths. The public is welcome for lunch and dinner.

Clausen Farms, Rte 20, Sharon Springs, 284-2527, offers spectacular views of the Mohawk Valley from the Casino, a Victorian Gentleman's Guesthouse, and from the grounds of this country estate. Full catering is offered for private parties and special events.

Cooper Inn, Main and Chestnut Sts, Cooperstown, (607) 547-2567, is a Federal style home near the foot of Lake Otsego. It is open all year for lodging and continental breakfast. Guests may use the additional facilities of the Otesega Inn.

Federal House Inn, Rte 102 Main St, Lee, Massachusetts, (413) 243-1824, is an early nineteenth century home which offers seven rooms for guests, each with private bath. An attraction is its restaurant which is one of the best in the Berkshires. Breakfast is included in the room rate.

Gregory House, Rte 43, Averill Park, 674-3774, is a twelve room country inn with private baths and an excellent restaurant which is open to the public housed in the old homestead. Breakfast is included in the room rate.

Inn at the Century House, Rte 9, Latham, 785-0931, provides lodging for sixty-eight guests. It is adjacent to the Century House Restaurant, known for its good food and service.

Horned Dorset Inn, Rte 8, Leonardsville, (315) 855-7898, is an 1860 Victorian house located in a small rural town. Four rooms two of which are suites with four-poster beds are available. All rooms are furnished to create a Victorian atmosphere. Breakfast, included in the room rate, is served in the guests' room. The Horned Dorset Inn Restaurant is next door for dining at its finest. Rte 20 W to Bridgewater, south on Rte 8, 4 miles. (one hour and forty-five minutes)

L'Hostellerie Bressane, Hillsdale, 325-3412, welcomes travelers to its charming ambiance. The superb restaurant occupies the main floor. All upstairs rooms have been redecorated to create a cozy warm interior. There are two rooms with private bath and four rooms with shared baths. Breakfast is not served.

Mansion Hill Inn, 115 Philip St, in downtown Albany, 465-2038, has fourteen rooms with private baths, individual heat, and air conditioning. Six suites have full kitchens and some have sundecks. The decor is charming and includes stained glass and Victorian style furniture in keeping with the architecture of the buildings. Full breakfast is included in the room rate. A four star restaurant occupies the lower floor.

Sedgwick Inn, Rte 22, Berlin, 658-2334, is a two-hundred-year-old Colonial house which serves as a charming inn. Five rooms in the main house are decorated with antiques and six rooms in the motel annex are styled with Cushman Colonial fabrics and furniture. Breakfast is included in the room rate.

Widow Kendall House, 10 North Ferry St, Schenectady, 370-5511, is a charmingly tipsy street-side house tucked away and conveniently located in the heart of Schenectady's Historic Stockade District. The circa 1790 building has three bedrooms furnished with antiques. Aromas of baking muffins and rich coffee start the morning, followed by a four course breakfast overlooking the gardens.

HOTELS AND MOTELS

Albany Best Value Inn
1579 Central Ave, Colonie, 869-8471

Albany Quality Inn
I90 and Everett Rd, Albany, 438-8431

Comfort Inn Airport
866 Albany Shaker Rd, Latham, 783-1900

Days Inn Albany
Rte 9W, Glenmont, 465-8811

Days Inn of Albany
16 Wolf Rd, Albany, 459-3600

Econolodge
1632 Central Ave, Albany, 456-8811

Econolodge Downtown
300 Broadway, Albany, 434-4111

Hampton Inn
981 New Loudon Rd, Rte 9, Latham, 785-0000
Wolf Rd, Albany, 438-2822

Holiday Inn
100 Nott Terrace, Schenectady, 393-4141

Holiday Inn Airport
946 New Loudon Rd, Rte 9, Latham, 783-6161

Holiday Inn Turf
205 Wolf Rd, Albany, 458-7250

Microtel Country Inn
3083 Carman Rd, Schenectady, 355-2190

Northway Inn
1517 Central Ave, Albany, 869-0277

Ramada Albany
1228 Western Ave, Albany, 489-2981

Ramada Inn Convention Center
450 Nott St, Schenectady, 370-7151

Red Roof Inn
I87 and Albany Shaker Rd, Albany, 459-1971

Rensselaer Inn
6th Ave and Fulton St, Troy, 274-3210

Sheraton Airport
200 Wolf Rd, Albany, 458-1000

Susse Chalet
44 Wolf Rd Colonie, 459-5670
Troy Rd (Rte 4) East Greenbush, 477-7984

The Ginger Man Restaurant, Albany

RESTAURANTS

One of the enjoyable mini-adventures of life is keeping up with the changing scene of newly-established restaurants and measuring the pleasantness and satisfactions of the longtime successful spots. In the years since the first edition of *IN AND AROUND ALBANY* in 1980, the number of restaurants in the area has flourished, providing a burgeoning—and fluctuating—variety of foods and atmospheres and an increased source of entertainment. The restaurants suggested here are those recommended to us or those we have found by experience at the time of publication of this volume to be rather consistently satisfactory. Since it is impossible to list all of the restaurants of all kinds in the enlarged Capital District, the absence of a restaurant listing below does not suggest that it is inferior; it's either new or missed. This listing can serve as a start to enjoy all of the many restaurants of the area. Since the level of prices and the hours of restaurants change often, including whether the restaurant serves lunch and dinner, or dinner only, we recommend that you call for this information. The listing of restaurants is organized in what we hope are fifteen helpful categories.

Fine Dining	**Chinese**	**Deli's and Food To Go**
Upscale	**Italian**	**Lunch Places**
American/Continental	**Japanese**	**Fish Fry**
Hotel Dining	**Taverns, Bistros,**	**Pizza Spots**
Seafood	**Pubs, and Light Foods**	
Ethnic	**Diners**	

For best use, try to identify the category of restaurant you are looking for and then see the listings in that category. Sometimes the categories are not mutually exclusive; for instance, many of the restaurants listed elsewhere are not listed in the Lunch Places category even though they may serve lunch. Enjoy your own mini-adventure of keeping up with the restaurant scene.

FINE DINING

Escoffier Room
Culinary Institute of America, Hyde Park, (914) 452-9600
Reservations necessary, the formal dining room at a school for chefs

Federal House
South Lee, Massachusetts, (413) 243-1824
One of the best in the Berkshires, European cuisine

Harrald's
Stormville, (914) 878-6995
Award winner, fixed price, reservations necessary

Horned Dorset
Rte 8, Leonardsville, (315) 855-7898
Historic house restored with architectural artifacts, excellent food, expensive

La Serre
14 Green St, Albany, 463-6056
Imaginative cooking, greenhouse dining room, outdoor terrace

L'Hostellerie Bressane
Rte 23, Hillsdale, 325-3412
Beautiful old brick house with award winning French menu, expensive

Ogden's
42 Howard St, Albany, 463-6605
Continental cuisine served with nouveau artistry

Siro's
168 Lincoln Ave, Saratoga Springs, 584-4030
Dine with the jockeys and the horse set, August only, excellent food and service, expensive

Suisse Hutte
Rte. 23 Hillsdale, 325-3333
Small country resort, Swiss owner/chef, excellent food

Summit Room
Rte 7, Duanesburg, 895-8907
Contemporary cuisine

UPSCALE

Auberge Suisse
1903 New Scotland Rd, Slingerlands, 439-3800
Regional Swiss French cuisine

Beverwyck
275 Lark St, Albany, 472-9043
Valet parking, creative preparations

Cafe Capriccio
49 Grand St, Albany, 465-0439
Italian and Mediterranean cooking, comfortable ambiance

Cafe Tamayo
89 Partition St, Saugerties, (914) 246-9371
Gourmet preparations, bistro style

Carlton
1605 Becker St, Schenectady, 393-0707
Clubby atmosphere, emphasis on service and presentation

Charleston
517 Warren St, Hudson, 828-4990
Locally grown produce and herbs, game offerings, seasonal menu changes

Culinary Institute of America
Hyde Park, (914) 452-9600
Training ground for world class chefs, four diverse restaurants, reservations necessary

DePuys Canal House
High Fall, (914) 687-7700
Creative international cuisine, old canal house

Dorato's
Western Ave and State Farm Rd, Guilderland, 456-5774
Award winner, nouvelle cuisine

Eartha's Kitchen
60 Court St, Saratoga Springs, 583-0602
Intimate grille and wine bar, mesquite cooking

Elms
Rtes 9 & 9P, Malta, 587-2277
Northern Italian, fresh pastas made daily

Four Chimneys
Rte 7E, Bennington, Vermont (802) 447-3500
Continental cuisine, master chef/owner

Friends Lake Inn
Friends Lake Rd, Chestertown, 494-4751
Vintage wines accompany finely prepared beef, seafood and veal

Glen Sanders Mansion
1 Glen Ave, Scotia, 374-7262
Popular for special dinners and receptions, on the Mohawk River

Gregory House
Rte 43, Averill Park, 674-3774
150 year old homestead with four candlelit dining rooms

Hail Columbia
Central Square, Chatham, 392-6950
Victorian ambiance, savory cuisine

Hilander
67 Haviland Rd, Queensbury, 793-6363
Grille and dining room, golf course setting

Inn at Osborne Hill
125 Osborne Hill Rd, Fishkill, (914) 897-3055
International cuisine in a country inn setting, good wine list

John Andrew's Restaurant
Rte 23, South Egremont, MA, 413-528-3469
New American cuisine

La Griglia
Windham, 734-4499
Northern Italian Renaissance dishes, casually elegant

La Rive
Old King's Rd, Catskill, 943-4888
Open Mother's Day through October, French country style

Mansion Hill Inn
115 Philip St, Albany, 465-2038
Located in the old south end neighborhood, elegant dinners, award winner

Merrill Magee House
2 Hudson St, Warrensburg, 623-2449
Greek revival house, food skillfully prepared

Michele Da Verona
1192 Western Ave, Albany, 482-0345
Diverse menu, well prepared food

Milano
594 New Loudon Rd Newton Plaza, Latham, 792-3334
Attractive modern decor, brick ovens, special desserts

Montcalm
Rte 9, Northway Exit 20, Queensbury, 793-6601
Cozy dining room, large variety

Nicole's Bistro at L'Auberge
351 Broadway, Albany, 465-1111
Very good food, choice of fixed price menus on the weekends

Old Mill Restaurant
Rte 23 South Egremont, Massachusetts (413) 528-1421
Fine restaurant and bar parlor

Palmer House Cafe
Main St, Rensselaerville, 797-3449
Contemporary food in a historic village setting

Red Lion Inn
Main St, Stockbridge, Massachusetts (413) 298-5545
Norman Rockwell setting; garden, tavern and formal dining areas

River St Cafe
429 River St, Troy, 273-2740
Excellent food, attractively restored building on the Hudson River

Stewart House
2 North Water (off Rte 9W), Athens, 945-1357
1883 restored river front Bed and Breakfast, bistro and formal dining

Stone Ends
Rte 9W, Albany, 465-3178
Progressive American cuisine with a European influence

Tai-Pan
Rte 9, Clifton Park, 383-8581
Attractive modern Chinese architecture, wide menu selections

Tory Tavern
Off I88 at Rte 30 and 443, Schoharie, 295-7128
Hearty American cuisine in Colonial setting

Underhill Inn
Hillsdale, 325-5660
Continental cooking with new age flair, eclectic furnishings

Yono's
289 Hamilton St, Albany, 436-7747
Indonesian cooking, internationally known top rated chef

Zanadu
Rte 20, New Lebanon, 794-8725
Eclectic, full of surprises, excellent food, unique menu

AMERICAN/CONTINENTAL

Algonquin Bar and Restaurant
Bolton Landing, 644-9142
Favorite spot on Lake George

Ash Grove Inn
Church St, Saratoga Springs, 587-1278
Seafood, veal, steak as you like it

Barnsider
480 Sand Creek Rd, Colonie, 869-2448
Beef and fish specialities, always busy

Basement Bistro
County Rd 45, Earlton, 634-2338
New American, 25 seats, call for reservations

Bear's
Rte 7, Duanesburg, 895-2509
Beef at its best, call ahead for reservations

Beekman Arms
Rtes 9 and 308, Rhinebeck, (914) 876-7077
America's oldest inn housing the 1766 Tavern, award winning

Berkshire Room
Rte 9, Castleton, 732-7744
Continental food, table smorgasbord

Butcher Block
1632A Central Ave, Colonie, 456-1653
Wide selection of beef and seafood, large salad bar

Canterbury
500 Union Ave, Saratoga Springs, 587-9653
Unique setting for regular dining or special parties

Century House
997 New Loudon Rd Rte 9, Latham, 785-0834
Fine American cuisine in an old Dutch farm house

Charlie Weaver's
698 North Pearl St, Menands, 462-1022
Good American food with Charlie as host

Cinnamon Tree
1254 Rte 9, Latham, 783-0376
Homemade soups and breads

Clare
817 McClellan St, Schenectady, 382-0108
Friendly neighborhood bistro

Cock N' Bull
Parkis Mills Rd, Galway, 882-6962
Rustic setting, good daily specials

Cranberry Bog
56 Wolf Rd, Colonie, 459-5110
Family owned, quality food, cranberry bread is a speciality

Crystal Palace
Rte 50, Ballston Spa, 885-8588
Consistently good food

Donovan's
Old Rte 146 and Plank Rd, Clifton Park, 383-2294
Fresh pasta, veal, seafood in a contemporary setting

Drummond's
Corey Rd, Hancock, Massachusetts (413) 738-5500
Charming, warm atmosphere at Jimminy Peak Ski Resort

Duncan's Dairy Bar
890 Hoosick St Rte 7, Troy, 279-9985
Troy institution, old fashioned roadside restaurant, home-cooking

Hattie's Chicken Shack
45 Phila St, Saratoga Springs, 584-4790
Southern fried chicken, simple food and surroundings

Hunters Inn
312 Oakwood Ave, Troy, 235-8997
Fine dining, Sunday brunch

Jimmy Casey's
Rtes 9 & 20 Schodack Center Plaza, Schodack, 477-8074
Relaxing neighborhood pub and good restaurant

Justin McNeil
301 Lark St, Albany, 436-7008
Unique selections, light menu at all times, jazz

Kirker's Steak and Seafood
959 Loudon Rd, Latham, 785-3653
Popular spot, fine food and grog

Krause's Restaurant and Grove
2 Beach Rd, Clifton Park, 371-0833
Scenic setting on the Mohawk River

Kristel Inn
654 Saratoga Rd, Burnt Hills, 399-4155
Daily specials, home made corn chowder

L'Ecole Encore
44 Fuller Rd, Albany, 437-1234
American bistro cuisine

Lillian's
408 Broadway, Saratoga Springs, 587-7766
Casual dining, cozy ambiance

Mario's Theater Restaurant
Campbell Ave, Troy, 274-3421
Good value, early specials

Mayflower Restaurant
209 Central Ave, Albany, 463-9071
Good homecooking for breakfast, lunch and dinner

My Way Cafe
Rtes 9 & 67E, Malta, 899-4196
Memorabilia and music of Frank Sinatra

Northway Inn
1517 Central Ave, Colonie, 869-0277
Consistently good food at reasonable prices

Old Daley Inn
499 2nd Ave, North Troy, 235-2656
Historic building, old time favorite, teriyaki specialities

Old Journey's End
Rte 43, West Sand Lake, 674-2701
Continental cuisine

Olde Bryan Inn
123 Maple Ave, Saratoga Springs, 587-2990
Restored 1773 inn, well prepared food, cozy ambiance

Olde Dater Tavern
130 Meyer Rd, Clifton Park, 877-7225
Old stagecoach stop, intimate dining

Olde Shaker Inn
1171 Troy Schenectady Rd, Latham, 783-6460
Relaxed dining in 18th century farm house

OTB Teletheater
711 Central Ave, Albany, 438-0127
Wager while dining

Parkwood La Galleria
Parkwood Plaza, Clifton Park, 371-5672
Varied menu

Parrot House
Main St, Schoharie, 295-7111
Reasonably priced menu and wine lists, game dishes

P.D. Ladd's
32 Dove St, Albany, 463-9892
Downtown neighborhood favorite, sidewalk cafe in summer, serves late

Pillars Carriage House
Rte 20, New Lebanon, 794-8007
Good food in a country setting

Pine Hill's
1108 Madison Ave, Albany, 489-8859
Good wine, freshly baked breads and desserts

Professor Moriarty's
430 Broadway, Saratoga Springs, 587-5981
In door and out door dining amongst art and antiques

Raindancer
Rte 30, Amsterdam, 842-2606
Quality food and service in a library atmosphere

Regan's Steak and Seafoood
Rte 4, North Greenbush, 283-9906
Popular eating spot

Saratoga Flat Track
Saratoga Springs
Open during racing season 7am-9am for breakfast, closed Tuesdays, arrive early

Scallions
404 Broadway, Saratoga Springs, 584-0192
Excellent food with a flair

Sedgwick Inn
Rte 22, Berlin, 658-2334
Historic country inn, limited weekly international menu

Shipyard
95 Everett Rd, Albany, 438-4428
Offers three different dining areas for your pleasure

Starr's
1 Key Corp Plaza, Albany, 432-1500
American bistro serving California Pop cuisine, outdoor greenhouse

Thacher's
272 Delaware Ave, Albany, 465-0115
Good food in a casual atmosphere

Tool's
283 Delaware Ave, Delmar, 439-9111
Long time favorite, casual

Van Dyke
237 Union St, Schenectady, 374-2046
Features nationally known jazz and blues musicians

Veeder's
2020 Central Ave, Colonie, 456-1010
Good food served family style

Victory Cafe
10 Sheridan Ave, Albany, 463-9113
Serving lunch and dinner, daily specials

Wishing Well
Rte 9, Saratoga Springs, 584-7640
Popular old roadside restaurant

HOTEL DINING

Adelphi Hotel Ballroon Restaurant
365 Broadway, Saratoga Springs, 587-4688
Open May through the fall, Victorian setting

Albany Omni Hotel
State and Lodge Sts, Albany, 462-6611
Sunday brunch at **Cinnamon's**

Best Western Copperfield Inn
224 Main St, North Creek, 251-2500
Excellent food

Desmond
660 Albany Shaker Rd, Albany, 869-8100
Simpson's Country Grille, Casual
Scrimshaw, Fine dining, Williamsburg like atmosphere
Temptations, Coffee shop

Econo Lodge
300 Broadway, Albany, 434-4111
The Senate Restaurant, pleasant atmosphere, casual, full service

Gideon Putnam Hotel
Saratoga Spa State Park, Saratoga Springs, 584-4300
The Georgian Room, Elegant dining, daily specials, Sunday brunch

Holiday Inn Turf
205 Wolf Rd, Albany, 458-7250
Turf House Grille, Casual, daily specials, seafood
Playfield's, Light fare, finger foods, pasta

Marriott Hotels and Resorts
189 Wolf Rd, Albany, 458-8444
Ashley's, Four star restaurant, formal dining
Market Bistro, Casual, varied menu

Ramada Renaissance Hotel
534 Broadway, Saratoga Springs, 584-4000
Sandalwood, Casual dining with elegant ambiance, nightly early bird specials, entertainment in lounge on weekends

Sagamore Hotel and Conference Center
Bolton Landing, 644-9400
Trillium Room, Elegant dining, formal diverse menu

SEAFOOD

Seafood is brought to the Tri-City area almost daily in refrigerated trucks from the docks in New York City and New England and distributed to markets and restaurants for your eating enjoyment. We recommend the following, but recognize that many of the other restaurants offer fresh seafood on their menus which is deliciously and tastefully prepared at your request.

Balcony Pier 9
612 Watervliet Shaker Rd, Latham, 783-7402

Cape House Seafood
254 Broadway, Troy, 274-0167

Jack's Oyster House
42 State St, Albany, 465-8854

Lobster Pound
Rte 9, Latham, 785-0061

Mac's Seafood
159 Bridge Ave, Cohoes, 237-8502

Ocean's Eleven
1811 Western Ave, Westmere, 869-3408

The Real Seafood Company
195 Wolf Rd, Colonie, 458-2068

Weathervane Seafood
Columbia Turnpike, East Greenbush, 479-3509
South Broadway, Saratoga Springs, 584-8157

ETHNIC

Among the most unusual and skillfully prepared dishes are those from the
"homeland." Owners take pride in their selection of menus, individual preparations and presentations to satisfy you, the customer. Call ahead for a special
request or for what is being offered for the day. You will be pleasantly
surprised.

Bavarian Chalet
Western Ave Rte 20, Guilderland, 355-8005
Wursts at their best

Brookside Inn
Rte 30, Esperance, 875-6972
German-American menu, small intimate dining, veal specialities

Cafe West
855 Central Ave, Albany, 482-7485
Southwestern cuisine, award winner

Chariot Restaurant
Western Ave Rte 20, Guilderland, 356-1116
Delicious Greek preparations

El Loco
465 Madison Ave, Albany, 436-1855
Good neighborhood Mexican Cafe

Garcia's
1673 Central Ave, Colonie, 456-4116
Large seating capacity, delightful decor, Mexican favorites

Halima's Homecooking
50 Oneida St, Cohoes, 237-9983
Authentic Polish dishes, specializing in Kielbasa, pierogys and golompke

Indian Dawat
2209 Central Ave, Albany, 370-4400
Vegetarian and non vegetarian dishes

Little Czechoslavakia
437 Geyser Rd, Saratoga Springs, 885-2711
Potato pancakes at their finest, excellent fare at a reasonable price

Mamoun's Falafel
206 Washington Ave, Albany, 434-3901
Middle eastern, good food

Margarita's
286 Lark St, Albany, 426-9757
392 Broadway, Saratoga Springs, 583-1106
Mexican fare, favorite night spot

Nature's Way
277 Washington Ave, Albany, 462-0222
Specializing in chicken, fish and vegetarian dishes

Nazarian's Courtyard
1000 8th Ave, Watervliet, 273-1104
Lamb dishes and other Armenian dishes

Scholtz-Zwicklbauer Hofbrau
Warners Lake, East Berne, 872-9912
German, old time and all time favorite

Sitar Indian Restaurant
1929 Central Ave, Colonie, 456-6670
Indian cuisine with Tandoori cookery

Spa Brauhaus
East High St, Ballston Spa, 885-4311
Extensive German menu

Taco Pronto
1246 Western Ave, Albany, 438-5946
Quick Mexican food, eat in or drive through

CHINESE

Chinese restaurants have flourished in this region and can be found on any highway, in any town, shopping center or out of the way place. Prices are moderate, with a wide menu selection. Eat in or take out. With advance notice, dishes can be prepared at your request. Regional Chinese cuisine can be found in most restaurants with Szechuan, Mandarin, Cantonese or Hunan among the favorites.

Amazing Wok
267 Lark St, Albany, 434-3946
726 New Loudon Rd, Latham, 783-5158

Chang's
250 Delaware Ave, Albany, 463-0667

China Garden
1028 State St, Schenectady, 370-0160

China Star
155 Wolf Rd Park, Albany, 438-9752
May select Peking Duck from menu

Dumpling House
120 Everett Rd, Albany, 458-7044

Eastern Dynasty
831 New Loudon Rd, Latham, 785-5028

Golden Dragon
2035 State St, Schenectady, 374-5773

Hunan Chinese Restaurant
1094 Madison Ave, Albany, 489-6966

Hunan Family Duck House
1579 State St, Schenectady, 370-0812
Duck specialties

Jade Fountain
1652 Western Ave, Albany, 869-9585

Peking
1100 Madison Ave, Albany, 489-0606
Also features Thai specialities

Plum Blossom
685 Hoosick Rd, Troy, 272-0036

Jack's
1881 Central Ave, Colonie, 456-5522

Yip's
117 Columbia Turnpike Rtes 9 & 20, Rensselaer, 449-2030

ITALIAN

Italian restaurants abound in the tri-city area perhaps due to the large number of Italians who settled here in the early 1900's. Ingredients are fresh and plentiful for all preparations. The bread and pasta vary and are always a surprise. We have included a few of our favorite places and suggest you explore to find others on your own. Most are casual, comfortable and crowded so call ahead.

Allegro Cafe
33 2nd St, Troy, 271-1942
Delightful trattoria, freshly made pasta

Caffe Italia
662 Central Ave, Albany, 482-9433
The place to eat and to be seen

Cavaleri's
334 2nd Ave, Albany, 463-4320
Veal specialities, very popular

Citone's
457 Elk St, Albany, 463-6199
Good neighborhood restaurant

D'Raymond's
269 Osborne Rd, Loudonville, 459-6364
Imaginative preparations

Elda's
122 4th St, Troy, 274-3532
Continental flair, pasta, seafood

Fannie's
472 Troy Schenectady Rd, Latham, 785-5404
Old time favorite

Figliomeni
1814 Western Ave, Albany, 456-0686
Family favorite

Italia
24 4th St, Troy, 273-8773
Tops on everyone's list

Italian American Community Center
Washington Ave Ext, Albany, 456-0292
Always a treat

La Trota
Rte 9, Malta, 587-5943
Three star favorite

Lombardo's
121 Madison Ave, Albany, 462-9180
Old Albany establishment, recently changed owners

LoPorto's
85 4th St, Troy, 273-8546
Manhattan atmosphere, serving four star Italian preparations

Lucia's
268 Saratoga Rd, Glenville, 399-2100
Modern decor, excellent food

Mangia
1562 New Scotland Rd, Slingerlands, 439-5555
Stuyvesant Plaza, Albany
Brick oven pizza, casual family restaurant

Maria's Bistro
123 1/2A Madison Ave, Albany, 434-4567
Freshly prepared food, inexpensive, cozy environment

Maurilio's Quackenbush House
Clinton and Broadway, Albany, 432-7607
Italian and Spanish cooking, award winning chef

Mona Lisa
1118 Central Ave, Albany, 459-3421
Good food, reasonable prices

Nicole's
556 Delaware Ave, Albany, 436-4952
Northern and Southern dishes, intimate atmosphere

95 Ferry Street
95 Ferry St, Troy, 274-5358
Authentic Italian

Pagliacci's
44 South Pearl St, Albany, 456-0001
Seafood, house specialties, homemade desserts

Paolo Lombardi's
104 West Sand Lake Rd Rte 150, Wynantskill, 283-0202
Ultimate in Italian cuisine with generous portions

Pasta Factory
492 Yates St, Albany, 438-2012
Pine Hills neighborhood restaurant, newly refurbished

Romano's
Albany Saratoga Rd, Halfmoon, 371-1650
Great for the whole family

Sam's
Rte 9W 125 Southern Blvd, Albany, 463-3433
Always busy, Northern and Southern preparations

Sorrento's
2544 Guilderland Ave, Schenectady, 377-2132
Old neighborhood favorite

Spiak's
1 Archibald St, Watervliet, 273-9796
Always busy, good food and moderate prices

Villa Valenti
369 West Sand Lake Rd Rte 150, Wynantskill, 283-1291
Family style restaurant, take home portions

Wheatfields
440 Broadway, Saratoga Springs, 587-0534
Fresh pasta made daily

Zia's
79 Washington Ave, Rensselaer, 477-9901
Cozy, good preparations

JAPANESE

Arita
192 North Allen St, Albany, 482-1080
Sushi bar and hibachi tables

Gasho of Japan
Rte 32, Central Valley, (914) 928-2277
400 year old farmhouse from Japan; hibachi tables

Hiro's
1933 Central Ave, Colonie, 456-1180
Table hibachis for personalized service

Mari's
2850 River Rd, Niskayuna, 374-8357
Authentic Japanese cuisine in a country setting

Suji's Japanese Restaurant
Rtes 20 and 22, New Lebanon, 794-8725
Old stone house, fine preparations

TAVERNS, BISTROS, PUBS, AND LIGHT FOOD

Boulevard Bookstore Cafe
15 Central Ave, Albany, 436-1505
Soups, bread, fruit, cheese, desserts, coffees

Bruegger's Bagel Bakery
Several locations
Fresh bagels with assorted fillings, eat in or take out, attractive shops

Buckshots Country Barb B Que
979 Troy-Schenectady Rd, Latham, 785-9291
Sleek bar, good food

Capital Park at Noon
Concession stands on State St and
Washington Ave; great fun for munching and lunching

Daily Grind Cafe
204 Lark St, Albany, 434-1482
Good selection of food and coffee any time of the day

Elena's Caffe
112 Central Ave, Albany, 434-2253
Excellent capuccino and subs

El Dorado
121 4th St, Troy, 272-0578
Simple food, comfortable atmosphere

Famous Lunch
111 Congress St, Troy, 272-9481
Little hot dogs with the works

Ginger Man
234 Western Ave, Albany, 463-5963
Beautiful bar with fine wine selection, light food or regular meals

Holmes and Watson
450 Broadway, Troy, 273-8526
Famous for the many labels of beer

Hot Dog Charlies
Several locations
Mini hot dogs with Charlie's own meat sauce

Hurley's Grill
613 Clinton Ave, Albany, 434-6854
Award winning chicken wings

Last Exit Cafe
461 Broadway, Troy, 271-8545
Sandwiches, desserts, fancy coffees in a literary setting

Lexington Grill
112 Wolf Rd, Colonie, 458-7300
Modern setting with good finger foods and spirits

Lionheart
258 Lark St, Albany, 436-9530
Good variety of menu selections

McGeary's
4 Clinton Square, Albany, 463-1455
Gathering place for those who enjoy good sandwiches and beverages

Parc V
661 Albany Shaker Rd, Colonie, 869-9976
Favorite with the young professional crowd, food and drinks in an attractive setting

Parting Glass Pub
40 Lake St, Saratoga Springs, 583-1916
"As Irish as it comes."

Plaza Grille
414 Broadway, Albany, 463-9439
A step into Old Albany; family owned since 1940

Purple Pub
50 Cohoes Rd, Watervliet, 273-9646
Very popular, good pizza

Quintessence
11 New Scotland Ave, Albany, 434-8186
Gourmet dining, late night dancing in an art deco diner

Scubber's
465 River St, Troy, 271-0368
590 New Loudon Rd, Latham, 786-1480
Wings as you like them

Sutter's Mill and Mining Company
1200 Western Ave, Albany, 489-4910
Award winning burgers

Tap Room Trojan Hotel
43 3rd St, Troy, 272-8200
Patrons meet to chat, eat and enjoy

Yorkstone Pub
79 North Pearl St, Albany, 462-9033
Saloon atmosphere, sandwiches, soups

DINERS

Good food, reasonable prices, specials daily, extensive variety, most bake on premises, families welcome, tempting desserts, most open all hours, favorite after-movie spots, easy parking.

Blue Ribbon Diner
1801 State St, Schenectady, 393-2600

Colonie Diner
1890 Central Ave, Colonie, 456-1550

East Greenbush Diner
751 Columbia Tpk, East Greenbush, 477-8483

Empress Diner
1619 Central Ave, Colonie, 452-0969

Farmer Boy Diner
1975 Central Ave, Colonie,456-2243

Gateway Diner
899 Central Ave, Albany, 482-7557

Glenville Queen Diner
210 Saratoga Rd, Glenville, 399-3244

Halfmoon Diner
231 Grooms Rd, Halfmoon, 371-1177

Jay Street Diner
118 Jay St, Schenectady, 382-8608

Jimmy's Luncheonette
93 Congress St, Troy, 273-4777

Menand's Diner
550 Broadway, Menands, 465-1869

Mike's Diner
3767 Carman Rd, Schenectady, 355-9868

Miss Glenmont Diner
Rte 9W, Glenmont, 462-3631

Miss Troy Diner
626 Pawling Ave, Troy, 273-7557

Mountain View Olympic Diner
Rte 9W, Ravena, 756-2558

Olympic Flame Diner
262 Brandywine Rd, Schenectady, 374-7404

Rick's Diner
Rte 150 and Millers Corner Rd, West Sand Lake, 477-1150

Ruby's Silver Diner
167 Erie Blvd, Schenectady, 382-9741

Scotia Diner
49 Mohawk Ave, Scotia, 382-9748

Spa City Diner
133 South Broadway, Saratoga Springs, 584-9833

Stagecoach Diner
855 Hoosick Rd, Troy, 279-1932

Village Diner
1090 Troy Schenectady Rd, Latham, 783-6005

Vivian's Diner
314 Columbia Tpk, Rensselaer, 434-3268

Voorheesville Diner
39 Voorheesville Ave, Voorheesville, 765-2689

DELI'S AND FOOD TO GO

Fresh ingredients sliced to order, imported products, exotic sandwiches, gourmet pizza, pasta and salads, eat in or take out, bread, bagels, rolls but rye is the favorite, often sandwiches cannot be finished—take home bags requested, some are only open for lunch.

Bagel Baron Inc
285 New Scotland Ave, Albany, 482-9264

BFS Deli and Imports
145 Western Ave, Albany, 452-6342

Colonie Deli
Colonie Center, Colonie, 459-1217

Cowan and Lobel
Stuyvesant Plaza, Albany, 458-2771

Debbie's Kitchen
290 Lark St, Albany, 463-3829

Deli Mill
33 Maiden Ln, Albany, 449-8340

De's Deli
256 3rd Ave, North Troy, 237-8663

Durlacher's New York Style Delicatessen
579 Delaware Ave, Albany, 465-3762

E Street Deli
25 Eagle St, Albany, 465-8768

Expresso Service
24 4th St, Troy, 273-8773

Genoa Importing Co.
430 Loudon Rd, Loudonville, 427-0078

Gershon's Deli
1600 Union St, Schenectady, 393-0617

Mother Goldsmith's
43 Phila St, Saratoga Springs, 584-9772

Platt's Place
44 Wolf Rd, Colonie, 459-7575

Sandwiches to Go
37 Maiden Ln, Albany, 434-0614

The Deli
Stuyvesant Plaza, Albany, 489-3354

Unique Catering
594 New Loudon Rd, Latham, 463-6223

Unlimited Feast
340 Hamilton St, Albany, 463-6223

LUNCH PLACES

Albany Center Art Galleries Cafe
23 Monroe St, Albany, 462-8587

Fo'Castle Farm Country Store
166 Kingsley Rd, Burnt Hills, 399-8322

Four Corners Luncheonette
2 Graves St, Delmar, 439-0172

Londonderry Cafe
Stuyvesant Plaza, Albany, 489-4288

Luncheon Gallery
Albany Institute of History and Art
125 Washington Ave, Albany, 463-4478
Closed in summer

Peaches 'N' Creme
Stuyvesant Plaza, Albany, 482-3677

Sign of the Tree
Empire State Plaza, Albany, 436-1022
Splendid view of the Plaza. M-Fri.

Sweet Nothings
Burlington Ave, Round Lake, 899-6480

Sweet Tooth Caterers
1624 Upper Union St, Schenectady, 393-5592

Yonder Farms
381 North Greenbush Rd, Rt 4, Troy, 283-4267
Rte 155, Albany, 456-6823

FISH FRY

Bob and Ron's Fish Fry
1007 Central Ave, Albany, 482-9747

Combo Fish Fry
865 Crane St, Schenectady, 377-6636

Deet's Fish Fry
187 5th Ave, North Troy, 235-0736

Fish Peddler's Fish Fry
1814 State St, Schenectady, 374-0772

Gallagher's Fish Fry
795 1st Ave, Watervliet, 273-4461

Gene's Fish Fry
Defreestville, 286-3767

Harbor House
Rte 9, Clifton Park, 371-3813

Nick's Subs and Fish Fry
1 Ferry St, Rensselaer, 434-0653

Off Shore Pier and Fish Market
Rte 4 & 43, Rensselaer, 283-9880

Ted's Fish Fry
636 New Loudon Rd, Latham, 783-3176
350 2nd Ave, North Troy 235-5552
447 3rd Ave, Watervliet 273-0232
700 Hoosick Rd, Troy, 272-0144

Two Cousin's Fish & Fry
1702 Chrisler Ave, Schenectady, 346-5331

PIZZA SPOTS

Pizza parlors and pizzerias are plentiful in this area. Many offer chicken wings, Italian dinners, salads, pastas and calzones as well as speciality pizzas to eat in, pick up or for delivery to your home. The following is a sampling of what is available or seek out the yellow pages for your own favorite spots.

De Fazio's Pizzeria
266 4th St, Troy, 271-1111

Fireside Pizzeria
1631 Eastern Parkway, Schenectady, 382-1616

Fountain Restaurant
283 New Scotland Ave, Albany, 482-9898

Jeff's
1038 Madison Ave, Albany, 489-2000

Knotty Pine Tavern
2301 15th St, Troy, 272-4557

Lou Bea's Pizza
376 Delaware Ave, Albany, 463-1992

Madison Restaurant
331 Madison Ave, Albany, 434-1938

Orchard Tavern
68 North Manning Blvd, Albany, 482-5677

Pizzeria Uno
Crossgates Mall, Albany, 869-3100

Red Front Restaurant and Tavern
71 Division St, Troy, 272-9241

Sovrana Grocery Bakery and Deli
63 North Lake Ave, Albany, 465-0961

Spinner's Pizza and Subs
Crestwood Shopping Plaza, Albany, 482-7311

Jean Lewis Maloy, Albany

SHOPPING

As in the rest of the United States, in the past several decades many stores have moved from concentrated areas in the business and professional section of the city to locate where people now reside, to shopping strips in residential suburban areas and to a number of shopping malls—some small and some major all-purpose centers with food courts and cinemas. Numerous stores have remained or have been established in city centers to serve those people who have chosen to live in the city and thus avoid the suburban commute. The expansion of shopping possibilities is also a result of the fact that Americans have turned shopping into an extraordinary entertainment industry, perhaps second only to television and the VCR. People of both sexes and all ages, it seems, love to shop. A survey of regional shopping arenas reveals a staggering array of merchandise and an impressive assortment of sales techniques.

This chapter is organized in sections focused on major shopping malls, suburban and neighborhood malls, outlet and discount stores, country stores, food stores, clothing stores, and stores providing particular or specialty goods.

The text is intended as a guide for the newcomer and long-time resident alike. It should be noted, however, that even as we write new stores will be opening and others will be closing or moving. We also recognize that it is impossible for us to list every store in every city and in every suburb. We apologize in advance to those not included and affirm that we do not in any way imply that those merchants not included are in any way unworthy. The annual Yellow Pages gives a complete listing of all merchants.

MAJOR SHOPPING MALLS

Clifton Country Mall
Exit 8 Northway (I 87N), Clifton Park, 371-7010
120 stores including J.C. Penney, Steinbach's and Caldor

Colonie Center
Central Ave and Wolf Rd, Colonie, 459-9020
120 retail stores with Macy's, Sears and Steinbach's as anchors

Crossgates Mall
Washington Ave Extension, Albany, 869-9565
160 retail stores including Jordan Marsh, J.C. Penney, Filenes and Caldor, Lord & Taylor (1993)

Latham Circle Mall
Rte 9 at Latham Circle, Latham, 785-6633
85 stores including J.C. Penney and Caldor

Mohawk Mall
Balltown Rd and Rte 5 West, Niskayuna, 374-3521
88 stores including Montgomery Ward, Addis and Deys, Bradlees

Northway Mall
1440 Central Ave, Colonie, 459-5320
50 shops including Montgomery Ward, Marshalls, Kids 'R Us, Silo

Rotterdam Square
Rte 890 at Campbell Rd, Schenectady, 374-3713
100 shops and services including K-Mart and Sears

Saratoga Mall
Rte 50, Saratoga Springs, 584-6255
56 shops including Montgomery Ward and Jamesway

Stuyvesant Plaza
Fuller Rd and Western Ave, Albany, 482-8986
62 fine speciality shops and restaurants

Wilton Mall
3065 Rte 50 (exit 15 I 87N), Saratoga Springs, 583-2138
68 shops, Addis and Dey, J.C. Penney, Sears

"Outside of the Ordinary"

*From M&M's to Godiva, bagels to Bearnaise,
Stuyvesant Plaza has a unique blend of
62 fine stores and restaurants to fit any budget.*

Open Monday thru Friday 10 to 9;
Saturday 10 to 6; Sunday Noon to 5.

Western Avenue, Albany where the Northway begins

SUBURBAN AND NEIGHBORHOOD SHOPPING MALLS

Bayberry Square
Rte 9 637 Loudon Rd, Latham

Carousel Village
Rte 50, Ballston Spa, 885-0615

Delaware Plaza
163 Delaware Ave, Delmar, 439-9030

Newton Plaza Center Shoppes
Rte 9, Loudonville

Parkwood Plaza
1812 Rte 9, Clifton Park, 371-0216

Rensselaer County Plaza
Rte 4, East Greenbush, Wal-Mart opening early 1993

Twenty Mall
Rtes 20 and 155, 2080 Western Ave, Guilderland

Windsor Plaza
Sand Creek Rd and Wolf Rd, Colonie

Wolf Road Shoppers Park
Wolf Rd, Colonie, 785-6611

OUTLETS AND DISCOUNT STORES

Cohoes Commons
55 Mohawk St, Cohoes, 235-8717
Cohoes Fashions, Dansk, Ralph Lauren, Lee Jay

Lake George Factory Outlets
A cluster of several outlets along Rte 9 between Queensbury and Lake George
known as the "Million Dollar Half Mile". They include:
   Adirondack Factory Outlet, 793-2161
   Corning, Bookware House, Barbizon, Linens 'N More
   French Mountain Commons, 792-1483
   Skyr, Fieldcrest, Pflatzgraf, Reebok
   Lake George Plaza Outlet, 798-7234
   Timberland, London Fog, Micki Separates
   Log Jam Outlet
   Maidenform, L'Eggs and Hanes, Gitano

Latham Outlet Village
Rte 9 north of Latham Circle, Latham
Lenox, Oneida, Harvé Benard

Lechmere
1440 Central Ave, Albany, 459-1500
Appliances, cameras, televisions, housewares

Manchester Village
Manchester, Vermont
Major designers and name brands including Brooks Brothers, Calvin Klein, and
Ralph Lauren. Shoppers paradise, worth the trip

Saratoga Village Factory Outlets
Malta Exit 12 Northway (I-87)
Diane Fries, Housewares Store, Royal Doulton, Adrienne Vittadini

Service Merchandise
Wolf Rd Shoppers Park 145 Wolf Rd, Colonie, 458-7501
Year round savings, housewares, gift items, luggage, outdoor furniture, catalog in house

Woodbury Commons
Exit 15 N.Y.S. Thruway (I 87)
Fine factory outlets, Mark Cross, Donna Karen, Leslie Fay

COUNTRY STORES

Country stores, an adventure in shopping for items out of the past.

Country Token
Sand Lake Village, 674-8481
Gourmet foods from England, sweets, dinnerware, lace, lamps

Fo'Castle Country Store
Burnt Hills, 399-8322
Baked goods, kitchen items, jams, penny candy

Little Country Store
427B Kenwood Ave, Delmar, 475-9017
All USA made, candles, tin, pottery, Shaker reproductions, quilts

Silo
Aviation Rd, Glens Falls, 798-1900
Cheeses, plants, candies, baked goods, maple syrup, gift items

Vermont Country Store
9203 Main St, Weston, Vermont (802)362-2400
Ovaltine, longjohns, pant stretchers, balms, cotton goods, cooking utensils, catalogue

Westheimer's Carrot Barn
Rte 30 2 miles south of Schoharie (exit 23 I 88), 295-7139
Bakery on premises, local crafts, gifts, April-December

Williams and Sons Country Store
Main St, Stockbridge, Massachusetts (413) 298-3016
Kitchen utensils, penny candy, glassware, Americana and folk prints, cards, cookbooks

Yonder Farms
381 North Greenbush Rd, Rte 4, Troy 283-4267
Rte 155, Albany, 456-6823
Plants, gifts, cards, food products

FOOD

Guide to Farm Fresh Foods may be obtained by writing to the Department of Agriculture and Markets, One Winners Circle, Albany, NY 12235 or call 457-9858. Regional guides to local pick-your-own farms, roadside farm markets and stands, community farmers' markets, wineries and maple-sugar farms are updated annually.

This section is dedicated to culinary wizards looking for ingredients and to syba-rites craving delicious food already prepared. The listings in the various sections outlined below should provide the source for all but the most elusive item, such as freshly dug morels.

Supermarkets

There are three major super markets in the area, **Grand Union, Price Chopper** and **Shop and Save**. Some of these are neighborhood stores while other are "super centers". Most of them carry food in bulk, a good selection of food to go, freshly baked bread and pastries, custom cut meats, fresh fish and a fine selection of cheese. Kosher products and meats are also offered in some of these markets.

Wholesale Food Warehouses

B.J. Wholesale Club Inc.
1440 Central Ave, Colonie, 438-1400
Goods and foodstuffs at discount prices, open 7 days a week, annual member-ship fee, membership card may be purchased at door

Deli Warehouse
132 Railroad Ave Ext, Albany, 482-5732
Wholesale/retail, cold cuts, bakery, party platters

Edwards Food Warehouse Store
711 Troy Schenectady Rd, Latham, 783-0912
Good value, package your own, frequently offers double coupons

Pusatere's Market
First and Adams Sts, Troy, 272-6520
Fresh produce and meats, retail food at wholesale prices, open daily

Sysco
71 Fuller Rd, Albany, 459-7679
New Skete cheesecakes, catering platters

Food Co-operatives
Honest Weight Food Co-Op
112 Quail St, Albany, 465-0383
Members and non-members may shop here, bulk natural foods, fresh vegetables, fruit, herbs, bread

Niskayuna Consumers Co-op
2227 Nott St, Schenectady, 374-1362
Good small supermarket with a selection of fresh fish, deli products and meats, luncheon foods and salads to go

Natural Foods
Earthly Delights
162 Jay St, Schenectady, 372-7580

Honest Weight Food Co-Op
112 Quail St, Albany, 465-0383

Miles Natural Foods
28 Central Ave, Albany, 462-1020

Uncle Sam's Good Natural Products
77 4th St, Troy, 271-7299

Convenience Store
Stewart's Ice Cream Company (584-8700) is headquartered on Route 9 in Saratoga Springs. Makers of fine ice creams, light ice cream, and sherberts; bottlers of milks, cream, sodas and juices; distributor of bread and donuts. There are over 65

Stewart's Shops in the Capital District which also serve sandwiches and coffee to eat in or take out. A popular gathering spot where one can "make your own sundae." Weekly specials on ice cream flavors, milk and soda. A quick stop for forgotten groceries.

Home Deliveries/Groceries and Pharmacies
Albany
Cardona's Market
340 Delaware Ave, Albany, 434-4838

Chazan's Pharmacy
31 New Scotland Ave, Albany, 462-0612

Crestwood Market
22 Picotte Drive, Albany, 438-1331

Delaware Pharmacy
374 Delaware Ave, Albany, 434-8213

Kessler's Pharmacy
538A New Scotland Ave, Albany, 482-1377

Schenectady
Arthur's Food Market
35 North Ferry St, Schenectady, 372-4141

Greulich's Market
3403 Carman Rd, Schenectady, 355-1530

Joseph's Pharmacy
2541 Albany St, Schenectady, 393-3644

Scholz' Market
1329 State St, Schenectady, 374-4477

Troy
DeVito's Pharmacy
447 Hoosick St, Troy, 273-8651

Lindsay Drug Co.
416 5th Ave, Troy, 235-2522

Rotelli Brothers Grocery
681 Hoosick Rd, Troy, 274-3974

Bakeries

Alfred Bakery
1600 Altamont Ave, Schenectady, 355-5170
Authentic German baked goods, European specialty cakes

Bagel Baron
285 New Scotland Ave, Albany, 482-9264
Bagels all varieties

Bella Napoli
Rte 9, Latham, 783-0196
721 River St, Troy, 274-8277
Fine Italian cakes and pastries, bread and rolls

Bruegger's
Many locations
Bagels, excellent flavor

Carosello's Bakery
72 Hurlbut St, Albany, 434-2449
197 Lark St, Albany, 434-1504
Bread, donuts and rum cakes

Civitello's
42 North Jay St, Schenectady, 381-6165
Italian cookies, pastries, rum cake, wedding cakes and trays

Corcione
37 Robin St, Albany, 463-4834
Excellent bread and rolls, sold in grocery stores only

French Confection
1042 Troy Schenectady Rd, Latham, 785-1486
Delicious croissants, French bread and pastries

Freihofer's Bakery
235-0710
Major local bakery, legendary chocolate chip cookies, sold in grocery stores

Fiorello Bakery
1180A Western Ave, Albany, 482-8171
Italian bread and rolls, crisp crust with soft thick center

Grandma's
1273 Central Ave, Albany, 459-4585
Good pies baked daily

J. & S. Watkins
1675 Rte 9, Clifton Park, 383-1148
Gourmet desserts and specialty cakes

Perreca's Bakery, Schenectady

Joan's Cake Chateau
Rte 155 (600 ft west of Exit 5 I-87), Colonie, 783-6442
Special design cakes, baked goods to order

Lee Fong's
579 New Scotland Ave, Albany, 438-2622
Unusual Chinese pastries and desserts

Leo's
28 Maple Ave, Albany, 482-7902
Full line of Kosher baked goods, whipped cream cakes, challah bread

Nino's
718 Central Ave, Albany, 489-6640
Italian bread and rolls, thick, rich and tasty

Perreca's
33 North Jay St, Schenectady, 372-1874
Excellent Italian bread, very popular, arrive early

Prediger's
98 Hudson Ave, Green Island, 273-3620
Good rye bread

Prinzo's Bakery
344 Delaware Ave, Albany, 463-4904
Popular neighborhood bakery, assorted rolls, rye bread

Rock Hill Bakehouse
Sprague Town Rd, Greenwich, (802) 442-7246
Retail sales at bakehouse Mon, Wed and Fri., excellent numerous sour dough breads available at Food Co-Ops, Two Cousins Fish Market, Michael Pellegrino's

Schuyler Bakery
637 3rd Ave, Watervliet, 237-0142
Miniature danish, hearty donuts, specialty cakes

Shady Lane Bake Shop
14 Saratoga Rd, Scotia, 399-6108
Wedding cakes, cream cakes, Italian pastries

Sweet Tooth
1624 Upper Union St, Schenectady, 393-5592
Gourmet desserts, breads

Villa Italia
3028 Hamburg St, Rotterdam, 355-1144
Italian cookies, pastries, cakes

Candy (Homemade)

The following merchants sell candies which meet the standards of the most demanding sweet tooth.

Candy-Kraft
2575 Western Ave, Guilderland, 355-1860
Famous for peanut butter ribbon candy, molded candies

Krause's Homemade Candy
622 Central Ave, Albany, 458-7855
41 South Partition St, Saugerties, (914) 246-8377
Hand dipped candies, nuts, fudge, peanut brittle

The Peanut Principle
Rte 9 Latham, 3 miles N. of traffic circle, 783-8239
Truffles, spice candies, nuts

Cheese

Cowan and Lobel
Stuyvesant Plaza, Albany, 458-2771

Deli Warehouse
132 Railroad Ave Ext, Albany, 482-5732

Hickory Farms
Colonie Center, Latham Center and Wilton Mall

Yonder Farms
381 N. Greenbush Rd Rte 4, Troy, 283-4267
Rte 155, Albany, 456-6823

Coffee and Tea

The following merchants carry and care for a good selection of fresh teas and coffees.

Coffee Beanery
Colonie Center Mall, Colonie, 783-1637

BFS Deli and Imports
1754 Western Ave, Albany, 452-6342

Daily Grind
204 Lark St, Albany, 434-1482
258 Broadway, Troy, 272-8658

Earthly Delights Natural Foods
162 Jay St, Schenectady, 372-7580

Pearl Grant-Richman's
Stuyvesant Plaza, Albany, 738-8409

Uncle Sam's Good Natural Products
77 4th St, Troy, 271-7299
Organic coffee beans

Fish

Captain Lee's Fish Market
9 Cobbee Rd, Latham, 783-1047
Brought in daily from New England waters, lobsters, whole Ipswich clams, home-made chowders

Ferrara's Fish Market
33 3rd Ave, Albany, 463-5873
Specializes in fish from Southern waters, whole fish (porgies, whiting, sea bass), will cut fillets

Off Shore Pier Fish Market
Rte 4 and 43, Rensselaer, 283-9880
Full line of fish from North Atlantic waters, live lobster in season, seafood salad is popular

Two Cousins Fish Market
581 Livingston Ave, Albany, 449-8830
1702 Chrisler Ave, Schenectady, 346-1798
Full line of fish

Lobster Pound Seafood Market
Rte 9 Albany Saratoga Rd, Latham, 785-5863
Fresh and frozen fish from East coast waters, lobsters year round, will prepare
(bake, broil, fry) while you wait

Fruits and Vegetables
Albany, Schenectady and Troy all host **Farmers' Markets,** a modern version of
the traditional weekly town square day. On designated days, farmers gather to
sell their wares directly to consumers from the backs of their trucks and cars. The
times and places of these wandering fairs are published in the local newspapers.

In addition to the usual commodities available at these markets, it should be
noted that the region produces its own exotica, Hand Melons, lush fruit har-
vested and sold only during August. (The fact they mature as the flat track opens
in Saratoga has linked them forever with thoroughbreds; predictably, they are all
the rage in Saratoga.)

Community Gardens
Community Gardens cater to those who wish to grow their own produce. Two
organizations assist personal gardeners:

Capital District Community Gardens
83 4th St Troy, 274-8685
Coordinates activity at 12 community garden sites in Rensselaer and north
Albany counties. A modest fee is charged for each person wishing to cultivate a
plot. The group deliberately keeps the fee low because the group cooperates in
several projects: growing food for regional food pantries, supervising youth gardening programs, publishing an informative newsletter and placing annual seed
and tree orders.

Community Gardens of Albany
Martin Rd in Voorheesville, 765-3500
Run by the Cooperative Extension of Albany County in cooperation with the City
of Albany. This group administers 7 garden sites, each with large and small plots
available for use by local residents.

Farm Markets

The following is a list of farm markets which are known for the freshness and variety of their produce.

Burhmaster Fruits and Vegetables
Saratoga Rd, Scotia, 399-5931

Engel's Farm and Market
Albany Shaker Rd opposite Desmond Hotel, 869-5653
Open June 1-Thanksgiving. Specialty is corn, also fruits, vegetables and home baked goods

Fo' Castle Country Store
Burnt Hills, 399-8322
Apple picking, baked goods

George Vogt
760 Troy Schenectady Rd, Latham, 785-0031
Garden vegetables, plants and flowers

Guptill's Farm
1087 New Loudon Rd, Boght Corners, 786-8633
Wild Maine blueberries

Indian Ladder Farms
Altamont, 765-2956
Farm stand, fruit picking, cider making, baked goods

Kolber Deerfield Farm
Rte 9, Selkirk, 767-3046
Fruits and vegetables in season, annuals, perennials and vegetable plants

Krugs Farm Stand
65 Everett Rd, Albany, 482-5406
Excellent corn, also fruits and vegetables, summer only

Lakeside Farm
Rte 2 Round Lake Rd, Ballston Lake, 399-8359
Cider mill, produce, baked goods, luncheon

Indian Ladder Farms, Altamont

LeVie's
Rte 85A, Voorheesville
Fresh produce, sweet corn, strawberries, summer only

Menands Market
Broadway in Menands just south of Menands Bridge. Largest group of vendors, wholesale and retail, open all year, early morning to early afternoon, fruit, vegetables and plants

Oronacah Farm
Vischers Ferry Road, 1½ miles south of Rte 146, Clifton Park, 383-6438
Thirty acres of berries of all varieties; fields of wild flowers for your picking

Samascott Orchards
Kinderhook
Large variety of fruit for picking

Shaker Shed
945 Watervliet Shaker Rd, Colonie, 869-3662
Farm stand, fruits and vegetables

W.F. Ryan
114 Railroad Ave, Albany, 459-5775
Broad selection in season and out, good prices, open all year

Yonder Farms
Rte 4, Troy, 283-4267
Rte 155, Colonie, 456-6823
Fresh fruit, berry picking, baked goods, cheese, plants and flowers

Westheimer's Carrot Barn
Rte 30 2 miles south of Schoharie (exit 23 I-88), 295-7139
Asparagus and raspberry picking

Fruit Baskets
Madison Fruit Garden
628 Madison Ave, Albany, 469-6973

Windrose Gifts Ltd
1663 Central Ave, Albany, 452-2100

Herbs and Spices

Cottage Herb Farm Shop
311 State St, Albany, 465-1130

Earthly Delights Natural Food
162 Jay St, Schenectady, 372-7580
Organically grown produce, spices, medicinal and fresh herbs

Gooseberry Farms
48 Wetsel Rd, Troy, 235-1068
Herb plants, honey, bee keepers

Cottage Herb Farm Shop, Albany

Honest Weight Food Co-Op
112 Quail St, Albany, 465-0383
Fresh herbs in season

Magik Herb
138 Jay St, Schenectady, 377-2873

Ice Cream and Frozen Confections
Ben and Jerry's
11 South Pearl St, Albany, 462-6588
579 New Scotland Ave, Albany, 482-1714
250 Lark St, Albany, 463-7182
Main Square, Delmar, 439-0113
1705 Union St, Schenectady, 346-0251
133 Wolf Rd, Colonie, 459-4425
All natural, 34 interesting flavors, Vermont made

Carvel
590 Newton Plaza, Latham, 785-4962
1321 Central Ave, Colonie, 459-7226
Frozen cakes a speciality

Civitello's Spumoni Shop
42 North Jay St, Schenectady, 381-6165
Bisque Tortoni, Spumoni, Italian Ices

Dahlia Supreme Ice Cream
858 Madison Ave, Albany, 482-0931
Homemade ice cream, soft serve yogurt

Gina's Gourmet Italian Ice Cream
1841 Van Vranken Ave, Schenectady, 370-7941
Ice cream cakes, Spumoni, Tortoni and assorted variety of frozen and non-frozen desserts

Kurver Kreme
1349 Central Ave, Albany, 459-4120
Cones, frosts, sundaes, soft ice cream, summer only

Peaches N' Creme
Stuyvesant Plaza, Albany, 482-3677
Assorted exotic flavors, ices year round

People's Choice
1836 Columbia Tpke, Schodack, 477-7867
Assorted flavors, soft ice cream

Toll Gate
1569 New Scotland Rd, Slingerlands, 439-9824
Handpacked assorted creams and sherberts, family favorite

Imported Foods and Ethnic Specialties

Because of the rich cultural mix represented within the population of the Capital District, foods native to other countries form a base for the regional diet and are widely available.

BFS Deli Imports
1754 Western Ave, Albany, 452-6342

Cowan and Lobel
Stuyvesant Plaza, Albany, 458-2771

Rolf's Pork Store
70 Lexington Ave, Albany, 463-0185

Russian and International Foods
153 N Allen St, Albany, 482-7120

Specialty World Foods
84 Montgomery St, Albany, 436-7603

Unique Catering
Newton Plaza, Latham, 783-3334

Indian Foods
Indian Spices
10 Fuller Rd, Albany, 489-3944

Italian Imports
Andy's and Sons
256 Delaware Ave, Albany 463-2754

De Fazio Imports
264 4th St, Troy, 274-8866

De Fazio Imports, Troy

Dominick's Italian Imports
122 Columbia Turnpike, Rensselaer, 463-6154

F. Cappiello Dairy Product
510 Broadway, Schenectady, 382-9045
Wholesale and retail

Genoa Importing
435 Loudon Rd, Loudonville, 427-0078

Munafo's Importing Company
961 Altamont Ave, Schenectady, 346-0389

Pellegrino, Michael
1117 Central Ave, Albany, 459-4472

Pellegrino Importing Co.
165 Madison Ave, Albany, 434-6695

Ragonese Italian Imports
409 New Scotland Ave, Albany, 482-2358

Ricciardi Produce and Italian Imports
1599 Union St, Schenectady, 374-7448

Roma Importing Co.
9 Cobbee Rd, Latham, 785-7480
131 South Broadway, Saratoga Springs, 587-6004

Oriental Foods
Kim's Oriental Shoppe
1649 Central Ave, Colonie, 869-9981

Nien-Hsuan
284 Troy Schenectady Rd, Latham, 783-0241

Meat
The following butcher shops offer superior meats and skilled service.

Cardona's Market
340 Delaware Ave, Albany, 434-4838

Rolf's Pork Store, Albany

Cowan and Lobel
Stuyvesant Plaza, Albany, 458-2771

Crestwood Market
22 Picotte Drive, Albany, 438-1331

Dichian's
300 4th St, Troy, 274-7623

Falvo Meats
Rte 85A, Slingerlands, 439-9273

Emil Meister's Market
329 Ontario St, Albany, 482-2556

Helmbold's
12 Industrial Park, Troy, 273-0810
Homemade hot dogs and sausages

Guertze Farm Market
Rte 9W, Selkirk,767-3345
Fresh chicken, eggs, lamb

Primo's Prime Meats
540 Clinton Ave, Albany, 465-2102

Rolf's Pork Store
70 Lexington Ave, Albany, 463-0185

Scholz'
1329 State St, Schenectady, 374-4477

Troy Pork Store
158 4th St, Troy, 272-8291

Catering
In addition to the speciality shops, the following businesses provide commendable catering services.

Barnsider's Catered Affair
480 Sand Creek Rd, Colonie, 869-0175

Brooks BarB.Q.
Rte 7, Oneonta, (607) 432-1782
Chicken and ribs

Capri Catering
RD 1 Box 66A, Earlton, 634-2338

Capriccio Banquet Theater
33 2nd St, Troy, 271-1942

Glen Sanders Mansion
1 Glen Ave, Scotia, 374-7262

Guertze's
Selkirk, 439-8777
Chicken and pig roasts

Kaye's Caterer's
22 Willow St, Albany, 438-5275
Kosher and non kosher

Michael's
Green Island, 273-2885

Old Daley Inn
499 2nd Ave, North Troy, 235-2656

Unique Catering
Newton Plaza, Latham, 783-3334

Unlimited Feast
340 Hamilton St, Albany, 463-6223

Specialty Stores

These stores offer ready-to-eat fresh and frozen foods, food stuffs and party foods.

Cowan and Lobel
Stuyvesant Plaza, Albany, 458-2771

BFS Deli and Imports
145 Western Ave, Albany, 452-6342

Cardona's Market
340 Delaware Ave, Albany, 434-4838

De Fazio
264 4th St, Troy, 274-8866

Expresso Service
24 4th St, Troy, 273-8773

La Stella
Main Square, Delmar, 475-0902
Rome Plaza Rte 9, Clifton Park, 373-9014
55 Church St, Saratoga Springs, 587-2782
Pasta shop, take out

Ragonese Italian Imports
409 New Scotland Ave, 482-2358

Unique Catering
Newton Plaza, Latham, 463-2203

CLOTHING

This section has various organizational headings—clothing for both men and women, for special sizes, for children, moderately priced for the family, and for shoes.

Clothing for Men
Kelly Clothes Inc.
886 New Loudon Rd, Latham, 785-3796

Kuppenheimer's
Sears, Colonie Center, Albany, 482-8508

Rodino's
348 Congress St, Troy, 274-1151

S. & K. Famous Brands
Marshall's Plaza, Niskayuna, 374-5555
Northway Mall, Colonie, 459-0022
Crossgates Mall, Albany, 464-5054
Off price merchandise

The Custom Shop Shirtmakers
Crossgates Mall, Albany, 456-7100

Clothing for Women
Ann Taylor
Crossgates Mall, Albany, 456-4433

Barbizon Fashion Discounters
Westgate Shopping Center, Albany, 489-5354
Shoppers World, Clifton Park, 383-8340
Wolf Rd Shoppers Park, Colonie, 459-5637

Casual Set
Stuyvesant Plaza, Albany, 482-7136

Entre-Nous
Stuyvesant Plaza, Albany, 482-1193

Grande Entrance
637 New Loudon Rd, Latham, 786-7704
Borrowing for special formal occasions

Harvé Benard
Latham Outlet Village, Latham, 783-0380

Honingsbaum's
Stuyvesant Plaza, Albany, 489-5564

Jean Lewis Maloy
Stuyvesant Plaza, Albany, 482-6260

Laura Ashley
Crossgates Mall, Albany, 452-4998

M. Solomon
Colonie Center, Colonie, 459-9070

Madame Pirie's Famise Corset and Lingerie Shop
255 Central Ave, Albany, 434-2600

Talbots
Stuyvesant Plaza, Albany, 482-0395

Talbots Sale Store
5 Metro Park Drive, Colonie, 482-4611

Town and Tweed
Delaware Plaza, Delmar, 439-4018

Clothing for Men and Women

Amore, Angelo Joe
123 State St, Albany, 434-4054
Custom and ready made

Anderson-Little Company
Mohawk Mall, Niskayuna, 370-4298
Northway Mall, Colonie, 459-5442
Rotterdam Square Mall, Schenectady, 374-2103
Saratoga Mall, Saratoga Springs, 587-0090

Banana Republic
Crossgates Mall, 452-5973

Cohoes Fashions
43 Mohawk St, Cohoes, 237-0524
Discounted

Day Break
22 Central Ave, Albany, 434-4302
Antique clothing, used furs

Hoffman's
626 New Loudon Rd, Latham, 785-9891
Largest selection of Pendleton woolens in the Northeast

Krall's Ltd
One Second St, Troy, 272-6621

Peter Harris
574 Columbia Tpke, East Greenbush, 477-2115
417 Kenwood Ave, Delmar, 439-9510
Mayfair Shopping Center, Scotia, 399-7267

Polo Ralph Lauren Factory Store
55 Mohawk St, Cohoes, 237-0307

Spectors
233 Central Ave, Albany, 434-0187

Sweater Venture
1090 New Loudon Rd Rte 9, Cohoes, 783-1932
Handknit woollens from around the world

T.J. Maxx
666 New Loudon Rd, Latham, 783-6813
Discounted

The Gap Stores
Clifton Country Mall, 371-6641
Colonie Center, 459-2254
Crossgates, 456-4173
Latham Shopping Center, 785-6006

Clothing for Special Sizes
Men
Casual Male Big and Tall
110 Wolf Rd, 482-9717

Marshall Ray
701 River St, Troy, 272-6700

Peter Harris Plus
952 Troy Schenectady Rd, Latham, 783-1938

Simon's Men's Wear
1671 Union St, Schenectady, 377-1182

Women
Half Size Shop
Woodlawn Plaza, Schenectady, 346-3402
Stuyvesant Plaza, Albany, 438-6637

Peter Harris Plus
952 Troy Schenectady Rd, Latham, 783-1938

Petite Sophisticates
Colonie Center Mall, Colonie, 438-5068
Crossgates Mall, 869-5099
Rotterdam Square Mall, 393-0815

Stylish Women Ltd.
Westgate Plaza, Albany, 459-7749
Latham Circle Mall, 785-3612

The Answer
43 Mohawk St, Cohoes Commons, Cohoes, 235-7673

Wonderfull Woman
Windsor Plaza at Shaker and Wolf Rds, Colonie, 482-1658

Clothing for Children
Babyland
1400 Central Ave, Albany, 459-7706

Cohoes Kids
43 Mohawk St, Cohoes, 2nd floor 237-0524 ext. 250
Discount clothing
50 Mohawk St, Cohoes, 237-0524 ext. 203
Discount furniture

Gingersnips
Stuyvesant Plaza, Albany, 459-3090
Makes and sells a full line of children's wear

Jean Lewis Maloy
Stuyvesant Plaza, Albany, 482-6260

Magic Toad
635 Loudon Rd, Latham, 783-9198

Peter Harris
574 Columbia Tpke, East Greenbush, 477-6837
Mayfair Shopping Center, Scotia, 399-7267
417 Kenwood Ave, Delmar, 439-9150

Rugged Bear
Stuyvesant Plaza, Albany, 482-8325
Offers outerwear and equipment for Juniors

Sears Roebuck
Colonie Center, Colonie, 454-3229

Talbots Sale Store
5 Metro Park Drive, Colonie, 482-4611

Tough Traveler
Stuyvesant Plaza, Albany, 438-1807
Child carriers, back packs, sleeping bags

The Gap for Kids
Crossgates Mall, Albany, 452-3077

Clothing for the Family, Moderately Priced
Adirondack Dan-Army Navy Store
59 North Pearl St, 434-3495

Burlington Coat Factory
664 Loudon Rd, Latham, 783-0464

Champion Factory Outlet Stores
Westgate Plaza, Albany, 489-8215
Crosstown Plaza, Schenectady, 381-4186

Cramer's Armory
Columbia and Main Sts, Cohoes, 434-3495
Uniforms for all professions

Lodge's
75 North Pearl St, Albany, 463-4646

Schaffer's Department Store
640 Central Ave, Albany, 482-8010

Standard Manufacturing Outlet
750 2nd St, Troy, 235-6097

Shoes

Cohoes Fashions
43 Mohawk St, Cohoes, 237-0524
Shoes for men and women at discount prices

Delmar Bootery
Stuyvesant Plaza, Albany, 438-1717
376 Delaware Ave, Delmar, 439-1717
Fine mens shoes

Manufacturer's Shoe Outlet
49 3rd St, Troy, 271-0921

Maxine Fine Footwear
110 Wolf Rd, Colonie, 438-4490
Discount designer shoes

Spectors
233 Central Ave, 434-0187
Men only

GOODS

This section provides a listing of shops providing a variety of goods in a wide range of specialty areas.

Antiques

During the year, there are many good auctions and antique shows which are advertised in the newspapers and which are well worth attending. The following list represents dealers who have permanent shops in the area.

Art and Antiques
462 Broadway, Saratoga Springs, 584-4876
Group of dealers

Black Sheep
Rte 20, Delanson, 895-2983
70 dealers in a group shop

Daybreak Antique Clothing
22 Central Ave, Albany, 434-4302

Dennis Holzman Antiques
2240 Washington Ave (2nd floor), Albany, 449-5414

Edward Jubic Antiques and Auction Service
1137B Central Ave, Albany, 459-5927

Empire State Antiques
20 Central Ave, Albany, 465-8823

Fred Johnston Antiques
Kingston, (914) 331-3979
Fine collection of regional antiques

Historic Albany Foundation Parts Warehouse
399 South Pearl St, Albany, 465-2987
Articles for rehabilitation; mantels, doors, hardware, architectural details

Hudson New York
See chapter Not Far Away

James VanDerVort
1691 Delaware Ave, Delmar, 439-2143

Kinderhook Antique Center
Rte 9H, Kinderhook, 758-7939

Mill House Antiques
Rte 6, Woodbury, Connecticut (203) 263-3446
Fine quality country furniture, see chapter Not Far Away

New Scotland Antiques
240 Washington Ave, Albany, 463-1323

Regent Street Antique Center
153 Regent St, Saratoga Springs, 584-0107

Sotheby's Restoration
Maple Ave, Claverack, 851-2544
Repair and restoration of fine antiques

Volbrecht Antiques
206 Lark St, Albany, 434-4732

Artist and Technical Drawing Supplies and Services

These shops carry a full range of equipment for the professional and give careful, competent advice to the amateur.

Arlene's
57 Fuller Rd, Albany, 482-8881

Crafts Plus
Stuyvesant Plaza, Albany, 438-7679

Hill's Stationery
451 Broadway, Troy, 274-3191

Northco Products Inc.
Rte 155 343 New Karner Rd, Colonie, 869-6056

Soave-faire
449 Broadway, Saratoga Springs, 587-8448

W.L. Coughtry
268 Central Ave, Albany, 463-2192
151 Erie Blvd, Schenectady, 374-1655

Books
General Bookstores

As in other parts of the United States, the Capital District marketplace for books is dominated by chains with branches in shopping plazas. **Waldenbooks** is in Clifton Country Mall, Colonie Center, Crossgates Mall, Latham Shopping Center, Mohawk Mall, and Rotterdam Square Mall. **B. Dalton Bookseller** is at Clifton Country Mall, Crossgates Mall, and Latham Circle Mall. All these branches carry great quantities of recent titles in the full range of popular interest. In spite of the power of these outlets, small stores maintained by rugged individuals persist, offering readers additional variety, quality and service.

Blackwood and Brouwer Booksellers
7 Hudson St, Kinderhook, 758-1232
Eclectic collections, large selection of regional cookbooks, mysteries, works by local authors and publishers, music tapes for children and adults, books on tape, rental club

Book House
Stuyvesant Plaza, Albany, 489-4761
All purpose, steady graceful growth over 15 years, well rounded, large stock, good depth of inventory, full special order service, good for browsing, chairs for reading

The Little Book House
Attached to the Book House, good selection of children's books and foreign language books for children, story telling on Saturdays

Book Mark
Rte 9 Newton Plaza, Latham, 785-7869
General book store with a large children's selection, will special order

Book Nook
1606 Union St, Schenectady, 346-0075
Located on upper Union St, specializes in local history and quality children's books, special order

Bookworks
456 Broadway, Saratoga Springs, 587-3228
General bookstore, children's books, periodicals

Boulevard Bookstore
15 Central Ave, Albany, 436-1505
Includes an art gallery and cafe, open late, center for Albany's literary and poetry scene, full schedule of concerts and readings

Burnt Hills Books
772 Saratoga Rd (Rte 50), Burnt Hills, 399-7004
Good selection for children, specializes in quilting books, large selection of Adirondack and local books

Chatham Bookstore
27 Main St, Chatham, 392-3005
Complete selection of books, personal touch, special order, will mail anywhere, relaxed atmosphere, children's books

Clapps
1032 Madison Ave, Albany, 482-4136
Old neighborhood bookstore with gifts, cards and stationery

Clapps
20 Mall, Guilderland, 456-5772
Large selection of books for cat lovers, also gifts and stationery

Critics Choice
365 Feura Bush Rd, Glenmont, 436-9673
New and used books, children's books

Empire Plaza Books
Empire State Plaza, Albany, 465-1807
General bookstore located in the north lobby of the Empire State Plaza, selection of African-American, children's, computer and travel books

Friar Tuck Bookshop
Located in the Delaware Plaza 439-3742, Saratoga 587-2632 and Wilton Malls 583-7821, at 99 Pine St Albany 462-0099, and Rte 9 Latham 783-6352, and The Discount Book Center shops at the Northway 482-3300 and Amsterdam Malls 843-4423, are all owned by Price Chopper.
General bookstores, customer oriented company, special order

Haven't Got A Clue
1823 Western Ave, Albany, 464-1135
Mystery, suspense and espionage (new and used books, games, children's mysteries, tee shirts and mugs)

ibd Ltd. (International Book Distributors)
Hudson St, Kinderhook, 1-800-343-3531
Dictionaries from publishers around the world, multi-language, many different fields, no store, call for information

I Love Books
Builders Square Plaza 1814 Central Ave, Colonie, 456-4275
General bookstore with children's books, special orders

Little Professor Book Center
Mayfair Plaza 262 Saratoga Rd, Scotia, 399-2665
General bookstore, customer service is important, special order, store has two popular cats

Museum Shop
New York State Cultural Education Center, Albany, 449-1404
Native American studies, science, nature and New York history, children's books

North River Books
386 Delaware Ave, Albany, 463-3082
General books new and used, feature local and New York State material, literature, history and philosophy

Northshire Books
Main St, Manchester Center, Vermont (802) 362-3565
A wonderful store for browsing, strong collection of literary titles

Open Door
136 Jay St, Schenectady, 346-2719
Unique with complete selection of titles for both adults and children, also unusual gifts, cards and tapes

Saratoga Science Fiction and Mystery Bookshop
454 Broadway-Mall, Saratoga Springs, 584-3743
New and used books, vintage paperbacks, horror, "best selection between NYC and Canada"

The Shop
Albany Institute of History and Art 125 Washington Ave, Albany, 463-8190
Featuring a wide selection of books for adults and children related to the history,
art and culture of Albany and the upper Hudson River Valley region, best sellers
include books on the New Netherlands and the Hudson River School of Art

Antiquarian Books
The Lyrical Ballad
7 Phila St, Saratoga Springs, 584-8779
Modern first editions, New York Statiana, equine books, superb fine art section,
large rare and out of print stock

Tintagel Books
East Springfield, (607) 264-3669
Located in the front rooms of a Victorian house near Cooperstown, specializing in New York Statiana, out of print art books and modern first editions;
owners are a young interesting couple, browsers welcome. Rte 88 to Exit 24
(Duanesburg) Rte 20 West 37 miles to East Springfield, watch for sign on the
right (1 hour).

Children's Books
Children's Book World
Crossgates Mall, Albany, 869-6379
Clifton Country Mall, Clifton Park, 383-8160

Hodge Podge Books
272 Lark St, Albany, 434-0238

The Little Bookhouse
Syuyvesant Plaza, Albany, 437-0101

Out of Print Books
W. Somers Bookseller
841 Union St, Schenectady, 393-5266

Used Books
Bryn Mawr Book Store
1 Spring St, Albany, 465-8126

Central Station
260 Central Ave, Albany, 463-4190

Dove and Hudson
296 Hudson Ave, Albany, 432-4518

Owl Pen
Riddle Rd, Greenwich, Washington County, 692-7039
Two barns full of books, open May through October

Costumes
The Costumer
1020 Barrett St, Schenectady, 374-7442
Northway Mall, Colonie, 458-2846
Clifton Country Mall, Clifton Park, 383-5373

Capitol Costumes
2313 Western Ave, Guilderland, 456-5754

Flowers and Plants
Floral Arrangements
The following florists seem particularly creative and responsive to special requests.

Blooms by Michael
290 Delaware Ave, Albany, 432-4293

Danker's
658 Central Ave, Albany, 489-5461
Stuyvesant Plaza, Albany, 438-2202
239 Delaware Ave, Delmar, 439-0971

Doris Remis Flowers
1740 Union St, Schenectady, 346-1271

Felthousen's Florist and Greenhouse
1537 Van Antwerp Rd, Schenectady, 373-4414

Larkspur
2 Franklin Square, Saratoga Springs, 587-3100

Nagengast, Emil
Ontario and Bensen, Albany, 434-1125

Silver Strawberry
830 Hoosick Rd, Brunswick, 279-1277

Surroundings Floral Studio
Shaker Pine Mall 145 Vly Rd Extension, Colonie, 464-1382

Verstandig's
454 Delaware Ave, Delmar, 454-4946

Flowers
Blossom Farm
Johnny Cake Lane, Greenville, 966-5722
Acres of cut-your-own of fresh, dry and wild flowers. Country bouquets, herbs, plants. Directions: Rte 32S to Greenville, right on Rte 81W, 1.8 miles to Old Plank Rd, take left for ½ mile.

Greig Farm
Pitcher Lane, Red Hook, (914) 758-1234
Acres of cut-your-own flowers, pick-your-own berries, herbs, spices. Directions: NYS Thruway South, Exit 19, over Kingston-Rhinecliff Bridge. Left on 9G. Go 2.8 miles, right onto Kelly Lane. Go one mile, turn left at stop sign. Pitcher Lane on right.

Oronacah Farms
Vischers Ferry Rd, 1½ miles south of Rte 146, Clifton Park, 383-6438
Fields of wild flowers for your picking.

Ralph Pitcher Nursery
Middle Rd, Rhinebeck, (914) 876-3974
Principal anemone growers on the east coast, dazzling colors line the greenhouses; bouquets available at wholesale prices.

Garden Plants
Brizzel's
562 New Loudon Rd, Newtonville, 783-6926
Open for Christmas, Easter, spring and fall, home grown plants, garden mums, wreaths

Cedar Hill Iris Garden
Rte 144 (6 miles south of Albany), 767-9608
Perennials with an emphasis on peonies and irises

Clatter Hill Nurseries
Business District, Spencertown, 392-3140
I-90E to Taconic Parkway; Rte 203E to Spencertown. 45 min.

Faddegon's Nursery
1140 Troy-Schenectady Rd, Latham, 785-6726

Helderledge Farm
418 Picard Rd, Altamont, 765-4702
Trees shrubs and plants, specializing in perennials, particularly day lilies,
Christmas shop, display gardens, design oriented use of material

Kolber Deerfield Farm
Rte 9W, Selkirk, 767-3046
Annuals, perennials, and vegetable plants

Menands Market
Broadway, Menands
Different vendors selling plants and bushes at low prices

Moreau Perennials
543 Selfridge Rd, Gansevoort, 792-6381
Thousands of varieties of day lilies, open for sales when lilies are blooming

Pigliavento's Greenhouses
3535 Lydius Rd, Schenectady, 356-9188
Annuals, perennials, herbs, vegetable plants

Siesel's Flower Farm
488 Loudonville Rd, Loudonville, 463-7937
Annuals and perennials, vegetable plants, summer only

Smalltown Perennial Gardens Inc.
161 Kingsley Rd, Burnt Hills, 399-5084
Hardy field grown perennials

White Flower Farm
See chapter Not Far Away
Specimen varieties of hard to find plants and bushes, display gardens, beautiful
instructive catalog

House Plants

All these stores carry a good selection of carefully nurtured plants.

Ann Scheeren Orchids

Verbeck Ave, Shaghticoke, 753-6315 greenhouse, 753-4044 home
Ten thousand orchid plants, 3 large greenhouses, plants in bloom throughout
year, retail sales. Rte 7E to Rte 40N to Village of Schaghticoke. Turn left on Rte 67
(at end of fairgrounds). First right.

Faddegon's Nursery

1140 Troy Schenectady Rd, Latham, 785-6726

Felthousen's Florist and Greenhouse

1537 Van Antwerp Rd, Schenectady, 373-4414

Mohawk Valley Orchid Estate

143 East Main St, Amsterdam, 843-4889

Price Greenleaf
14 Booth Rd, Elsmere, 439-9212

Schultz Greenhouse and Garden Center
136 Wolf Rd, Colonie, 458-7957

Valoze Greenhouses
Rte 9 north of the Latham Circle, 785-4343

Verstandig's
454 Delaware Ave, Delmar, 439-4946

Garden Equipment and Supplies

Probably because summer months in the Capital District are ideal for the development of productive gardens, the region is replete with stores providing equipment, supplies and plants for the gardener. The list below surveys the area, noting the special strengths of each merchant.

Agway Cottage
1158 Troy Schenectady Rd, Latham, 783-0084
Wholesale and retail farm and garden supply; bird food

Faddegon's Nursery
1140 Troy Schenectady Rd, Latham, 785-6726
All around garden supplies, plants and equipment, landscaping available

Garden Shoppe
Feura Bush Rd, Glenmont, 439-8169
3699 Carman Rd, Schenectady, 356-0442
All around garden supplies, plants and equipment, landscaping available

Price Greenleaf
14 Booth Rd, Elsmere, 439-9212
Excellent selection of bulbs, good tools, plants, and bushes

Russell Nursery
Rte 9, Malta, 584-1355
Greenhouse, horticulture center, landscaping services

Schultz Greenhouse and Garden Center
136 Wolf Rd, Colonie, 458-7957
All around garden supplies, greenhouse plants, garden equipment

Greenhouse Faddegon's Nursery

Story's Nursery
Freehold, 634-7754
Trees, shrubs, unusual and dwarf specimens, perennials, annuals, tropical house plants, (45 minutes)

Troy Bilt Factory Store
102nd St and 9th Ave, Troy, 237-8430
Power equipment, Troybilt rototillers

Utica Seed Co.
Menands Market Broadway, Menands, 434-6521
Wholesale and retail, bulk seed, supplies for farmers, backyard gardeners and hobby greenhouse owners

Yunck's Nursery
Rte 9, Latham, 785-9132
Large selection of perennials, bushes and trees

Gifts
These shops carry interesting, good quality gifts for the home or individual.

Balcony
1328 Van Antwerp Rd, Schenectady, 374-1333
Gift items, home accessories

Clearly Yours
588 Newton Plaza, Latham, 783-1212
Personalized gifts (picture frames, photo albums, towels, children's gifts)

Cohoes Fashions
43 Mohawk St, Cohoes, 237-0524
Imported pottery, glass, stuffed toys, books for the home, cards

Cottage Herb Farm Shop
311 State St, Albany, 465-1130
Imported and handmade gifts, teas, herbs and spices

Crabtree and Evelyn
Stuyvesant Plaza, Albany, 489-0038
Toiletries and cosmetics for men and women

Dansk Factory Outlet
50 Mohawk St, Cohoes, 235-9906
Decorative cookware, glass and tableware all discounted

DeAnna's Country Gift Shop
West Sand Lake Rd, Wynantskill, 283-6252
Folkcraft, decorative Americana, jewelry, chocolates

Frank Adams Jewelers
58 N. Pearl St, Albany, 463-3278
China, crystal, silver, fine traditional jewelry

Guess What
Stuyvesant Plaza, Albany, 482-5619
Handcrafted American artist designs

Import Specialty Gifts
595 Newton Center, Latham, 785-1932
Imported gifts, jewelry, oriental accessories

Iron Horse Gifts
Rte 9, Latham, 785-3735
Imported toys and dolls, collectors items

Judy's Cards and Gifts
Parkwood Plaza, Clifton Park, 371-0769
Gift wrap, greeting cards, candles, party supplies

Larkspur
360 Broadway, Saratoga Springs, 587-3200
2 Franklin Square, Saratoga Springs, 587-3100
Distinctive and unique gifts, household items, floral arrangement, plants, jewelry

Maisonette
265 Osborne Rd, Loudonville, 438-4302
Beautiful selection of home accessories

Malawee Asian Imports
5 Broadway, Troy, 273-8358
Food items and gifts from Asia

New York State Museum Shop
Cultural Education Center, Albany, 449-1404
Natural artifacts, baskets, books, stationery, prints, jewelry

Nostalgia
436 Broadway, Saratoga Springs, 584-4665
Decorative home furnishings, accessories and gifts

Open Door
136 Jay St, Schenectady, 346-2719
Unusual gifts, cards and tapes

Owl's Nest
164 Jay St, Schenectady, 374-2803
Jewelry , chocolates, crystal, paper goods

Pearl Grant-Richman
Stuyvesant Plaza, Albany, 438-8409
Bridal Registry, china, linens, furniture, cookware, glass, cards

Pier One Imports
120 Wolf Rd, Colonie, 459-5304
Imported housewares, clothing, candles, home furnishings

Pink Kitty
Red Lion Inn, Stockbridge, Massachusetts (413) 298-5545
Lamps, waste baskets, cards, children's wear, lingerie

Pleasant Valley Gallery and Gifts
2739 Pleasant Valley Rd, Knox, 872-0394
Wide variety of collectibles for the home, imported goods, jewelry

Rensselaer County Historical Society Shop
59 2nd St, Troy, 272-7232
Museum related gifts plus toys, books, gifts for the home

Schenectady Museum Shop
Nott Terrace Heights, Schenectady, 382-7890
Souvenirs, reproductions from around the world, books on nature, science and cooking
The Gallery Shop has juried arts and crafts by regional artists and craftsmen.

Sumptuous Settings
Lakeshore Drive at Trout Lake Rd, Bolton Landing, 644-3145
Vintage fabrics, Victorian and French trims, laces, antiques, collectibles

Sutton's
Rte 9, Glens Falls, 798-1188
Cards, candies, gourmet items, Americana and folk art, restaurant

Romeo's Gifts
299 Lark St, Albany, 434-9014
Unique gifts, glass, stationery

Tara's Florist and Gifts Ltd.
RD3 Brunswick Rd, Troy, 279-3082
Christmas villages, Irish imports and collectibles

The Difference Is
118 South Ferry St, Schenectady, 382-7600
Women's sportswear, gifts, stationery, children's gifts

The Shop
Albany Institute of History and Art 125 Washington Ave, Albany, 463-8190
Museum related gifts, books, cards, jewelry, reproductions

Toad Hall
358 Broadway, Saratoga Springs, 583-0149
63 Pioneer St, Cooperstown NY (607) 547-2144
Furniture, gifts, folk art

Tri-City Luggage
1645 Central Ave, Colonie, 869-9221
Stuyvesant Plaza, Albany
Desk accessories, travel kits, leather goods, pens

Verstandig's
454 Delaware Ave, Delmar, 439-4946
Decorative items, imported gifts

Village Shop
Delaware Plaza, Delmar, 439-1823
Home furnishings, cookware

Wits End Giftique
Parkwood Plaza, Clifton Park, 371-9273
Wide variety of merchandise and price ranges, music boxes, crystal, country kitchen

Windrose Gifts
1663 Central Ave, Albany, 452-2100
Speciality gift baskets, floral arrangements, collectibles

Handi-Craft Supplies
These well stocked shops cater to the person actively engaged in making objects by hand as well as those seeking a hobby.

Crafts Plus
Stuyvesant Plaza, Albany, 438-7679

Deco-World
Rte 146N, Guilderland, 355-5745
South Broadway, Saratoga Springs, 584-3193
North Greenbush Rd, Troy, 283-7203

For Craft Sake
65 Canvass St, Cohoes, 237-6360

Hobby Shop
351 Altamont Ave, 346-6500
Radio controls, doll houses

Leisure Times Arts and Crafts
Country Dollar Plaza, Clifton Park, 383-2824

Mohawk Valley Railroad
2037 Hamburg St, Schenectady, 372-9124
Operating layout, model train suppplies, railroadiana

Ye Olde Yarn & Gift Shoppe
1204 Eastern Ave, Schenectady, 393-2695

Home Accessories, Decorating and Repairs
Electrical Supply
Loyal Supply
156 Railroad Ave, Albany, 438-6891

Meginniss Electric Supply
370 Broadway, Albany, 463-3103

Wolberg Electrical Supply
118 Erie St, Schenectady, 381-9231
35 Industrial Park Albany, 489-8451

Hardware Stores

There are scores of good hardware stores in the Captial District. This selection has been divided into major and neighborhood stores. If you are a hardware buff, Spags and the Old Forge stores are worth seeing.

Major Hardware Stores

A. Phillips Hardware
(formerly Terminal Hardware) 294 Central Ave, Albany, 274-7019

Builders Square
1814 Central Ave, 452-7081
Emporium for building supplies

Hometown Hardware
898 Troy-Schenectady Rd, Latham, 785-3690

Lindy's Hardware Inc.
Canal and 2nd, Troy, 272-0761

Old Forge Hardware
Old Forge, (315) 369-6100

Shaker Lumber and Hardware
607 Watervliet-Shaker Rd (Rte 155), Latham, 785-9052

Spags
Rte 9, Shrewsbury, MA

Trojan Hardware
96 Congress St, Troy, 272-7330

Wallace Armer Hardware and Home Center Stores Inc.
225 Erie Blvd, Schenectady, 381-6666

Neighborhood Hardware Stores
Adams Hardware Store
333 Delaware Ave, Delmar, 439-1866

Andy's Colonie Hardware Inc.
1789 Central Ave, Colonie, 869-9634

Bridgeford Hardware
388 Delaware Ave, Albany, 465-8276

Robinson Hardware Corp.
1890 Western Ave, Albany, 456-7383

Home Decorating

Brookstones
Crossgates Mall, Albany, 869-1908
Fancy cabinetry hardware, reproductions of hard-to-find accessories, lighting and bathroom items

Country Curtains
The Red Lion Inn Main St, Stockbridge, Massachusetts (413) 298-5565
Made to order, and in-store selections

Decorating Den
1683 Western Ave, Albany, 456-3153
Custom designed draperies, wall coverings, carpeting

Deitcher's Wallpaper Factory Outlet
188 Remsen St, Cohoes, 237-9260
Complete interior design, slipcovers, upholstery, window treatment, flooring, first quality wallpaper discounted

Fred Sisto Associates
5 Sherman St, Albany, 436-4339
Drapes, upholstery, custom made furniture, repairs and refinishing

Home Fabric Mills
443 Saratoga Rd, Scotia, 399-6325
All varieties of home decorating fabrics

Huck Finn's Warehouse
Tivoli St off Broadway, Albany, 465-3373
Home furnishings

Interior Alternative
5 Hoosac St, Adams, Massachusetts (413) 743-1986
Savings on famous brand seconds of decorative products

Kermani Oriental Rugs
3905 State St, Schenectady, 393-6884
98 Wolf Rd, Albany, 459-9656
Fine selection of Oriental carpets

Laura Ashley
Crossgates Mall, Albany, 452-4998
Wallpaper and fabrics

Old Stone Mill
Adams, Massachusetts (413) 743-1015
Factory seconds of decorator wallpaper

Miller Paint
296 Central Ave, Albany, 465-1526
1681 Rte 9, Clifton Park, 371-1649
Free delivery

Passonno Paint
1438 Western Ave, Albany, 489-1910
500 Broadway, Watervliet, 273-3822
Locally manufactured paints and stains

Racklyn/Capitol Wallpaper Paint and Hardware
1721 State St, Schenectady, 372-5964

Riverside Sales and Upholstery Company
683 Broadway, Watervliet, 274-6442
Furniture repair, custom upholstering

Household Accessories
Bed Bath and Beyond
32 Wolf Rd, Albany, 437-0147
Linens, stack shelving, bathroom accessories

Different Drummer's Kitchen
Stuyvesant Plaza, Albany, 459-7990
Cooking equipment and supplies

Lee Jay
Crossgates Mall, Albany, 869-0346
Linens, bedding, towels, at a reasonable price

Lee Jay for the Home
43 Mohawk St, Cohoes, 237-8400
Discount outlet for linens, bedding, towels

Linens and Lingerie by Johnston Inc.
300 Bennett Pl, Medina, (716) 798-0170
Fine quality for special occasions, by private appointment only

Linens by Gail Ltd.
406 Kenwood Ave, Delmar, 439-4979
Bedspreads, blankets, table linens

Pearl Grant-Richman's
Stuyvesant Plaza, 438-8409
Bathroom accessories, linens, china, crystal, quilts

Polo Ralph Lauren Factory Store
55 Mohawk St, Cohoes, 233-0307
Towels, comforters, sheets, pillows

Tablecloths For Granted
1956 Watt St, Schenectady, 346-7647
Rental tablecloths and napkins

Village Shop
Delaware Plaza, Delmar, 430-1823
Kitchen accessories, knives, cookware

Household Appliances and Repair
Algen Sales and Service
300 Kenwood Ave, Delmar, 439-3323
Appliance sales and major appliance repairs

Cornwell Appliance Company Inc.
1357 Central Ave, Colonie, 459-3700
44 years of merchandising and repairing

Green's Appliances
Several locations
Noted for variety of major household appliances

Jacoby Appliance Parts
1656 Central Ave, Colonie, 869-2283
One million parts in stock, wholesale and retail

Lake Electronic Service Inc.
1650 Central Ave, Colonie, 869-8424
Parts and service for all portable appliances

Lexington Vacuum
562 Central Ave, Albany, 482-4427
Three generations of selling and servicing all makes of vacuum cleaners, large inventory of bags and parts, trade-ins

Jewelry

These reputable jewelers specialize in selling, repairing and appraising beautiful ornaments. Some of these jewelers offer custom designs.

American Indian Treasures
2558 Western Ave, Guilderland, 456-3324

Carr's Mfg Jewelers Inc.
10 Russell Rd, Albany, 438-5733

Drue Sanders Custom Jewelers
Stuyvesant Plaza, Albany, 438-2090

Fritze Jewelers
1659 Central Ave, Albany, 869-7880

Frank Adams
58 North Pearl St, Albany, 463-3278

Harold Finkle
217 Central Ave, Albany, 463-8220

Hummingbird Designs
29 3rd St, Troy, 272-1807

Kelly's Jewelers
Kimberly Square Osborne and Albany Shaker Rds, Latham, 438-8175

Naughter's Diamond Guild
201 Central Ave, Albany, 465-3814

Schauer Jeweler
630 Central Ave, Albany, 489-4014
Watch, clock and jewelry repair

Music
Recorded Music
Blue Note Record Shop
156 Central Ave, Albany, 462-0221
Every hit record since 1948, sing along (karoke) tapes, no used records

Central Station
260 Central Ave, Albany, 463-4190
Used records and tapes with collectors in mind

Lechmere
1440 Central Ave, Albany, 459-1500
Large selection of tapes, and CD's

Record Town
20 Wolf Rd, Colonie, 459-6247
And all major malls

The Music Shack
65 Central Ave, Albany, 436-4581
Alternative music, rock, reggae, rap, records, tapes and CD's

Records 'N Such
Delaware Plaza, Elsmere, 439-2449
Folk and blues section
Greenbush Plaza, East Greenbush, 477-7846
Stuyvesant Plaza, Albany, 438-3003
Large classical section

Tape World
Colonie Center, 458-8135
Crossgates Mall, 869-2214
Rotterdam Square Mall, 374-1856
Offering the Top 200 hits

Sheet Music
Van Curler Music Co.
296 Delaware Ave, Albany, 465-4576

Schenectady Van Curler Music
Proctor's Arcade, Schenectady, 374-5318

Musical Instruments
Drome Sound
3486 State St, Schenectady, 370-3701
321 Central Ave, Albany, 436-4000
Keyboard instruments, drums, recording equipment, guitars, amplifiers

John Keal Music Company
819 Livingston Ave, Albany, 482-4405
Band and orchestral instrument rental, sales and repairs

Newspapers and Magazines
Colonie News
1787 Central Ave, Colonie, 869-0441
Open 24 hours

Coulson's News Center
454 Delaware Ave, Albany, 465-4232
Newton Plaza Latham, 785-6499, foreign newspapers
420 Broadway, Albany, 449-7577 open 24 hours
1506 Altamont Ave, Schenectady, 356-2921

Finnegan's Convenience Store
122 Quail St, Albany, 463-5570

Fowler's
196 Lark St, Albany, 436-7076

Ned Abbot Newsroom
185 Hoosick St, Troy, 272-9753

News Stand Amtrak Train Station
Rensselaer, 449-8097
Open 5:30am to 11pm, foreign and a variety of U.S. papers

Westmere News and Variety
1823 Western Ave, Albany, 456-4223

Newspapers from New York City Delivered
Taylor News
Albany, 482-1730

Party Supplies and Services
Alternatives to Sending Flowers
Cookie Bouquet
31 Broadway, Waterford, 237-0682
Cookies made in the form of long stem roses or floral arrangements, made to order, will deliver

Cookie Creations
Castleton, 732-2119
Three dimensional cookie creations made to order for any occasion, also chocolate brownie pizza, will deliver

Balloonage
594 Loudon Rd, Latham, 783-0748

Balloons Plus
131 Lark St, Albany, 449-5223

Zing-A-Gram
432 2nd Ave, Albany, 462-1703

Party Supplies
Albany Party Warehouse
76 Fuller Rd, Albany, 458-1144
Shoppers World Plaza, Clifton Park, 383-6146

Let's Party
1400 Altamont Ave, Rotterdam, 356-6889

Rayge Display Inc.
91 Broadway, Menands, 434-6910

Party Services
Cranberry the Clown
31 South Lake Ave, Troy, 272-6486
Entertainment for parties, shows, magic, ventriloquist

Old Curiosity Shop
409 16th St, Watervliet, 273-1374
Magician for special occasions

Pet Boarding
Pinebush Kennels
274 New Karner Rd, Albany, 456-0700

Supernal Pet Motel
480 Hudson River Rd, Rexford, 235-2103

Picture Framing
Clement Frame and Art Shop
39 2nd St, Troy, 272-6811
204 Washington Ave, Albany, 465-4558

Deck the Walls
Crossgates Mall, Albany 869-0976

Frame and Art Shop
1789 Western Ave, Guilderland, 456-5615
715 Columbia Tpk, East Greenbush, 479-4130

Ferguson's Frame House
932 State St, Schenectady, 370-1481

Gidley's Fine Framing
1712 Union St, Schenectady, 393-6311

Greenhut Galleries
Stuyvesant Plaza, Albany, 482-1984

Northeast Framing
243 Delaware Ave, Delmar, 439-7913

South Street Framers and Gallery
377 Delaware Ave, Delmar, 439-5579

Shoe Repair
Albany Quick Shoe Rebuilders
297 Central Ave, Albany, 463-0954

Delmar Bootery
376 Delaware Ave, Delmar, 439-1717
Stuyvesant Plaza, Albany, 438-1717

Empire Shoe Rebuilders
32 Maiden Ln, Albany, 465-3067
Empire State Plaza, Albany, 432-6972

Troy Quick Shoe Repairing Co.
81 3rd St, Troy, 274-2431
Shoe dyeing

Sporting Goods
Five stores cater to the general needs of the athlete; these are supplemented by recommended merchants who carry an in-depth selection of equipment for a few sports.

General Stores
Anaconda Kaye Sports Inc
44 State St, Schenectady 382-2061

Cahill's
26 4th St, Troy, 272-0991

Goldstocks Sporting Goods
121 N. Broadway, Schenectady, 382-2037

Herman's
20 Wolf Rd, Colonie, 459-1350

Johnny Evers Co. Inc.
330 Central Ave, Albany, 463-2211

Specialty Stores

Berwick Ltd, Tack and Tennis
1669 Western Ave, Albany, 456-2955

Down Tube Cycle Shop
466 Madison Ave, Albany, 434-1711

Jerry's Bike Shop
463 Sand Creek Rd, Colonie, 869-7800

Kemp's Hockey Shop
Rte 9, Latham, 785-5279

Klarsfeld's Schwinn Cyclery
1370 Central, Ave Albany, 459-3272

Mike DeRossi Sports Inc.
1823 Western Ave, Albany, 456-7630
Hockey, lacrosse

Mountaineer
Rte 73 Keene Valley, 576-2281

Orvis
Rte 7, Manchester, Vermont (802) 362-3750
Fly fishing

Orvis Outlet
Union St, Manchester, Vermont (802) 362-3881
Fly fishing

Phoenix Ski Shop
1057 Troy Schenectady Rd, Latham, 785-0501
Ski equipment, hybrid and road bicycles

Ski Market
600 Troy Schenectady Rd, Latham, 785-5593
Ski equipment, bicycles, tennis racquets, car racks

Soccer Unlimited
1520 Rte 9, Clifton Park, 383-1026
391 Sand Creek Rd, Colonie, 458-8326

Taylor and Vadney
303 Central Ave, Albany, 472-9183
Hunting, fishing, camping

Tough Traveler
1476 State St, Schenectady, 393-0168
Stuyvesant Plaza, Albany, 438-1807
Well-known local manufacturers of luggage, back packs and carryalls for adults and children. Upscale outdoor clothing, camping, climbing and hiking equipment.

Stationery and Office Supplies

These shops have the best selection of items essential to make the office and the home function efficiently.

Compose Yourself
57 North Pearl St, Albany, 436-9882
Computer access studio, rent computers for in-store use, color and black and white

Gavit and Company Inc.
50 Trinity Pl, Albany, 434-1400
Fine engraved stationery, printing, thermography

Hill's Stationery
451 Broadway, Troy, 274-3191

Johnson Stationers Inc.
239 Delaware Ave, Delmar, 439-8166

Kinko's Copies
110 Wolf Rd, Albany, 482-9094
Fax, photocopy, in-house computer rentals, blueprint and poster copies, open 24 hours

Office Max
1814 Central Ave, Colonie, 452-3371
79 Wolf Rd, Colonie, 438-0086
Rtes 9 and 155, Latham, 783-0430
Discount

Paper Mill
Delaware Plaza, Delmar, 439-8123

Paper Cutter
19 Clifton Country Rd, Clifton Park, 383-4033
1892 Central Ave, Albany, 456-2296
Westgate Plaza 911 Central Ave, Albany, 482-1834
Mohawk Mall, Niskayuna, 370-0537

Schatz
Latham Circle Mall, Latham, 785-3550
Colonie Center, Albany, 459-7384
Greenbush Fair Shopping Center, East Greenbush, 477-7257

Toys
Duane's Toyland
Westgate Shopping Center, Albany, 482-8429
3901 State St, Schenectady, 393-7330

Toymaker
318 Delaware Ave, Delmar, 439-4880
595 New Loudon Rd, Latham, 783-9866

Toys R Us
38 Wolf Rd, Colonie, 459-5561

Iron Horse Gifts
Route 9, Latham, 785-3735

Miscellaneous Goods
The following four stores, all different in character, are worth noting.

Armadillo Games
2263 First St, Schenectady, 355-6517
Adventure games, board games, military and historical reference books

Backyard Birds
1481 Rte 9, Clifton Park, 383-4048
Everything pertaining to the backyard bird, seed, houses, baths, books, tapes

Knights Designer Fabrics
265 Osborne Rd, Albany, 482-9088
High quality apparel fabrics, patterns

Old Curiosity Shop
409 16th St, Watervliet, 273-1374
Magic tricks, supplies, lessons, books, magician for special occasions, retail and mail order

The Farmers' Market, Empire State Plaza

"Little Peasant" or "The First Grief " by Erastus Dow Palmer, Albany Institute of History and Art

MUSEUMS

The Museums and Historic House Museums presented in this chapter are within the Capital-Saratoga region. Other museums are covered in the chapter *Not Far Away.*

Albany Institute of History and Art, 125 Washington Ave, Albany, 463-4478, is the oldest museum in New York State and one of the oldest in the country, tracing its founding to 1791. This regional museum's collection focuses on the history, art, and culture of the Upper Hudson Valley and includes Hudson River School paintings, Albany-made silver, early portraits, and other decorative arts. There are changing exhibits throughout the year. The museum's facilities include the McKinney Library, a rich source for historical research, with a collection of over 50,000 manuscripts and documents. The Institute offers a wide range of educational programs, lectures, tours and art classes. There is a suggested donation for admission. Open: Tues-Fri 10-5, Sat-Sun 12-5. Closed Mon.

Crailo State Historic Site, 9 1/2 Riverside Ave, Rensselaer, 463-8738, was the house of the descendants of Kiliaen Van Rensselaer until the mid-19th century when it served as a school for boys and as a church rectory. It is now a New York State historic site and houses a museum on the history of Dutch culture in the Hudson River Valley. Free. Open: Apr-Dec Wed-Sat 10-5, Sun 1-5. Tours every half hour. Call for off-season hours.

Empire State Aerosciences Museum, 130 Saratoga Rd (Rte 50), Scotia, 377-2191, at the Schenectady County Airport is an educational facility presenting the aviation heritage of New York State and exploring the scientific principles of flight. It includes airplanes, models, dioramas, photos, and 'please touch' exhibits. Individual and family admission is free. There are special tours for groups. Open: Tues-Sat, 10-4.

Hall of History Foundation, in Schenectady is a non-profit volunteer organization dedicated to collecting and preserving the artifacts and the documentary heritage of the electrical industry. The collection includes over 600 artifacts, including turn-of-the-century appliances, photographs, and the private papers of noted investigators. The collection is housed in General Electric Building 28, 1 River Rd, Schenectady. Open: Mon and Thursday 10-4. Take the NY Thruway to Schenectady, then to I 890 to GE sign. Visitors must obtain a pass from the GE Main Reception, Building 3, before going to the Hall of History. GE Main Reception will provide directions to Building 28 and instructions for parking. For information, call 385-1104.

The Irish-American Heritage Museum, in East Durham in Greene County, NY, 634-7497, is dedicated to the preservation and promulgation of Irish-American culture. Its main exhibition space is in a renovated 1850s farmhouse in East Durham, which features exhibits on Irish-American history, art, language, music, literature, and dance. The museum also sponsors its research library in the College of St Rose. Library inquiries should be addressed to Mary Ann Lanni at the library, 454-5180. The main headquarters and offices for the museum are located at 19 Clinton Ave, Albany, 432-6598.

National Bottle Museum, Verbeck House 20 Church Ave, Ballston Spa, 885-7589, has a display of antique glass bottles, early glass making tools, and related items representing the 18th and 19th century industry of making bottles and jars by hand. The museum is housed in an 1889 Victorian mansion undergoing restoration. Open: 10-4 daily from June to Oct, and weekdays from Oct to June. Fee.

The National Museum of Racing, Union Ave, Saratoga Springs, 584-0400, is entertaining for the entire family. On display are such artifacts from thoroughbred racing as trophies, portraits of great horses and famous owners, and the costumes and equipment of leading jockeys and renowned stables. The explanatory notes throughout the museum tell of the role of Saratoga in the growth of racing in America and describe the impact of various people of wealth on the sport. A gift shop with items pertaining to horses is in the museum. There is an admission charge. Open: Sept thru Apr, Tues-Sat 10-4, Sun 12-4:30; May-July 28, Mon-Sat 10-4:30, Sun 12-4:30; July 29-Aug 31 (racing season) Mon-Sun 9-5. Directions: Take Northway to Exit 14. Take Union Ave (Rte 9P) west to museum, which is opposite the Flat Track.

National Museum of Dance, South Broadway, Saratoga Springs, is described in the chapter The Arts.

Intriguing

Inspiring

Incomparable

Informative

Innovative

Join 'In'

Discover 200 years of the region's
treasures at the…

Albany Institute of History & Art

125 Washington Avenue
Albany, NY 12210 |518| 463-4478

The New York State Museum, Empire State Plaza, Albany, 474-5877 (474-5843 for group tour information), is dedicated to preserving and interpreting the natural and cultural history of New York State. Life-like human figures in realistic settings enhanced by video presentations and historic photographs allow visitors to step back in time and see how people lived in past centuries in the Empire State. Open: Daily 10-5, except Thanksgiving, Christmas and New Year's Day.

Adirondack Wilderness shows how humans have impacted on the region from a prehistoric wilderness 5,000 years ago to a major recreation area in the 20th century. Visitors experience the natural setting of wildlife and the impact of human settlements and industry through life-size dioramas that recreate moments from the past.

New York Metropolis shows the emergence of the city of New York from a forested island before the arrival of Europeans to a major world center of commerce, art, and finance. Visitors explore how human activities have transformed the natural harbor into a bustling port, open spaces into sky-scrapered canyons through dioramas which recreate memorable places like 19th century Delmonico's Restaurant, 18th century South St Sea Port, Chinatown, Broadway, Ellis Island and even Sesame St.

Birds of New York features mounted specimens of 170 species commonly found in New York State, all placed in environmental settings. The exhibit hall rings with the beautiful and melodic calls of New York's bird species.

Upstate New York, Native Peoples of New York features life- size recreations of the extinct Mastodont and New York's Native Peoples in realistic settings that take the visitor back thousands of years to the Ice Age and before European contact in New York State.

Fire Fighting Exhibit features old and rare fire-fighting apparatus from the perilous world of the fire fighters. Included are several fully restored antique fire trucks and fire fighting equipment.

Bitter Hope: From Holocaust to Haven documents the story of 982 Jewish refugees given temporary haven in Oswego, New York, from the terrors of Hitler's Nazi war machine during World War II.

Dinosaur Discovery Center features puzzles, computers, stencils, books, fossils, models and more for hands-on fun and learning for the whole family. Parents and children ages 3 to 12 can enjoy exploring the wonders of science and prehistory together in this interactive exhibit. Saturdays and Sun 10-4:30; Mon-Fri 2:30 to 4:30.

Changing Exhibits Changing exhibits feature highlights from the Museum's own extensive collections of historic and scientific treasures of New York State, as well as fine arts and crafts from museums and collections throughout the country.

Special Programs Outstanding programs feature hands-on activities for youngsters and adults, as well as lectures, workshops, films and more for all ages and tastes. For more information on programs call 474-5842.

Pharmacy Museum, located in the Albany College of Pharmacy, 106 New Scotland Ave, Albany, is an authentic restoration of a nineteenth century drug store moved to Albany from Schoharie. Visitors can look through the store window to see the original fixtures and setting, including the stove, cuspidor, labeled drawers with porcelain pulls where herbs and medicines were stored, pharmacy posters, and glass bottles. Open: Mon-Fri, 9-4. Call 445-7211.

Rensselaer County Junior Museum, corner Fifth Ave and 106th St North Troy, 235-2120, is a wonderful little spot. Permanent collections include snakes, "touch me" objects and a fascinating sand pendulum and visitors can launch into outer space by visiting the "Our Place in Space" exhibit. A small planetarium is housed downstairs in this converted firehouse, and temporary exhibits open from time to time. The Museum also sponsors a science festival, weekend workshops, and a Grafton Summer Program. Suggested donation. Open: Sat-Wed 1-5.

Saratoga Harness Hall of Fame, 352 Jefferson St, Saratoga Springs, 587-4210, traces the history of Saratoga's harness track through photographs from its beginnings in 1941. There is also a blacksmith room, a sulky room, a Hall of Fame and a reference library. Call for hours. Free.

Schenectady County Historical Society, 32 Washington Ave, Schenectady, 374-0263, is both a museum and a center of research. On display are artifacts of early life in the area—paintings, dolls, guns, costumes, furniture, and household goods. Of particular interest are the doll house which belonged to Governor Yates' family, the letter-books, notes, and memorabilia of electrical wizard Charles Steinmetz, and collections of beautiful objects of prominent Schenectady families over the years.

The Society houses books, manuscripts, maps, photos and recordings and invites the general public to do research on regional history. Over the years slide-tape programs have been developed which are available for use by individuals and groups. Suggested donation. Open: Mon-Fri 1-5. Closed holidays.

The Schenectady Museum and Planetarium, Nott Terrace Heights, Schenectady, 382-7890, features exhibits of science, technology, history and art as well as several annual events—the Crafts Festival, Festival of Nations and Museum Ball. The planetarium offers three public shows on Saturday and Sunday for a nominal fee: a show for young people, a constellation show, and a feature show. The museum has two shops. One is a traditional museum shop; the other offers juried arts and crafts by regional artists and craftspeople. Admission to museum free for members, minimal fee for non-members. Open: Tues-Fri 10-4:30; Sat-Sun 12-5. Directions: Rte 5 (State St) to downtown Schenectady. Turn right onto Nott Terrace, then turn right onto Nott Terrace Heights by the locomotive.

Scotia-Glenville Children's Museum, 102 North Ballston Ave, Scotia, 346-1764, is a travelling museum within a fifty mile radius of Schenectady featuring art, science, and local history. The museum's programs are offered to district schools, nursery schools, and day care centers. There is a fee.

Watervliet Arsenal Museum on Broadway (Rte 32) in Watervliet is housed in Major Mordecai's 1859 cast iron storehouse in Greek Revival style, a historic landmark. The museum features artifacts about cannon development and the history of the Arsenal. Free. Access for the handicapped. For scheduled tours call 266-5805.

HISTORIC HOUSE MUSEUMS

Cherry Hill, South Pearl St, Albany, 434-4791, is a charming colonial building built in 1787 by Philip Van Rensselaer and lived in by his family until 1963. It offers the visitor a rare opportunity to see the continuum of life in Albany for over two hundred years. As each generation passed, it handed down the possessions it had accumulated; thus the house acquired vast collections of furniture, portraits, china, documents, textiles and other items. The accumulation of belongings came to possess a great deal of interesting variety and historic value. When Emily W. Rankin, the last member of the family, died in 1963, she left the house and its contents to Historic Cherry Hill, which opened the museum in 1964. The visitor will enjoy the warm, inviting atmosphere of this pleasant museum. On a Sunday early in December the house is decorated with family ornaments and toys, and refreshments made from family recipes are served. Admission. Open: Tues-Sat 10-3, Sun 1-3; closed in January and on some holidays. Tours on the hour.

Hart-Cluett Mansion, 59 Second St Troy, 272-7232, is owned by the Rensselaer County Historical Society. This late Federal style townhouse, built in 1827, has on display for the public an important collection of early 19th century furnishings and artifacts including works by Phyfe, Galusha, Hidley and Moore. Family and

Hart-Cluett Mansion, Troy

adult self-guided tours focus on the social history of urban living, including the roles of family members and household staff. The adjoining building houses changing exhibits, a museum shop, and a meeting room. The library holds maps, genealogical sources, broadsides, and photographs. Suggested donation. Open: (Museum, Shop, and Library) Tues-Sat 10-4.

Schuyler Mansion State Historic Site, Clinton St between Catherine St and Fourth Ave, Albany, 434-0834, is the once splendid home of Philip Schuyler, general in the Revolution. Known in its day as "The Pastures,"the brick building was once surrounded by ten to twelve acres of rolling lawns and carefully tended gardens through which strolled many heroes of the Revolution and "Patricians" of the era, most notably LaFayette and Alexander Hamilton, son-in-law of the general. Visitors may walk through the house, which contains beautiful furniture, a unique stairway, portraits and accessories of the time. Behind the building is an herb garden duplicating that once tended by the Schuylers. The visitor's center, next to the mansion, has an orientation exhibit. A parking lot is available behind the building. Free. Open: Apr-Oct Wed-Sat 10-5; Sun 1-5. (Phone for winter hours). Closed holidays except Memorial Day, Independence Day and Labor Day. Directions: Drive east on Madison Ave, turn right on Eagle St, left on Morton Ave, right on Elizabeth St and then left on Catherine St.

Ten Broeck Mansion, 9 Ten Broeck Pl, Albany, 436-9826, a beautiful home of the Federal period, was built as a residence for Abraham Ten Broeck and his wife Elizabeth Van Rensselaer in 1797-8. Ten Broeck was a member of the Colonial Assembly, a delegate to the Continental Congress, Brigadier General in the Revolutionary Army in the battle of Saratoga, member of the State Senate, mayor of Albany and first president of the Bank of Albany. The house, also called Arbor Hill, served for a short time as a boys' school and then was reconverted to a private home by the Olcott family, who occupied the house for four generations. In 1948 the Olcotts presented this lovely mansion to the Albany County Historical Association. Suggested donation. Open: Wed-Fri 2-4, Sat-Sun 1-4, Closed: Jan-Feb and holidays.

New York State Museum

"The Billboard" by George Segal, Empire State Plaza

THE ARTS

One of the most endearing characteristics of the Capital District is that in all the arts—music, theater, dance, art, and film—residents are welcome to produce their own work, to participate in an ensemble, or to serve as members of an audience. Throughout the year, local individuals and groups actively engage in creating artistic products, and season after season—with particular flamboyance in summer—internationally acclaimed artists come to display their talents. The visits are frequently short-lived, so the lover of the arts must be vigilant.

INFORMATION ABOUT THE ARTS

City of Albany Arts Commission works to promote and encourage the arts to flourish in the region.

Jazz Calendar for the Capital District is published every two months by A Place for Jazz, 1221 Wendell Ave, Schenectady 12208, 374-6912.

Local Newspapers offer detailed listings of cultural events each week. Refer to the newspaper listings in the Sources of Information chapter.

Mayor's Office of Special Events, (Albany) 60 Orange St, 434-2032, sponsors events and provides assistance with others including The Empire State Regatta, The Tulip Festival and First Night.

Arts Organizations

Albany-Schenectady League of Arts, 19 Clinton Ave, Albany, 449-5380, is a regional arts service organization which provides financial, legal, promotional, and administrative services to independent artists and art organizations as well as to the general community. It provides a bi-monthly calendar of events.

RCCA: The Arts Center, 189 Second St, Troy, 273-0552, is an arts advocacy organization which sponsors exhibits, a large selection of classes in the arts for adults and children, and a series of outreach programs for the disadvantaged and underserved.

Performing Arts Centers

Cohoes Music Hall, 58 Remsen St, Cohoes, dates back to 1874 and is one of the few pre-1900 American theatres in operation today. Seating 250 persons it is the home for Heritage Artists, performers of off-Broadway style musicals. Box office 235-7969.

Empire Center at the Egg is located at the Empire State Plaza between Madison Ave and State St. It houses the Kitty Carlisle Hart Theatre seating 950 persons and the Lewis A. Swyer Theatre, seating 450 persons. Box office 473-1845.

Knickerbocker Arena, 52 South Pearl St, Albany, is a 15,000 seat arena which hosts sporting events and is easily converted to traveling musicals, ice shows, circus performances and popular groups, including U2 and the Grateful Dead. Charge-by-phone 476-1000.

Palace Theater, Clinton Ave and North Pearl St, Albany, is a circa 1930 art deco, 2,900 seat performance center which formerly served as a vaudeville and movie house. Currently it is the home of the Albany Symphony Orchestra and the Berkshire Ballet and it also offers other concerts and fundraisers. Box office 465-4663.

Proctor's Theater, 432 State St, Schenectady, is beautifully restored and host to first rate events including Broadway shows, concerts, operas, dance groups and classic movie films. Subscription series and individual tickets. Box office 382-1083.

Saratoga Performing Arts Center, commonly referred to as SPAC, is located within beautiful Saratoga Spa State Park, Saratoga Springs. It has presented for over twenty-five years the fine performances of the New York City Opera in June, the New York City Ballet during July, and the Philadelphia Orchestra in August.

"Figures" by Mary Buckley, NYS Legislative Office Building

SPAC also hosts major popular musical performers throughout the summer. Tickets for seats at these performances often sell out hours after the box offices open, but there are thousands of lawn seats. These are held until the day of the performance unless the security forces anticipate that the demand will create a safety problem. At this point a ceiling is placed on lawn seats which are offered in advance. Over the years SPAC has earned a reputation for careful, thoughtful handling of crowds.

SPAC welcomes support through several levels of membership and rewards that participation by benefits, including advance mailing and priority ticket orders. It is also possible to request the season program and announcements by paying a small one-time fee to have your name placed on the Preferred Mailing List. Write SPAC, PML Saratoga Springs NY 12866. Information: 587-3330. Box office: 584-9330. Credit card charge: 584-7100.

Steamer #10, West Lawrence between Madison and Western Aves, Albany, produces and presents quality entertainment for children and families known as **Kids Fare** and for adults as **Live at Steamer #10.** The theater is in a renovated firehouse. 438-5503.

Troy Savings Bank Music Hall, 32 Second St over the Troy Savings Bank presents fine musicians from far and near to perform at this center. Box office 273-0038.

Tickets

Ticketmaster is a nation-wide computerized ticketing service with a number of ticket centers in the Capital District. For Ticketmaster site information call 427-0700. For charge by phone, call 476-1000.

Special Programs Embracing All the Arts

The Half Moon Cafe, which hosts readings, presentations, and musical performances, is described in the chapter Other Things to Do.

Institute for Arts in Education is a program for area teachers who want to include the arts in their teaching. Co-ordinated through the College of Humanities and Fine Arts of the University at Albany, SUNY, and run by an independent Board of Directors, the Institute's program includes two-week teacher workshops, performances, and artistic sessions in the classroom. Information available at Ten Broeck 107 Dutch Quad University at Albany 12222, or call 442-4240.

The Kennedy Center Imagination Celebration in Albany is one of ten regional Imagination Celebrations throughout New York State. The Albany celebration, encompassing eleven counties, includes the active participation of students, teachers, parents, artists, and members of the general public in providing experiences for youth in music, dance, theater, visual arts, poetry, storytelling, inventing, creative and journalistic writing, videography, holography, puppetry and magic. The celebration is usually held in the spring. For information, call the Cultural Education Center: 473-0823.

New York State Summer School of the Arts is a state-sponsored summer experience for students 14-18 years old. It consists of eight schools—visual arts, media studies, dance, ballet, jazz studies, orchestral studies, theater and choral study—each held on a campus within New York State. Information about programs and the application procedure is available at the State Education Department (Room 685) Albany 12234, 474-8773.

Tri-State Center for the Arts, Box 712 Pine Plains 12567, 398-7528 or (203) 364-5626, a community-based organization with the goal of advancing the performing and visual arts, is made up of professional and local talent, including high school students. The group sponsors theater productions in the summer and workshops throughout the year. The Center recently obtained a building for a permanent home from the Carvel Foundaton.

MUSIC

Orchestras

The Albany Symphony Orchestra offers a fine program each year, including various subscription series at the Palace Theater and at Troy Savings Bank Music Hall. Information is available at 465-4755. Tickets can be purchased at the Palace or by mail—Albany Symphony Orchestra, 19 Clinton Ave Albany 12207. The orchestra is assisted by an auxiliary group, Albany Vanguard.

The Boston Symphony makes its summer home in Lenox, Massachusetts, a renowned center of music education. Concerts of the full orchestra are conducted generally on weekends. Saturday morning rehearsals are open for an admission fee. During the week, performances by music students of the Tanglewood Music Center—a school for talented young musicians from all over the world—are scheduled, along with contemporary music concerts, and popular artists concerts. There is also a weekend of jazz, and a Boston Pops concert.

The full BSO summer calendar is printed mid-Spring in the arts section of The New York Times or may be obtained before June 1 through Symphony Hall, Boston, Massachusetts 02115 and subsequently through The Box Office, Tanglewood, Lenox, Massachusetts 01234, (413) 637-1940. Lawn seats are available and picnicking is something of a tradition. There is a gift shop and an excellent music store on the grounds. Beverages and food are also available. Tickets are available at the box office or by phone and charge at Ticketmaster (1-800-347-0808 or 476-1000). On the day of a concert children under twelve may get free lawn tickets.

Empire State Youth Orchestra, founded in 1979, is made up of talented musicians through high school age from the greater Capital District Region. The orchestra plays regularly scheduled concerts in Albany, Troy, and Schenectady and travels to other cities for festivals and performances. The Youth Orchestra also sponsors the Empire State Chamber Orchestra, Empire State Repertory Orchestra, Empire State Percussion Ensemble, and the Empire State Jazz Ensemble. The Youth Orchestra has been so successful that **The Junior Orchestra** was formed in 1981 to accommodate more players and to serve as a training ground for the Youth Orchestra. Both are funded by private donations. Auditions are held yearly. Information about all the activities of these groups is available at **ESYO,** 432 State St, Suite 217, Proctor's Theatre, Schenectady, 12305, 382-7581.

The Philadelphia Orchestra makes its summer home at the Saratoga Performing Arts Center. This orchestra is internationally acclaimed for its extraordinary discipline and cohesion. The program is available in early spring at SPAC Saratoga Springs 12866, 587-3330.

Tickets are available at the box office, either in person, by mail or by telephone if using a credit card, 584-7100, or at Ticketmaster locations. Children under twelve are admitted without charge to the lawn for most concerts; these tickets are available at the Box Office two hours before the concert. Regular lawn seats are available at the time of, or in advance of the performance. Because of the coolness of evenings, those selecting lawn seating should dress warmly.

Schenectady Symphony Orchestra is a community orchestra which annually presents four full concerts and one children's concert at Proctor's Theater. The League of the Schenectady Symphony, a volunteer agency, holds previews, sponsors the children's concert, and helps to raise money for the orchestra and for a musical scholarship. Information is available at 111 South Church St, Schenectady, 372-2500.

St. Cecilia Orchestra, founded in 1987 and made up of local musicians, sponsors three subscription concerts a year, playing each performance at four locations: Canfield Casino in Saratoga, Chancellor's Hall in Albany, Troy Savings Bank Music Hall in Troy, and Union College Memorial Chapel in Schenectady. In addition to the concert series, the orchestra accompanies area choruses and works as collaborators with other performing groups. For information, call 346-7996 or 433-9513.

Chamber Music

Capitol Chamber Artists present about 25 performances each year in concert halls throughout the region. Albany and Troy performances take place at the Troy Savings Bank Music Hall. The members design programs deliberately mixing new and old, well-known and unknown. Subscriptions are welcome. Information is available at 263 Manning Blvd Albany, 458-9231.

Friends of Chamber Music Inc in Troy has delighted music lovers for over 40 years by offering well-known chamber ensembles in concert six times each year. The performances are given in Kiggins Hall at Emma Willard School, 285 Pawling Ave, (Rte 66), Troy. Information is available at 274-2098.

International Festival of Chamber Music, sponsored by the Schenectady Museum and Union College, presents concerts featuring some of the most renowned ensembles in chamber music. Performances are given in the lovely Union College Memorial Chapel. Tickets are available at the door on the night of the concert; subscriptions and single tickets are available through Schenectady Museum, Nott Terrace Heights Schenectady 12308, 382-7890.

L'Ensemble, Suite 508 11 North Pearl St, Albany, 436-5321, is a core group of local musical artists who perform less frequently offered works of chamber music. The group presents a series of concerts at the Albany City Arts Building at the corner of Chapel and Orange Sts, Albany, and a summer series at the L'Ensemble Chamber Music Center, Rte 22, Cambridge, 677-5455. Directions: Rte 7 east to Rte 22 north. The center is two miles north of the village. The trip takes about an hour from Albany. The summer concerts are informal. Light suppers and brunches with the artists are available.

Renaissance Musical Arts Ltd., presents concerts during the year with musicians from major orchestras and music schools, and hosts lecture series on selected composers and their music. Money raised through these endeavors supports a scholarship program for area students to attend The Boston University Tanglewood Institute. All events are open to the public. 46 Holmes Dale, Albany, 482-5334 or 449-1217.

Concert Series

Music at Noon at the Troy Savings Bank Music Hall, 32 Second St, 273-0038, sponsored by the Troy Savings Bank Music Hall Corporation, is a monthly series on the second Tuesday of the month, September through June. Admission is free.

Music at the Hall series, at the Troy Savings Bank Music Hall, 32 Second St, 273-0073, sponsored by the Troy Savings Bank Music Hall Corporation, promotes jazz, ethnic, folk and classical music.

Siena College Music Series presents concerts of vocal and instrumental artists performing solo or in small groups. Information about these on-campus concerts is available through Siena College, 783-2300.

Troy Chromatics Concerts is a series of four superior musical performances scheduled throughout the fall, winter, and spring. The acoustically superb Troy Savings Bank Music Hall, State and Second Sts, Troy, functions as a stage for the concerts. Information and subscriptions available: P.O. Box 1574, Troy 12181 or call 235-3000 or 273-0038.

Choral Music

Albany Pro Musica is a semi-professional community chorus specializing in repertory for choir, especially Baroque, Romantic, and Contemporary. The group presents three major concerts a year. Information is available at 228 Placid Drive Schenectady, 12303 or call 356-9155.

Burnt Hills Oratorio Society, Box 76, Burnt Hills, 12027, a choral group that has been in existence for over twenty-one years, is open to those interested, without audition. It is a group of mixed singers—with a cross-section of talent and age—who want to learn and enjoy music. There are two sessions each year; September-November, and January-May. Two concerts of serious choral music, sometimes with orchestral accompaniment, are held each year in southern Saratoga and northern Schenectady counties. For information, call Rand Reeves at 885-5472.

Capital Hill Choral Society, a community chorus, presents concerts of classical choral music each year. Tryouts for new members are advertised in the newspaper. For information call Virginia Bowers at 463-7022 evenings or write Box 64 Albany 12201.

Mendelssohn Club of Albany is an all male glee club with singers from the larger Capital District. Formed in 1909, it presents performances of light music throughout the year at Chancellors' Hall. Information available at 395-8863.

Octavo Singers, established in Schenectady in 1933 as a community chorus, presents a minimum of three concerts a year—two with an orchestra. The group, composed of 80-100 vocalists, presents concerts of classical sacred music at Proctor's Theater or at Memorial Chapel on the campus of Union College. For information contact George Moross at 381-9444.

Schenectady Choral Society is a small community chorus of mixed voices which performs classical and contemporary works at two concerts a year. This organization, like so many of the other musical groups, has been in existence for more than half a century. Information is available at 377-7198.

Thursday Musical Club is a women's choral group which meets Wednesday mornings and sings classical and contemporary music, performing two concerts a year. No auditions necessary. Babysitting available. Call Judy Kilby 383-5399 for information.

Troy Musical Arts is a member chorus established in the Thirties as a women's choir. Since 1978 it has been a mixed chorus of male and female voices. One of their goals is to bring to their audience musical selections not usually performed by other groups or played on the radio. The society gives two or three concerts a year. For information call Terence Hegarty at 235-4772.

Opera

Glimmerglass Opera has become a major summer festival in the area. Performances are at the festival's Alice Busch Opera Theater, which itself is a distinctive architectural edifice. The theater is on Rte 80, two miles south of Rte 20, or eight miles north of Cooperstown. Tickets are available at the Opera Box Office, Mon-Sat 10-5, (607) 547-2255.

Lake George Opera Festival, which celebrated its thirtieth anniversary in 1991, is a July and August offering of operas performed in English at the festival auditorium and a musical cruise featuring selections from operas and musicals. Information is available from Lake George Opera Festival, P.O. Box 2172, Glens Falls 12801, Box office number: 793-3866. Directions: Take I-87N to Exit 19. Turn left onto Aviation Rd., Queensbury High School Auditorium is on right.

The New York City Opera in 1986 became the third company, along with the New York City Ballet and the Philadelphia Orchestra, to perform at SPAC in the summer. There are usually performances of two operas in the course of one week near the end of June. For information call SPAC, 587-3330. Tickets are available with credit cards by calling 584-7100 or at Ticketmaster locations. Children twelve years old and under are admitted free to the lawn for most performances. These tickets are available two hours before the performance.

Opera Excelsior, a regional repertory company performs main stage opera for adults using local talent. Their program for children serves the area schools by educating young children about opera through works with themes such as drugs and safety. For information call 372-4278 or write Box 3543 Executive Park Tower, Albany 12203.

WAMC (90.3 FM) broadcasts the Metropolitan Opera live on Saturday at 2:00 during the season.

Organ Music

Cathedral of All Saints, Swan St at the corner of Elk in Albany, presents concerts at 4:30 each Sunday November-April (except at Easter). There is no charge for admission.

First Methodist Church, 603 State St, Schenectady, 374-4403 sponsors three or four free public concerts by virtuoso organists. Receptions with the organists follow.

First Presbyterian Church, Glens Falls, 793-2521, hopes to have its newly installed large Reuter pipe organ—with 7,000 pipes, two consoles, four manual, 120 ranks—used as a concert instrument for the community.

The King of Instruments Concerts sponsored by the Eastern NY Chapter of the American Guild of Organists brings organists of national and international prominence to perform on the best instruments in the area. Recitals occur at different places throughout the year. For information call 861-5370.

Proctor's Theater puts its Golub Mighty Wurlitzer Organ to use throughout the year with live accompaniment to silent films, organ concerts and lively sing-a-longs.

The Round Lake Organ, an 1847 Ferris Tracker pipe organ located in the Round Lake Auditorium, is an historical artifact as well as an extraordinary musical instrument. Each summer the Round Lake Historical Society sponsors recitals Sunday evenings during July and August. Information is available at 899-5726. Directions: (I-87N) to Exit 11. Go one half mile east to Round Lake.

St Peter's Episcopal Church, 107 State St, Albany, 434-3502, offers organ concerts for one half hour at noon on Fridays from Sept-May.

Other Items of Interest Regarding Music

A Place for Jazz, 1221 Wendell Ave, Schenectady, is an organization with two goals: to enlarge the audiences for jazz—a synthesis of African and European musical traditions, and to support jazz musicians in the area. The organization sponsors a concert series in the fall at the First Unitarian Society in Schenectady and year-round lectures and workshops in schools. For information, Call Butch Conn, 374-6912.

Caffe Lena is described in the chapter Other Things to Do.

Capitaland Chorus of Sweet Adelines International is a non-profit eighty member award-winning chorus of women who sing barbershop style in four-part harmony. They perform at many public functions. New members are welcome. There is an annual dues for members. The group rehearses weekly at the Redeeming Love Gospel Church, 42 Woodward Ave, Troy. For more information, call 237-4384.

The Carillon in Albany's City Hall has an interesting history described by William Gorham Rice in a booklet, "The Albany Singing Tower," available in the McKinney Library. Most of the sixty bells are named after their donors, and many bear inscriptions such as that on bell thirty-eight—

O Albany! O Albany!
Far fairer city shall you see
Yet non that seems so fair to me.

The bells of the carillon chime gallantly over the city each noon.

Eighth Step Coffee House is described in the chapter Other Things to Do.

Luzerne Music Center is a summer program for youth ages 11-19. It combines supervised recreational activities with serious study of music. Orchestra, chamber music, and theory are taught by members of the Philadelphia Orchestra and faculty from area colleges. Recreation is supervised by students from major music schools or graduate music students who are skilled in sports or recreation. Student campers prepare to perform, either alone or in ensemble. They watch members of the Philadelphia Orchestra rehearse and perform. Public concerts by students, faculty, Philadelphia Orchestra members, and free-lance professionals are held Fri, Sat, Sun, and Mon. Information is available from Apr 15-Sept 1 at P.O. Box 35, Lake Luzerne, NY 12846, or call 566-1475; and from Sept. 1-April 15 at 4739 Harvest Bend, Sarasota, Florida 34235, or call 800-874-3202.

Monday Musical Club has been a viable factor in the community since 1903 when it was formed as a "forum for the enjoyment of music." The society sponsors workshops at which members preside, holds member artist performances, supports a women's chorus, and sponsors a young musicians forum for High School students studying voice or instrument. Information is available from Nancy Frank at 438-3735.

Schenectady Etude Club is a group of women from the tri-city area, well-trained in music, who are interested in performing at monthly meetings or at public events. Membership is open for instrumentalists and vocalists by audition only. Information is available from Lillian Roe at 374-8705.

WAMC (90.3 FM and with a booster signal at 89.9 FM) is a listener-supported station affiliated with National Public Radio. Its principal focus is classical music with some jazz, folk, and opera (as well as strong news, commentary and arts features).

WMHT (89.9 FM) is a listener-supported station devoted to continuous classical music. Members receive a monthly program and may participate in the listener request program each Saturday.

THEATER

Albany Civic Theater, 235 Second Ave, Albany, 462-1297, resides in a converted turn of the century fire house. In this intimate theater all seats are orchestra seats, and every audience member can appreciate fully the sounds and actions occurring on stage. The theater offers four productions each year. Each production is presented on Friday, Saturday, and Sunday for three weeks. Seats may be reserved by phone. Early reservations are suggested.

Capital Repertory Company is a professional resident theatre located at the Market Theatre, 111 North Pearl St, Albany. The annual program is ambitious and challenging; Capital Rep is a company willing to take risks. Each year's schedule includes at least one classic, one contemporary work, and a new play. Subscriptions are available for the full season, and patrons may arrange to sponsor particular performances or bring groups to the theater. The Company also makes attractive Before Theater dinner arrangements with various downtown restaurants. Information is available at 462-4531.

Heritage Artists Ltd, (HeArt), a non-profit arts organization founded in 1983 to revitalize and restore significant national landmarks and stimulate the cultural, educational and economic climates of regions, has taken as its principal enterprise the support of a professional music theater repertory company at the Cohoes Music Hall, a national landmark building. Subscriptions, group sales or tickets are available through the box office at 58 Remsen St, Cohoes, 235-7969.

Kupperberg Morris Movement Theater rehearses at the Performing Arts Loft, 286 Central Ave, Albany, 432-1639. The group creates works of movement theater, combining mime, dance, and clown theater. Further information can be obtained from Ann Morris at 674-8715.

The New York State Theatre Institute is an internationally acclaimed professional and educational regional theatre producing quality theatre for family audiences of the region and the state.

Proctor's Theater, Schenectady, hosts short runs of major theater productions by first rate road companies. The presentations, many of plays still running on Broadway, are excellent. In addition, it is fun being part of a large and appreciative audience in this grand old theater. Proctor's publishes its schedule in the spring for the season which runs from September to May. Tickets are sold at the box office. Information is available at 382-1083; tickets and information about season subscriptions are available at 346-6204.

Schenectady Civic Players is a community theater group celebrating in 1992 its 64th season. It mounts five varied productions annually, presenting seven performances of each offering. The players vary their material, taking on a range of types of plays and musicals. Tryouts for all roles are open to anyone interested in auditioning. Information is available at 12 South Church St Schenectady, 382-2081.

The New York State Theater Institute

Schenectady Light Opera Company is a volunteer group which produces four Broadway shows each year. Tryouts for all shows—open to the public—are advertised in the local papers. The company grants two awards each year to young members of the community who are aspiring singers. Information is available at 826 State St Schenectady, 393-5732.

Schenectady Theater for Children is a not for profit adult volunteer group dedicated to bringing professional quality theater to area children during the school day. It visits over 36 schools throughout the community and has the strong support of the Schenectady school system. Information may be obtained through the Schenectady Museum 382-7890.

Theater Voices mounts fully staged readings of quality but often neglected plays at the City Arts Building or at Steamer #10 at Madison and Western Aves in Albany. There are four free shows a year, with two weekend performances of each. For information, contact Eleanor Koblenz at 489-2086 or Judy Rettig at 439-6404.

Summer Theater

In June, July, and August the area hums with summer theater. The offerings are rich and varied and are available no matter which direction you go from the city.

Actors Shakespeare Company is a professional summer theater company which invites local actors, stage technicians, and other theater experts to develop and display their skill by presenting a rotating repertory of Shakespeare and other classics. The productions, usually two a summer, are presented out of doors on the parade grounds in Washington Park in Albany in July and August at 8 pm, Tuesdays through Sundays, free of charge. Information is available at 783-1971.

Albany Public Theater produces a single production of either contemporary or classic drama performed in July on Wednesdays through Sundays at 8 pm at the Academy of Holy Names, 1065 New Scotland Rd, Albany, in an outdoor, intimate setting.

Berkshire Theater Festival, East Main St, Stockbridge, Massachusetts, includes a main stage, the Unicorn theater in an adjacent building, and a children's theater in a tent, all in use from the last week of June to the last week of August. The main theater performances are traditional plays, usually four plays, one of which is a musical. The box office number, after June 1st, is (413) 298-5576 or (413) 298-5536.

The Little Theatre, Saratoga Performing Arts Center, offers a changing program each summer in drama, chamber music, and dance in a 500-seat theater. For information call 587-3330. For tickets with credit card charge, call 584-7100.

The Mac-Haydn Theater presents lively renderings of the most popular Broadway musicals from the past and the present. Plays are produced "in the round" in a rustic theater situated on a hill just outside Chatham. Also, musical adaptations of popular children's stories are performed for children of all ages on Friday and Saturday mornings in July and August. Tickets are reasonably priced. Information is available at the theater, Rte 203, Chatham 12037, 392-9292.

Park Playhouse Inc. provides free outdoor shows and musical entertainments each summer, Wednesdays through Sundays, at the Lake House in Washington Park. Information, 434-2032.

Shakespeare and Company, located at The Mount—Edith Wharton's home in Lenox, Massachusetts—is a summer theater company producing plays by Shakespeare, adaptations of works by Edith Wharton and Henry James, and other modern works. The Company uses two inside and two outside theaters and has extended its season into the fall and Christmas season.

The Mount, which is described in detail in the chapter "Not Far Away," offers tours in summer. For information call (413) 637-1197 or (413) 637-3353 for the Box Office.

Starlight Music Theatre, Latham, 783-9300, welcomes summer stock companies and a series of musical performers from June to September. Subscription prices are available.

Williamstown Theater Festival is considered one of the finest regional summer theaters in the East. This judgment is based on the nature of the plays undertaken as well as the quality of acting and directing. The theater has been the springboard of many famous theatrical figures, some of whom return each summer to contribute to the continuing excellence of the festival. Information and tickets are available at P.O. Box 517 Williamstown, Massachusetts 01267, (413) 597-3400.

DANCE

The Andrea Isaacs and Moving Images Dance Company, based in the Emma Willard School in Troy, came to the Capital District from Chicago in 1986. The company offers performances in various locations, lecture-demonstrations, workshops and classes, and features works which translate archetypal feelings into movement combining accomplished technique with spontaneous invention. For information, write the company at 285 Pawling Ave, Troy, 12180, or call 272-1557.

Berkshire Ballet Company performs regionally throughout the year. One of the highlights of the winter season is the Christmas presentation of THE NUT-CRACKER SUITE, for which the company recruits area students of the ballet to complement the regular ensemble. Programs and tickets are available through the Ballet, 25 Monroe St, 426-0660 or the Palace Theater.

Dance Behind the Scenes, National Museum of Dance, Saratoga Springs, 584-2225. Backstage tours for children 6-16 before and after matineee performances of NY City Ballet. Reservations required.

eba Center for Dance and Movement, eba Theater, 351 Hudson Ave Albany, 465-9916, offers classes for adults and children in ballet, jazz, modern dance and creative movements; there are also programs for health and fitness. The teachers are members of MAUDE BAUM AND COMPANY DANCE THEATRE, a resident professional touring dance company, which also performs locally.

Jacob's Pillow, Box 287 Lee, Massachusetts 01238, is a summer dance festival featuring major dance companies from around the country. As the oldest such festival in the country, Jacob's Pillow offers a wide spectrum of dance events and attracts some of the world's finest dancers. The performances are held in the Ted Shawn Theater, the first stage in America designed specifically for the dance. Schedules and reservations are available at the above address or at (413) 243-0745 after May 1. Directions: Take I-90 East to Massachusetts Turnpike. Take Turnpike

Berkshire Ballet Company

Exit 2. Take Rte 20E eight miles. Go left onto George Carter Rd. Theater is seven-tenths of a mile down this road.

The School of Dance at Jacob's Pillow, which functions during the festival, of-fers training in ballet, jazz, and modern dance for qualified students from around the country. Students live in rustic cabins and study with prominent artists. The schedule of the school runs concurrent with the dance festival, so students also have informal access to leading dancers. Auditions are held around the country in the spring. Call (413) 637-1322 for information.

National Museum of Dance South Broadway (Rt 9) Saratoga Springs, 584-2225, was conceived in 1984 to be headquartered in rehabilitated Washington Baths at Saratoga Spa State Park. The purpose of the museum is threefold: first, to estab-lish a center for the preservation and display of artifacts and memorabilia about dance; second, to make films, books, and records on the dance available to those studying this complex art form; third, to recognize outstanding contributions by principals in dance in the United States. The museum sponsors various displays, modern dance exhibitions, and master classes. It is under the direction of SPAC. The Lewis A. Swyer School for the Performing Arts—with three dance studios, is part of the Museum. There is a museum shop. The museum is open from May to October with a small admission charge. Memberships, which entitle free en-trance, are available.

The New York City Ballet takes up residence at SPAC, in Saratoga, during the month of July, presenting a mixed program which includes established favorites as well as world premiers of new or re-written works. The Corps is famous for its discipline, and among the principals are some of the world's greatest dancers. Much of the repertory derives from the work of its former director, the late George Balanchine. Children twelve years old and under are admitted free of charge to most performances; galas and matinees are not included. Tickets are available at the Box Office two hours before performances. For information, call SPAC at 587-3330; for tickets with credit card charge, call 584-7100.

ART

The Capital District has access to a wide variety of art collections, many of them located within easy traveling distance. They are described in the chapter "Not Far Away" and listed in the index.

Bennington Museum
Clark Art Institute
The Hyde Collection

Munson Williams Proctor Institute
Norman Rockwell Museum
Storm King Art Center
Wadsworth Atheneum
Williams College Museum of Art

(And, of course, the many superior museums of Boston and New York which are also listed in the chapter Not Far Away.)

Galleries

Albany Gallery, Stuyvesant Plaza, Albany, 482-5374, emphasizes American art, and specializes in Hudson River School, Impressionism and Modernist art.

Albany Center Galleries, 25 Monroe St (at the corner of Chapel St), Albany, 462-4775, is dedicated to presentation of the best of area artists in all media. Since its opening in 1977, the gallery has mounted 94 major comprehensive exhibitions. A non-profit enterprise supported by the City of Albany, local businesses and corporations, individuals, and sales, the gallery is a social gathering place, and is available for use for a variety of activities. Most works on display are available for purchase. Memberships and mailings available. Open: Mon-Sat 10-5:30, Sun 12-4, closed Sat. The gallery restaurant is open on weekdays from 11 to 2.

Bridge Gallery, Malden Bridge Art Center, Hoose Rd, Malden Bridge, 766-3616, hosts various exhibits in July and August, including that of the Malden Bridge Art League. Directions: I-90 East to Exit 12; turn right on Rte 9; go approximately one mile; turn left onto Rte 32; go five miles; turn left on Rte 66; take first left. (About one-half hour from Albany.) Open, Fri-Sun 12-5 and by appointment.

Dietle Gallery at Emma Willard School, 285 Pawling Ave, Troy, 274-4440, hosts ten exhibits from September to June of visual art by regional artists. Open daily 9-9, except school holidays.

Five Points Gallery, Sheridan House, Rte 295, East Chatham, 392-5202 focuses on artists living in Columbia County and the surrounding region. Open Tues-Sat, 12-5 by appointment. Directions: I-90 East to Exit 2B (Taconic Pkw and Rte 295); after toll about 100 yards take exit to right (Commercial traffic, to Rte 295); after 3/4 mile turn left on Rte 295; gallery is in center of East Chatham.

Greenhut Galleries, Stuyvesant Plaza, Albany, 482-1984, is a full service art gallery. As its primary function it displays and sells original works of art of regional and internationally known artists. It also offers a broad selection of art posters and reproductions, provides art investment counseling as well as corporate and

Tiffany Window, First Church in Albany

residential wall decor and space planning, and museum quality custom framing. They will send an expert to hang the works to insure that it is done appropriately.

McLean Gallery, 231 Lark St, Albany, open Tues-Fri 11-4, Sat 10-3 and by appointment, sells 19th and 20th century American and European paintings. The gallery specializes in Hudson River School, Post Impressionism, and Modernism.

The Nelson A. Rockefeller Empire State Plaza Art Collection is an assemblage of the art—paintings, sculptures and tapestries—of the New York State School from the 1960's and 1970's commissioned or chosen by a panel of experts appointed by the government of the State of New York. The stated purpose of the collection is to "symbolize the spirit of free inquiry and creative integrity which are so vital to modern society—the duty of governments everywhere to protect and promote the right of the creative individual to live and work in freedom." Owned by the citizens of New York State, they represent some of the most important American artists of the 20th century, many of whom lived and worked in New York State. Ninety-three of the works are on display throughout the parks, public spaces, and offices of the Plaza.

Each piece is well marked and annotated for both the casual visitor and for those interested in learning about contemporary arts via this extensive collection. The focal point of the collection is the newly installed Corning Tower Gallery, which highlights a selection of important New York State artists of this century. The Plaza level of the tower contains a sculpture gallery with works of David Smith, Louise Nevelson, and others. The Concourse level holds a collection of paintings, including those by Helen Frankenthaler, Franz Kline, Morris Louis, and Jackson Pollock. A catalog of the entire collection, prints, and postcards are available through Curatorial Services or at the NYS Museum Shop in the Cultural Education Center. A free pamphlet—The Empire State Collection—which also includes directions for approaching and parking at the Empire State Plaza and information on tours for individuals and groups and on the film series offered in the spring and fall is available at Curatorial Services, New York State Office of General Services, 29th Floor Room 2937 Corning Tower Empire State Plaza, Albany 12242, 473-7521. Tours, films, and lectures are scheduled throughout the year.

RCCA: The Arts Center, 189 Second St, Troy, 273-0552, sponsors exhibits of one person or group shows by artists from the region; work is largely experimental. Open Wed-Sat, 11-4.

Rice Gallery at the Albany Institute of History and Art, 135 Washington Ave, Albany, 463-4478, sponsors five yearly exhibitions of regional and New York State artists. It also has a sales/rental gallery. Open Tues-Sat, noon-5 during exhibitions.

University Art Gallery, Art Building, University at Albany, State University of New York, 1400 Washington Ave, Albany hosts exhibits of contemporary art in all media by artists throughout America, along with graduate theses and faculty exhibits. The skilled staff prepare handsome, helpful brochures and pamphlets to guide the visitor through the exhibits. To reach the gallery, drive into the University's main entrance on the Washington Ave side of the campus, park in the visitors' lot immediately south of the Collins Circle (the large grass plot), and walk onto the podium through the central opening (directly in front of the fountain and bell tower). The Art Building will be on your left. For information on exhibitions, openings, and tours call 442-4035. Usual hours: Tues-Fri 10-4, Thurs 10-8, Sat-Sun 1-4.

Exhibition Space

Several institutions provide exhibition space for artists' work.

Albany Institute of History and Art 463-4478
Art at the Boulevard Book Store 436-8848
College of St. Rose (at the Picotte Gallery) on State St in Albany 454-5185
Congregation Beth Israel Education Center in Schenectady 377-3700
Emma Willard School in Troy 274-4440
Key Corp Tower Lobby, Nacan Sculpture Court .463-4478
RCCA: The Arts Center in Troy 273-0552
Rensselaer Newman Foundation Chapel and
    Cultural Center at RPI in Troy 274-7793
Russell Sage College in Troy 270-2395
Sage Junior College (Rathbone Gallery) 445-1778
Schenectady Museum 382-7890
State Museum of New York in Albany 474-5877
Union College in Schenectady 370-6201

Art Classes and Clubs

In addition to the places described for patrons to view or purchase art, several centers cater to those who wish to learn more about art, and to develop their own artistic talents.

The Albany Artists Group, 455 State St, Albany, 463-8659, established and chartered in 1945, is a membership interested and involved in artistic pursuits, paintings, drawings and sculptures and in displaying these works. All members need not be working artists but should include those who are interested in the distribution and promotion of works of art, as well as art in general in our community. To join or for inquiries call the above number.

"Explorers Clubbing" at the Albany Institute of History and Art

The Albany Institute of History and Art Museum Art Classes,125 Washington Ave, Albany, 463-4478, serves adults and children by running various programs of instruction in art, crafts, and museum skills. Schedules of upcoming events are mailed to those who have placed their names on the mailing list.

Albany Print Club, Box 6578, Albany, 459-2674, founded in 1933, has commissioned a print each year since then by a nationally known artist for print club members. It has a permanent collection and sponsors a national print exhibit and public lectures.

Art Colonie, 215 Old Loudon Rd, Latham, 785-8220, offers lessons in oil painting and water color for children and adults.

The Malden Bridge School, described in the chapter "Not Far Away,"offers summer workshops in drawing and painting.

RCCA: The Arts Center, 189 Second St, Troy, 273-0552, sponsors workshops and classes in many art forms throughout the year.

Sage Summer Art, Sage Junior College, 140 New Scotland Ave, Albany, 445-1717 presents a summer art program in the month of July for students grades 9-12. Offerings include drawing, painting, photography, ceramics, 3-D sculpture, computer graphics and commercial art. Information is available at 445-1717.

Schenectady Museum, Nott Terrace Heights, Schenectady, 382-7890, offers arts and crafts instruction during two segments coinciding with the two semesters of the school year.

FILM

The Capital District now has dozens of screens showing the latest the American film industry has to offer. In addition to these theaters, all listed daily in local newspapers, are other cinemas and sources of films.

Scotia Cinema, 117 Mohawk Ave, Scotia, 346-5055 and **Madison Theater,** 1032 Madison Ave, Albany, 489-5431 offer second-run movies at inexpensive prices.

Spectrum Theater, 290 Delaware Ave, 449-8995 offers art, foreign, commercial, and independent films in four theaters. The theater publishes a monthly schedule. In addition to popcorn, candy, and soda, the concession offers coffee, tea, cake and ice cream. Call for movie information and show times.

In addition to the commercial movie houses, area film buffs can turn to several other sources.

The Council of Libraries has an impressive collection of 16mm films and VCR tapes available for home use for no charge to those who pay a small annual film-borrower fee. A catalog of their own film holdings is available at the main desk of the main branches of the public libraries as are the listings of other sources from whom films are available through interlibrary loan.

Area Colleges have film clubs which periodically show second run box office smashes, "golden oldies," or foreign films.

Proctor's, State St, Schenectady, runs film festivals periodically throughout the year. In summer, internationally respected virtuosos of theater organs bring life to classics of the silent screen by performing live on the Golub Mighty Wurlitzer Organ. In winter, film festivals featuring major stars or directors run whenever the theater is available. There is usually a film festival at Christmas time. Information is available at 382-1083.

Art Gallery, University at Albany, State University of New York

Knickerbocker Arena, Albany

SPORTS & RECREATION

The location of the Capital District at the confluence of two rivers (the Mohawk and the Hudson) and in the juncture of three mountain ranges (the Adirondacks, the Catskills, and the Berkshires) makes it a natural paradise for the lover of sport. The abundance of lakes, ponds, and rivers makes water sports—from sailing to ice fishing—possible year round. The hills and mountains allow for woodland sports—from hunting to snowshoeing—January to December. The Knickerbocker Arena provides the area with a large site for a variety of spectator sporting events. In addition, the fieldhouses, playing fields and gymnasiums of area colleges and universities serve as excellent arenas for area players and fans. Probably because of the long tradition of regional spectator and participant sports, area residents have also insisted that their civic parks and playgrounds be carefully tended. As a result, the system of state recreational sites in New York is extraordinary, the three area cities take justifiable pride in their beautifully landscaped, immensely enjoyable parks, and suburban towns continually upgrade their recreational facilities.

This chapter has two major parts. The first describes sports; the second deals with general recreation and use of the land. Throughout, emphasis is placed on facilities available to all citizens. Therefore, the excellent facilities maintained by suburban communities for their own residents are not described.

The Albany Foundation for Sports and Special Events, Inc. is a non-profit corporation designed to attract, promote, develop and sponsor amateur sports and other special events in the Capital Region. Housed at the offices of the Albany-Colonie Regional Chamber of Commerce, 540 Broadway, Albany, 434-1214, the foundation will assist in securing and staging statewide, regional and national sporting competitions and special events for the Capital District as well as serving as a liaison between organizational groups and promoters with the local entities that control the necessary facilities. Established in 1992 the Foundation will continue to work toward the common goal of increasing revenues and enhancing the image of Albany, Rensselaer, Schenectady and Saratoga counties.

SPORTS

Auto Racing

Fonda Speedway is a half-mile dirt track located on the Fonda Fairgrounds in Fonda, New York. The speedway features modified and street stock car racing every Saturday night from April to September. The schedule of specific events is available at P.O. Box 231, Fonda NY 12068, 853-4235. Directions: Thruway to Exit 28; 1/4 mile along Mohawk River.

Lebanon Valley Speedway and Dragway in West Lebanon, 794-9606 features stock car races every Saturday night from the end of April to the middle of September and drag races every Sunday from early April to late October. Special events (like demolition derbys) highlight the program occasionally, drawing enthusiastic spectators who love the tension, glamour, and noise. Directions: I-90 East to Exit 11 East; left on Rte 20; 11 miles to West Lebanon.

Baseball

Because the Capital District is equidistant from Fenway Park, Shea Stadium and Yankee Stadium, area fans used to fall into fairly even camps—Red Sox fanatics, Mets maniacs, and Yankee devotees. No more. In 1985, with a new Yankee farm team in town, the scale appears to be tipping in favor of the Bronx Bombers. The newcomers are the **Albany-Colonie Yankees,** an Eastern League minor league franchise. They play at the Heritage Park on Watervliet Shaker Rd (adjacent to the Albany County Airport).

In addition to taking pleasure watching professionals, area afficionados play the game themselves in a variety of leagues. Each city and town has Little League and Babe Ruth League ball and dozens of semi-organized sandlot groups. Information about these activities is available at the nearest city office of Parks and Recreation.

Basketball

The **Capital District Pontiacs,** a minor league affiliate of the New York Knickerbockers, is a community-supported team begun in 1981. The team's home court is at Knickerbocker Arena in Albany. Schedules, season tickets and individual tickets are available at the box office, 487-2000.

In addition to professional ball, the region is filled with superior college and high school play. Siena, SUNYA, and Union generally post winning seasons in seriously competitive leagues and combat each other fiercely in an annual Christmas tournament. The regional high school council pits the best area players against one another in play which draws enthusiastic fans throughout the season.

Biking

Bike paths in Albany, Colonie, Cohoes, Niskayuna, and Schenectady follow along the Mohawk and Hudson Rivers for forty-two miles, terminating in Rotterdam Junction. Signs mark the paths. Most of the paths are Class I; however, there are occasional detours onto paved streets.

The Town of Colonie guides peddlars along its section of the trail with an excellent booklet—complete with identification of flowers, birds and wildlife likely to be encountered. Call 783-2760.

The Uncle Sam Bikeway (Class I) in Troy runs through North Troy. It can be found by going east on 125th St and watching for signs.

The Hudson-Mohawk Wheelmen is a touring bicycle club. During the season it runs several rides each day on weekends and on some weekdays during the summer months. Weekend trips, a picnic, and a Century Weekend (100 mile event) are offered as well as quick, tour, and casual ride with varied pace and difficulty. Information is available at area bike shops and through Betty Lou Bailey, 4029 Georgetown, Schenectady, 12303, 355-0604, or call The Ride Line, 437-9579.

Boating

The Capital District is a haven for boating enthusiasts. Lake George and the Mohawk and Hudson Rivers accommodate sizeable vessels, and lakes suitable for small craft abound.

Boat launching sites are listed and described in a brochure free for the asking from the New York State Parks and Recreation Bureau, Empire State Plaza 12238, 474-0456.

Maps of New York State Inland Waterways are sold by the State Office of Parks and Recreation and Historic Preservation: CHARTS State Parks Albany, NY 12238, 874-0456.

Competitive rowing is described later in this chapter.

Bowling

The presence of over three dozen local bowling lanes testifies to the regional popularity of this year-round sport. Many of the facilities are reserved regularly for league bowling, so occasional bowlers should call ahead. Knowledgeable advice on the current bowling scene is available at Daubney's Bowling, Billiards, and Golf, 601 New Loudon Rd, Latham, 785-3555, or Albany Bowling Center, 104 Watervliet Ave, Albany, 438-4478.

Cricket

The Tri City Cricket Club, (formed from the Albany Cricket Club), founded in the early 1970's, is open to anyone who wishes to play cricket or learn about the game. The club, though not part of any formal league, hosts matches against opposing teams from throughout New York, Connecticut, Massachusetts, and Canada. Practices are scheduled regularly for 5:30 Friday afternoon from May through September, with games set for Saturdays and Sundays. Spectators are welcome at any time. The club welcomes Commonwealth citizens visiting our area to play any time. In addition to fielding its own team, the club conducts a clinic once a week, supervises exhibition matches, and runs a Cricket Field Day. All events take place at Cook's Park in Colonie. Information is available from Deochand Persaud, 456-8390, or Cecil King, 456-1879.

Curling

Curling, the game in which two teams of four players each slide special "stones" over a stretch of ice toward a circular target, is enthusiastically played and watched at two area centers:

Schenectady Curling Club, Balltown Rd, Schdy 372-4063
Albany Curling Club, McKown Rd, McKownville 456-6272

Fishing

Some of the best trout fishing in the country is found along the Battenkill, Kaydeross, and Kinderhook Creeks and the Ausable River. Salmon, small mouth bass, trout and pike can be fished from Lake George. Pike run in Saratoga Lake, and large mouth bass inhabit all major lakes in the area. For good advice about wise use of all facilities in the Catskills and Adirondacks, check Taylor-Vadney 303 Central Ave Albany, 472-9183 or Goldstock's 121 N. Broadway Schdy, 382-2037.

Superior advice, instruction, equipment and expert fishing "chat" are available at Orvis Co Inc, Manchester Vermont, (802) 362-3622. The experts here are renowned for their knowledge of fly-fishing techniques and equipment. They also provide a commentary on daily fishing conditions.

Football

Albany Firebirds, one of the twelve teams in the pro football Arena League, play at the Knickerbocker Arena drawing thousands of spectators to enjoy this indoor sport. Inquiries from 487-2222 or box office 476-1000.

The **Metro Mallers,** an Empire Football League team, play home games at Bleecker Stadium in Albany in a season running from July through October. Information about the team's schedule is available at 356-4417.

Area college and high schools field respectable teams in an intensely competitive Fall season of Saturday afternoon games.

Golf

In part because the Capital District enjoys such pleasant summers, golf thrives. Ardent enthusiasts swing their clubs on sunny April mornings and push the season well into October. As is the case elsewhere, a network of members-only clubs features the sport and hosts serious competition. In addition, the region maintains competitive public courses—some government sponsored, some run for profit. The following is a list of these courses, presented in alphabetical order.

Name	# Holes	Open	Shop	Rentals	Comments
The New Course at Albany New Scotland Ave 438-2208	18	dawn-dusk	yes	Clubs/ pullcart	Pro shop restaurant
Colonie Town 418 Consaul Rd Schdy. 374-4181	27	8 am-7 pm	yes	yes	
Eagle Crest Golf Club Rte 146A Ballston Lake 877-7082	18	dawn-dusk	yes	yes	Driving range

Name	# Holes	Open	Shop	Rentals	Comments
Frear Park Oakwood Ave Troy 270-4553	18	dawn-dusk	yes	yes	Putting green/ driving range
Hiawatha Trails State Farm Rd Guilderland 456-9512	18	7 am-dark	yes	yes	3 par
Schenectady Muni Oregon Ave Schenectady 382-5155	18	dawn-dusk	yes	yes	
Stadium 333 Jackson Schenectady 374-9104	18	dawn-dusk	yes	yes	
Sycamore Rte 143 Ravena 756-9555	18	dawn-dusk	yes	yes	Practice range/ putting green
Saratoga Spa Saratoga Spa St Pk Saratoga Springs 584-5006	27	7-7 weekdays 6-7 weekends	yes	yes	Championship park
Western Turnpike Rte 20 Guilderland 456-0786	27	dawn-dusk	yes	yes	Driving range/ putting green

Golf Driving Ranges

For those who enjoy swinging a club for a short time and sharpening their drives, a bucket of balls is available at a number of area driving ranges:

Clifton Park Driving Range
1759 Rte 9, Clifton Park, 371-3112

Evergreen Country Club
1400 Schuuman Rd, Castleton, 477-6224

Hoffman's Playland
Rte 9, Latham, 785-3842

Mill Road Acres Golf Course
30 Mill Rd, Latham, 785-4653

Saratoga Spa State Park
Rtes 9 or 50, Saratoga, 584-2006

Stadium Golf Course
333 Jackson Ave, Schenectady, 374-9104

Horseracing

Harness Racing

Saratoga Harness Track hosts trotters Mon-Sat from mid-April to mid-November, and Thurs-Sat from January to March. The track has a comfortable enclosed grandstand and a pleasant dining room. Post time is 8:00, but the grandstands and restaurant open at six. For dining room reservations, the number is 584-2110. Directions: Northway (87) to Exit 13N; Rt 9N to second blinker; turn right and follow signs.

Thoroughbred Racing

Saratoga Race Track, the nation's oldest track, merits the lavish praise it receives. The splendour of the grounds, the accessibility of the paddocks, and the pervasiveness of tradition make a visit to the track an exciting and pleasurable experience. Races are held from the end of July to the end of August (closed Tuesdays), featured events being the eighth race on Saturday. The first of nine races begins at 1:00. Call 584-6200 for information. Even those who do not like to bet will enjoy spending an afternoon watching magnificent animals, proficient jockeys, and unpredictable spectators.

In addition to the actual racecard events, Saratoga's morning activities provide a source of interest and pleasure. From 7:30 to 9:30 each morning, there are starting gate demonstrations, backstretch tours, and paddock talks open to all. Near the finish line, visitors may listen as an expert comments on the lineage, performance record, and idiosyncracies of each horse taking morning warm-up on the track. Afterwards, lectures on horse care and betting techniques are given. (Those who visit the track at this early hour must then exit and re-enter for the day's races.)

Saratoga Flat Track

Patrons may have breakfast at the track while enjoying the morning workout. Information about this is in the chapter on Restaurants.

Horseback Riding

A surprising number of area residents train, maintain, and show horses. Most stables which board horses also make several of their own available for public use with instruction. All the stables listed below offer boarding services and riding lessons (English saddle) for adults and children. Some run summer programs.

Dutch Manor
2331 Western Ave, Guilderland, 456-5010

Horsemen's Choice
5940 Veeder Rd, Slingerlands, 869-1196

Pine Bush Equestrian Club
175 Rapp Rd, Albany, 452-7755

Rolling Meadows Farm
White Rd, Ballston Spa, 885-1655

Hot Air Ballooning

Two regional centers provide rides, lessons, or equipment for this thrilling sport. **Adirondack Balloon Flights** (P.O. Box 65 Glens Falls; 1-793-6342) offers 45 minute to one hour journeys in a valley between the Adirondack Mountains and the Green Mountains every day from May through October. **Fantasy Balloon Flights,** 3 Evergreen Ln, Middleton, at Randall Airport, (914-856-7103). Daily April-December. This company also sponsors **Bungee Jumping,** a free fall from a hot air balloon (800-3Bungee). **Spacious Skies Balloon Co.,** Schenectady, 356-0954, offers gift certificates, personal instruction, and scenic rides over Balloon Meadows in Valatie as well as the Burnt Hills area.

On the third weekend in September, hot air balloon enthusiasts (spectators as well as flyers) gather for a festival at Warren County Airport, Glens Falls. The assemblage of colorful balloons floating gracefully above the field makes a wonderful backdrop for picnics and family gatherings.

Hunting

Experts at Taylor-Vadney 303 Central Ave, Albany, 472-9183, and Goldstock, 121 N. Broadway, Schenectady, 382-2037, can provide up-to-date information about seasons and regions for those who enjoy hunting animals with weapons.

The genteel sport of pursuing dogs who are in turn pursuing another animal is organized by two groups: the traditional mounted English fox hunt is conducted with great flourish by the Old Chatham Hunt Club, the oldest fox hunting club in the country. (The hunt is open to members.) Kindred spirits, the members of the Old Chatham Beagle Hunt Club, engage in beagling adventures—mad chases on foot after beagles pursuing rabbits. (This hunt, too, is open only to members.)

Lacrosse

The **Mohawk Lacrosse Club** organizes a league which uses the playing fields of University at Albany (SUNY) for its summer schedule. The newspapers report on recruiting and playing activities. Information may be obtained from Mike DeRossi Sports, 1823 Western Ave, Albany, 456-7630, and Anaconda-Kaye Sports, 440 State St, Schenectady, 382-2061.

Ice Hockey

Hockey is an intensely popular winter sport in the area. On the professional level, the **Adirondack Red Wings,** an NHL team, make their home at the Glens Falls Civic Center. The **Capital District Islanders,** a farm team for the New York Islanders of the National Hockey League, play forty of its seasons total of eighty

Hot Air Ballooning, Lincoln Park, Albany

games at home at the Houston Field House on the Rensselaer campus in Troy. Information: 272-6262.

On the college level, RPI and Union put excellent teams on the ice.

A 40,000 square foot Albany County facility serves as home ice for the US Olympic team, located on Albany Shaker Rd across from the Albany airport. A multi-purpose facility, it is used for public skating, speed and figure skating, and other hockey events such as youth hockey. Public skating is encouraged. Open daily. Information available by calling the Albany County Hockey Training Facility, 452-7396.

Youth Leagues

Capital Youth Hockey Association, 237-5528 or 785-7796, open to players four to seventeen years old, sponsors playing and training at the Albany County Hockey Training Facility on Albany Shaker Rd.

Schenectady Youth Hockey Association, 355-3538, sponsors learn to skate, house league, and travel team programs which are available to youths from three to sixteen years of age.

Troy Youth Hockey Association, with an 800 youth membership, practices and plays in Troy at Frear Park rink 270-4557 and at the Knickerbacker Facility Rink 235-0113 and at the rink at the Albany Academy.

Adult Leagues

Clifton Park Old-Timers Hockey Club, 756-8258 or 439-5714, is for players forty-five years and older, and plays recreational hockey—with non-checking and no slaps—beginning each November at the Clifton Park Arena on Tuesday and Thursday nights.

Hudson Valley Hockey League, made up of varied age groups, play pick-up games at the Frear Park Rink and Knickerbacker Facility in Troy.

Mohawk Valley Hockey League, 393-9719 or 583-3913, is a men's non-checking league.

In addition to these formally organized leagues, there is fine pick-up hockey played wherever amateurs find a bit of frozen water during December and January. Many town and city custodians mark off areas on ponds described in the section on iceskating to protect recreational skaters from injury should they intrude on the fast paced play of these games.

Ice Skating

Ice skating is an increasingly popular winter sport in the area, and facilities are expanding to keep pace with the demand.

Artificial Ice is maintained at the following sites, listed in alphabetical order:

Name	Open	Comments
Achilles Rink Union College Schdy 370-6134	Oct-Mar M-Sat 1-3 Sun 1-2:30; 3-4:30	Faculty and students only
Albany County Hockey **and Team USA Facility** Albany-Shaker Rd 452-7396	Mon-Fri 11 am-1 pm Mon, Wed, Thur, Fri 8-10 pm Sat-Sun 12-2 pm, 3-5 pm Sun 7:30-9:30 pm	Training room No skate rental
Center City Rink 433 State St Schdy 382-5104	Oct 15-Mar 31 Mon-Sat noon-1:30 Thur-Fri 7-8:30 Sat 3:30-5 & 10-11:30 Sun 3:30-5	Rentals available Lessons and programs Weekend parking in rear
Frear Park Rink Park Blvd Troy 270-4557 (rink) 270-4553 (shop)	Nov 1-Mar 31 Call for hours	Rentals Instruction Sharpening
Houston Field House RPI Peoples and Burdett Ave Troy 276-6262	Depends on practice schedule of team Call for info	Rentals
Knickerbacker **Recreational Facility** 103rd St and Eighth Ave Lansingburg 235-7761	Year round	Rentals
Saratoga Springs **Youth Community Rink** Excelsior and East Ave 587-3550	Oct thru March Call for information	Figure Skating Club Winner Speed Skating Club Adult Hockey Club May be reserved

Name	Open	Comments
Swinburne Park Clinton Ave at Manning Blvd Alb 438-2406 (rink) 438-2447 (office)	Nov thru March Call for information Th 10-12 for Senior Citizens	May be reserved for parties Rentals
Veterans' Memorial 2nd Ave & 13th St Watervliet 270-3824	M-F 12-4:30 Sat 12-2; 9:30 -11 for adults Sun 3-6	No rentals

Natural Ice at the following areas is tested for safety and plowed:

Albany:
Buckingham Pond (also called Rath's Pond) at Berkshire Blvd between Western and New Scotland Aves off Euclid.

Washington Park Lake on the south side of Washington Park.

Colonie:
Colonie maintains 14 natural skating sites. Ann Lee Pond, adjacent to the Albany County Airport, is one of the best in the area. For information and conditions for all Colonie sites, call 785-4301.

Loudonville/Menands:
Little's Lake, Van Rensselaer Blvd near Menands Rd (Rte 378).

Saratoga:
Two rinks (recreational and hockey) at Saratoga Spa State Park. Open Mid-Nov to Mid-Mar. Lighted at night. Free. Rentals and sharpening are available at recreational rink. For information call 584-2535.

Schenectady:
Iroquois Lake in Central Park and Steinmetz Lake in Steinmetz Park (near Lenox Rd).

Troy:
Beldon's Pond, near the junction of Rtes 2 and 66; and Knickerbacker Park at 103rd St and 8th Ave

Mountain Climbing

Adirondack Mountain Club, founded in 1922, has approximately 18,000 members and twenty-eight chapters. The Albany chapter, its largest with 1200 members, offers varied activities throughout the year, including trips, and seminars on wilderness skills, backpacking, and map and compass usage. Members receive the quarterly magazine, *The Cloud Splitter.* The group participates in volunteer effort in support of trail maintenance, wilderness cleanup, and in support of conservation efforts, especially as they relate to New York State wilderness areas. Monthly meetings are held in October through June on the second Tuesday of each month. For further information, call 899-2725.

Parasailing

In this exciting new sport, bold novices sail hundreds of feet above a body of water, held aloft by a parachute drawn by a motorboat. The sensation is gripping, the view spectacular. Rides are available May 15 through October 15, 9 am to dark, weather permitting. There are three parasailing companies on Lake George: **National Watersports** and **Watersports,** located in the village and **Sun Sports Unlimited in** Bolton Landing. **Aqua Sports Plus** is located on Saratoga Lake. Details are available at Information Centers.

Polo

Polo is a serious sport in the Capital District. Two organizations maintain facilities and supervise competition:

Saratoga Polo Associations Ltd., P.O. Box 821 Saratoga Springs, presents some of the best high goal polo in the world during the month of August. Top players from England, Argentina, and the U.S. contend in sponsored cup matches. The association welcomes spectators and encourages them by having the narrator explain the sport throughout play. The matches are played on fields famous for their quality. (From 1901-1935, the sport was popular in the area. Then it declined. In 1978 the field was redone and polo promoted once more.) Matches—which last about 1 1/2 hours—are played on Tuesdays, Fridays and Sundays at 5:30. Local newspapers note any variation in schedule. Picnic facilities are available.

Owl Creek Polo Club, 123 Hetcheltown Rd, Glenville, 399-4804, was established in 1966 by Paul Kant. It is the only year-round polo club within 200 miles of the Capital District. Lessons in the sport are held regularly. Practice on Tuesday and Thursday at 5pm. Games played on Saturday at 3 pm and Sunday at 1 pm.

Rafting

Adirondack Wildwaters Inc., Box 801, Corinth, offers rafting on the Hudson River Gorge and the Sacandaga River. There are two levels:

For high adventure (passengers must be 15 or older), rafting during spring runoff (April and May) starts at Indian Lake.

For pleasant family outings in summer (passengers must be 9 or older), rafting starts at Lake Luzerne. The numbers to call for information are: summer 696-2953; winter 654-2640.

Hudson River Rafting Co., Rte 28 North Creek (just before south entrance to North Creek, at Cunningham's Ski Barn), offers rafting on the Hudson River Gorge from the first weekend in April through the first weekend in June. The 17 mile trip takes from four to five hours. It is open to rafters age 12 and up. In summer, this company runs rafts on the Sacandaga River and the Black River at Watertown. Information is available at 251-3215 or 251-2466.

Roller Skating

Residents of the Capital District have taken the 50's sidewalk sport and converted it into a challenging entertainment practiced indoors and out. The following is an alphabetical list of centers for skating.

Guptill Arena Inc, Rte 9, Latham, 785-0660, the largest indoor arena in the area, hosted skaters long before the coming of the modern vinyl- wheeled skate. Open W-Sun, Guptill's offers a wide variety of skating programs. Musical accompaniment may include live organ selections as well as top 40, disco and rock. Adjacent to the arena is a disco with a lighted dance floor. Information on programs and parties is available at 785-4214.

Rollerama, 2710 Hamburg St Schenectady, 355-2140 or 355-2410, offers an interesting array of programs, of which this is just a sampling:

Sun and Tues:	skate-dancing to live organ music
Jan-April:	special girl scout skating
4th Mon of month:	skating to Christian music
Thurs 7-9:30:	family night

Open: Tues 8-10:30 (adults)
Wed 7-10 (everyone)
Thur 7-9:30 (family rate)
Fri 7-11:30
Sat 10:30-12:30; 2-4:30; 7:30-midnight
Sun 2-4:30; 7-9:30

Starburst Roller Skating, Rte 146 P.O. Box 441, Clifton Park, 371-1567, Open to public as well as for private parties. Rentals available.

Open: Thur 7-10 family night
Fri 7-11:30
Sat 1:30-4:30; 7:30-midnight
Sun 1-5:30; 7-10

Rowing

Rowing, the traditional Hudson River sport which had disappeared in the twentieth century, has staged a comeback. A boat launch site (including a boat house and docks) is located near the Colonie St section of the Corning Riverfront Preserve. Individuals and groups have purchased sculls and are sponsoring teams. To forward the progress of the sport, the Empire State Regatta Committee promotes open regattas to lure the world's best rowers to the site. For information write City Hall, Volunteer Services, Albany 12207, or call 434-5100.

Empire State Regatta is a two day weekend event held in early June at the Corning Preserve in the Hudson River. The world-class races, sponsored by the City of Albany and local businesses, are free. Food and entertainment are provided and there are fireworks on Saturday night. For information, call the Office of Special Events of the City, 434-2032.

The Knickerbocker Regatta, the New York State Intercollegiate Rowing Championships, is a one-day event held in spring at the Corning Preserve on the Hudson River. The regatta draws the crew teams of almost twenty colleges and universities from across the state for this exciting event.

Rugby

This sport has grown in popularity in recent years, both for participants and spectators. Local city and college clubs, all members of USARFU (the United States of America Rugby Football Union) play in spring and fall. The **Windover Rugby Club** plays at Windover Park, Grooms Rd, Clifton Park. This park has 10 fields and hosts many rugby clubs in games, tournaments, and national events. Information about all rugby events is available through Tom Selfridge, 120 S. Church St, Schenectady 370-3155.

Running

Running enthusiasts can use college campus paths and the riverfront bike and pedestrian paths for safe, predictable running. Those who enjoy running with others or training for competition can contact **Hudson Mohawk Road Runners**

Club (HMRRC) on the information hotline, 273-3108 The group publishes a monthly magazine, "The Pacesetter", on area running events and helps organize three major runs:

HMRRC Half Marathon (13.1 miles) from Schenectady to the University at Albany campus, held in early April.

The Stockade-athon, a 5K and a 10K held in Schenectady, on the 2nd Sunday in November.

Freihofer's Run for Women, a 10K held in spring organized by the Adirondack TAC.

Of course many area runners train for the traditional marathons in nearby New York or Boston.

Skiing/Downhill

The Capital District is in the enviable position of being surrounded by the Adirondacks, Catskills, Berkshires, and Vermont Mountains. As a result, the community of accomplished skiers in the region expects and receives comprehensive services.

There are four telephone numbers for current ski conditions:

For New York State ....1 (800) CALLNYS
For Catskills (24 Hour) 1 (800) 852-5500
For Massachusetts 1 (800) 342-1840
For Vermont 1 (800) 229-0531

Printed material is available for New York State at 474-4116 and for Vermont at SKI VT, 134 State, Montpelier 05602. The following is a list of popular ski centers presented according to driving distance from the Capital District. [Rentals and snow making are standard at all sites. Those which feature night skiing are preceded by an asterisk (*)].

One Hour or Less

*Brodie Mountain, Rte 7 New Ashford, Massachusetts, (413) 443-4752 or (413) 443-4753 (for conditions). Directions: I-90 East to Exit 7 (Defreestville). Turn left on Rte 43 to New Ashford.

*Catamount, Hillsdale, 325-3200. Directions: Taconic State Parkway south to Hillsdale Exit onto 23 East; 11 miles to Catamount.

*Jiminy Peak, Hancock Massachusetts, (413) 738-5000 Directions: I-90 East to Exit 7 (Defreestville); left on Rte 43 to Hancock Massachusetts; right at Jiminy Peak sign to Brodie Mountain Rd (Jiminy is 1/4 mile on right.)

*Maple Ski Ridge, Rte 159 Rotterdam (4 miles west of Schenectady), 381-4700. A great place to learn to ski in classes conducted by the Schenectady Ski School. Double and triple chair lifts, three rope tows, rentals.

Open: T-Sat 6:30 pm-10
       Sat-Sun 9-4:30
       Holidays 9-4:30

*West Mountain, R.D. 2 West Mt Rd Glens Falls 793-6606. Night skiing Monday through Saturday; West closes Sun at 6:00. Ski school and rentals. Directions: Northway (87) to Exit 18; left on Corinth Rd; three miles to sign on right; entrance is 3/4 mile on left.

*Willard Mountain, R.D. 3 Greenwich 692-7337. Beginner packages, lessons, rentals. Directions: Northway (87) to Exit 9 (Clifton Park); left on 146; right on 67 in Mechanicville; left on 40N; 3-4 miles to Willard. (25 minutes from Clifton Park.)

Ski Windham, Windham. Directions: Thruway to Exit 21, to Rte 23 West. For information, 1-800-342-5116.

One and One Half Hours

Gore Mountain, Box 470 North Creek, 251-2411, managed by the Olympic Regional Development Authority, also offers cross-country skiing. Directions: Northway (87) to Exit 23; bear right; 9N to Warrensburg; left onto 28; proceed 18 miles; left onto Peaceful Valley Rd; Gore is 1 mile on right.

Hunter Mountain, P.O. Box 629 Hunter 263-4223. Directions: Thruway to Exit 21; east on 23 and 23A West. Alternate directions: Thruway to Exit 21B; 9W South to Catskill; 23A East to Hunter.

Two to Two and a Half Hours

Bromley Mountain, P.O. Box 1130 Manchester Center, Vermont (802) 824-6915. Directions: NY Rte 7 to Rte 9 in Bennington to Vermont Rte 7; at Manchester, right onto Rte 11; two miles into Peru and Bromley.

Killington, 400 Killington Rd, Killington, Vermont (802) 773-1500. Directions: Northway (87) to Exit 20 (Fort Ann, Rutland); NY 149 East to US 4; left on 4 East to Killington (12 miles east to Rutland).

Mount Snow, 100 Mountain Rd, Mount Snow, Vermont (802) 464-3333 Directions: Rte 7 East to Bennington, Vermont where it becomes 9; Rte 9 to Wilmington, Vermont; left at stoplight onto 100 North; nine miles to Mount Snow.

Stratton, Stratton Mountain, Vermont 1-800-843-6867 This site has 92 trails, 12 lifts, an indoor sports center, a cross-country center, and Village Square shopping and dining. Directions: Vermont Rte 7 North to Manchester, Vermont; north to Rte 11 to Rte 30 South to entrance in Bondville; follow Stratton Mountain Rd 4 miles to ski area.

Whiteface, Rte 86, Wilmington 1-800-462-6236. Whiteface is managed by the Olympic Regional Development Authority. Cross-country skiing in village. Directions: Northway (87) to Exit 30; left onto Rte 9; follow signs to Whiteface.

Three to Three and a Half Hours

Stowe, Stowe, Vermont (802) 253-3000. (Cross country skiing also.) Directions: Northway (87) to Exit 20; Rte 149 East to Ft. Ann; US 4 North to US 4 East at Whitehall; crossing into Vermont at Fair Haven, take 22A North to Vergennes; north on US 7 to Burlington; Interstate 89 South to Exit 10; left onto 100N; 9 miles to Stowe.

Sugarbush Valley Ski Resort, Sugarbush Valley, Vermont (800) 451-5030 or (802) 583-2381. (Indoor sports center and cross-country trails as well.) Directions: Northway (87) to Exit 20; 149 East to Whitehall; on Rte 4 go eight miles past Rutland; left on Rte 100 North to Sugarbush.

Skiing/Cross-Country

Capital District residents have access to excellent cross-country skiing facilities. It is important to note that detailed information on cross-country skiing is available from the following sources.

NYS Department of Environmental Conservation Bureau of Preservation, Protection and Management, 50 Wolf Rd Albany, 457-7433, publishes an excellent booklet, *Nordic Skiing Trails in NY State,* complete with maps and thorough information on each site.

Albany County Department of Public Works, Rte 85A Voorheesville 12186, will provide information about opportunities in the immediate vicinity.

Capital Area Ski Touring Association (CASTA), P.O. Box 388, Latham, NY 12110, 438-5815, is a membership organization of Nordic skiing enthusiasts. All abilities are welcome. It organizes tours and publishes a newsletter and a valuable booklet describing almost 100 skiing areas.

N.B. The following downhill sites, described in the previous section, offer cross-country skiing as well: Gore, Stowe, Stratton, Sugarbush, and Whiteface.

Skiing Less than an Hour Away

(These sites do not offer rentals unless otherwise marked):

The New Course at Albany, New Scotland Ave, Albany, 438-2209. Open: daylight in season. Free. Directions: First left after Whitehall Rd when headed west.

Beebee Hill State Forest, Austerlitz, has three miles of expert ski trails. Free. Four miles southwest of Exit 3 on the Berkshire spur of the NYS Thruway, north on route 22 to Osner Rd, left beyond Barrett Pond.

Burden Lake Country Club, Totem Lodge Rd, Averill Park, 674-8917. Rentals. Open weekends. Nominal charge. Directions: Totem Lodge Rd is south of 150 at Sliters Corners.

Featherstonhaugh State Forest, a novice ski area with two miles of flat trails, is popular with families. Free. Nine miles west of Schenectady on Lake Rd near Mariaville.

Five Rivers Environmental Education Center, Game Farm Rd, Delmar, 475-0291. Open daily, dawn to dusk. Free. Directions: Off Rte 443, eight miles from downtown Albany.

Glens Falls International Ski Trails, Crandall Park, 624 Glen St, Queensbury. Includes lighted trails. Open: daily till 11 pm. Free. Rentals. Information may be obtained through the Inside Edge Ski and Bike Shop, 793-5676. Directions: Northway (87) to Exit 19; right to main intersection; right onto 9S (at third light); 1/2 mile down on 9S.

Helderberg Family, R.D. 1 Box 400A Voorheesville, 872-2106. Rentals and instruction. Open: Sat and Sun 10-dusk. Nominal charge. Directions: Rte 443, bear right to East Berne 1/8 mile; turn right on Pinnacle Rd, county Rte 303; 2 miles on left.

Howe Caverns, Rte 7 Howes Cave, 296-8990. Rentals and instruction. Open: daily. Nominal charge. Directions: Thruway to Exit 25A; I 88 West to Howes Cave exit; right onto Rte 7 and follow signs.

Indian Ladder Farms, Rte 156, Voorheesville, 765-2956. Hot cider and warm cider donuts in barn. Open seven days a week. Nominal charge. Directions: Rte

20 to 155 South; at end of 155 bear right on Maple Ave in Voorheesville; right onto 156; Indian Ladder 2 1/2 miles on left.

Lapland Lake, R.D. 2 Northville, 863-4974. Rentals, sales, and instruction. Lodging available. Open: daily. Nominal charge. Directions: Thruway to Exit 27; Rte 30N to Northville; west on Benson Rd for 6 miles.

John Boyd Thacher State Park, 872-1237. Six miles of ungroomed trails. Open: daily. Free. Directions: New Scotland Ave (Rte 85) to Rte 157 to Park. From Schenectady take Rte 146 South to Rte 156 in Altamont, go up the hill. Turn left on Rte 157A. Go to end, turn left on Rte 157.

Oak Hill Farms, R.D.1, Box 324, Esperance 12066, 875-6700. Nominal fee. Directions: 3 miles east of I-88, exit 23.

Partridge Run Wildlife Management Area, Sickle Hill Rd Berne, (607) 652-7364. (Cited by CASTA to have the most reliable snow conditions locally.) No restrictions on hours for skiing. Free. Directions: Rte 443 through Delmar to 146 through Altamont; west on 157 through Knox and south on 156; at Berne Knox Central School bear left and go one half mile; right onto Sickle Hill Rd; at top of steep hill, turn onto High Point Rd or Beaver Rd (just past church ruin) to Partridge Run.

Pine Ridge, County Rte 40, 12 miles east of Troy, 283-5509. Nominal fee.

Saratoga Spa State Park, Saratoga Springs, 584-2535. Rentals, sales, service, and lessons. Several miles of lighted trails. All trails well-groomed. Open: daily in daylight. Nominal charge. Directions: Northway (87) to Exit 13N; left onto 9N to left on Ave of Pines.

Saratoga National Historic Park, between Rte 4 and Rte 32, Stillwater, 664-9821. Open: 9-5 except Thanksgiving, Christmas, and New Years. Free. Directions: Northway (87) to Exit 12; follow signs to park, using routes 9N, 9P, 423 and 32.

Schenectady Municipal Golf Course, Oregon Ave Schenectady, 382-5153. Some lighted areas open till 10. Free. Directions: Thruway to Exit 25 to Rte 7; right onto Golf Rd at fourth light; left onto Oregon Ave.

Town of Colonie Golf Course, 418 Consaul Rd Schenectady, 346-5940 or 783-2760. Free. (Small fee for adults on weekends). Rentals. Well-groomed trails.

Tree Haven Trails, County Rte 45, 15 miles west of I-87, Galway 882-9455. Nominal fee.

Whispering Pines Golf Course, 2208 Helderberg Ave Schenectady, 355-2724. Rentals and sales. Open weekends in daylight. Nominal charge. Directions: Thruway Exit 25 to Rte 7 West (Curry Rd) for 3 miles; left onto Helderberg Ave; Whispering Pines is 1 mile on left.

Two Hours

Cunningham's Ski Barn–North Creek, 251-3215. Rentals, instruction, guided tours. Open: daily in season. Trail fee. Directions: Northway (87) to Exit 23; north on Rte 28. (Cunningham's is 20 miles NW of Warrensburg on Rte 28.)

Garnet Hill Ski Touring Center, North River, 251-2821. (Ten miles from Gore for those who enjoy Alpine and Nordic Skiing.) Rentals, instruction, guided tours, varied trails. Open: daily including night skiing. Nominal fee. Directions: Northway (87) to Exit 23 (Warrensburg); north on Rte 9 for 4 1/2 miles; northwest on Rte 28 for 20 miles to North River; left on 13th Lake Rd to Garnet Hill.

Two and a Half to Three Hours

Mount Van Hoevenberg, Olympic Regional Development Authority, Olympic Center, Lake Placid, 523-2811. Snowmaking capability. Site of 1980 Olympics and annual competitions; has 40km of groomed trails. Also site for luge, bobsled, and ski-jumping. Rentals, instruction, tours. Open: daily in season. Nominal charge. Directions: Northway (87) to Exit 30 east on Rte 73 to seven miles east of Lake Placid.

Sagamore Lodge And Conference Center, Sagamore Rd Raquette Lake (315) 354-5311. Cross-country skiing recreation weekends include instruction, guided tours, evening entertainment, moonlight skiing. Rentals available. Skiing free. Charge for meals and lodging. Nominal charge. Directions: Northway (87) to Exit 23 (Warrensburg); North on 28 to Raquette Lake. Reservations required.

Skiing/Special Cross-Country

Wilderness ski tours are two three or five day excursions in which skiers leave a Central Adirondack lodge in the morning and travel to another point, staying at a different lodge or wilderness cabin each night. Fees include meals, lodging, guides, and the transfer of luggage between lodges. Information is available at **Adirondack Hut to Hut,** R.D. 1 Box 85 Ghent 12075, 828-7007.

Skydiving

Sky Diving Club at Duanesburg Airport, Duanesburg, at intersection of Rte 7 and Rte 20. For information on lessons and dives, call 895-8140 or 895-8900.

Sports Cars

The **Mohawk-Hudson Region of the Sports Car Club of America** meets at the Lebanon Valley Speedway Clubhouse on Rte 20, Lebanon. For information, call 786-3118.

Swimming

There are numerous supervised swimming facilities in the region, some seasonal and others year round. Pools in outlying districts usually restrict use to verified residents. Information regarding hours and rules for these pools is available at the appropriate village or town hall. The three major cities open their facilities to the general public. Information about swimming opportunities and programs in the three cities is available at the following numbers:

Albany 438-2447
Schenectady 382-5152
Troy 270-4600

Swim School Inc, 1700 Seventh Ave, Troy, 274-8677, gives lessons on all levels—from competitive racing and synchronized teamwork to exercise, therapy and recreation. Pool is also available for pool parties.

Some area hotels and motels quietly open their pools to the general public through **Swim Clubs,** informal arrangements whereby local residents may pay an annual fee and swim when the pool is open. Details are available at each facility.

State Supervised Parks and Private Beaches: Because specific information on state run parks and private beaches open to the public is not so easy to find, the remainder of this section will present details.

Parks with Lakes: State Operated

These parks are free but a modest fee is charged for parking.

Cherry Plain State Park, off Rte 22 north of Stephentown is open 10-6 daily from late June through Labor Day.

Grafton Lake, Rte 2, Grafton, is open 10-6 daily late June through Labor Day. CDTA (482-8822) runs a bus to and from this park on a regular schedule.

Minekill State Park, off Rte 30 south of Middleburgh, is open 10-6 daily late June through Labor Day.

Moreau State Park, Exit 17S off Northway (87). Moreau is open 10-6 late June through Labor Day.

Thompson's Lake Camping Area, Rte 157 off Rte 85 Berne-Knox, 3 miles northwest of Thatcher Park, is open 10-6 daily late June through Labor Day. There is also a pool here.

Taghkanic State Park, 11 miles south of Hudson Rte 82 at Taconic State Parkway, is open 10-6 daily, late June through Labor Day.

Parks with Lakes: Privately Operated

Brown's Beach, Saratoga Lake. Open Memorial Day through Labor Day.

Scholz-Zwicklbauer Beach, Warners Lake, Berne, 872-9912. Open daily 11 am-dark July 4 through Labor Day.

Tifft's Bathing Beach, Rte 66, Glass Lake, 674-8912. Open 10-dusk Memorial Day through Labor Day.

Parks with Pools

John Boyd Thacher State Park, Voorheesville. Open 10-6 late June through Labor Day. Modest fee.

Saratoga Spa State Park, Rte 9 Saratoga Springs [Exit 13N off Northway (87)]. There are two pools here, the Victorian Pool and the larger Peerless Pool. Open 10-6 late June through Labor Day. Car gate fee and pool fee.

Tennis

The three cities maintain and oversee tennis courts at various locations, some lighted. The numbers to call for information are:

Albany 434-4181
Schenectady 382-5152
Troy 270-4600

Schenectady offers league tennis in Central Park. It is open to all Schenectady residents. A yearly outdoor summer event in Schenectady is the OTB tennis tournament, which attracts top-seeded players. It is the only major tennis tournament in the world that does not charge admission.

Tennis is played throughout the year at several indoor clubs. Membership, which is open to the public, entitles members to full use of the facilities and participation in leagues and tournaments. However, non- members are welcome to rent available courts. These clubs are listed in the telephone directory.

15 Love, sponsored by the Capital Region Youth Tennis Foundation, 95 Livingston Ave, Albany, 432-LOVE, aims to reach out to youth in the Capital District by using tennis as a medium to involve youths in positive, healthy choices by building character, developing self esteem, and promoting good health habits. The program was established through the collaboration of the Ashe-Bollettieri Cities Program, Hope House, and the Eastern Tennis Association. The program takes place at sites in Albany at Arbor Hill and Lincoln Park, in Troy at Russell Sage College and Prospect Park, and in Schenectady at the Michigan Ave Courts. Seven suburban communities have satellite programs.

Water Racing

White Water Derby on the Hudson River is an annual event guaranteed to provide exhilaration to contestants and spectators alike. The race, sponsored by the Hudson River White Water Derby Co., takes place the first full weekend in May in North Creek. The first day of the two day contest is the slalom; the second day is downriver.

Most spectators and photography buffs gather at Spruce Mt. Rapids where the boats must maneuver with great skill to stay upright. Directions: Northway (87) to Exit 23; Rte 28 to North Creek. (One and one half hours.)

GENERAL RECREATION

Sources of Information

The New York State Office of Parks, Recreation and Historic Preservation and the New York State Department of Environmental Conservation operate dozens of historic sites, parks and preserves. All are centered in beautiful locations and maintained with scrupulous attention to preservation and comfort. The two agencies split their duties thus: EnCon oversees the Catskill and Adirondack Forest Preserves; Parks and Recreation oversees all other state supervised parks. The addresses and telephone numbers are as follows:

NYS Parks, Recreation and Historic Preservation
Agency Bldg 1,
Empire State Plaza
Albany 12238
474-0456

Ask for the pamphlet
A GUIDE TO NYS PARKS, RECREATION, AND PRESERVATION

Environmental Conservation
50 Wolf Rd
Albany 12233
457-2500
(For fish and wildlife—457-5690)

An **Empire Passport** offers unlimited year-round entry to all NYS parks and recreational facilities. It is sold at all state parks or by mail from Passports, State Parks, Albany NY 12238.

A **Golden Park Pass** is free to NYS residents 62 or over, providing lifetime free admission for day use of state parks (M-F, except holidays.) It is available at the address listed above.

An **Access Pass** is available for state residents with permanent physical disabilities. It provides free vehicle access to state parks and historical and recreational facilities. It is available at the address listed above.

State Parks

There are two Adirondack Park Visitors Interpretive Centers which are open year round every day except Thanksgiving and Christmas. Free.

Rte 28N Box 101, Newcomb, New York 12852, 582-2000

Rte 30 Box 3000, Paul Smiths, New York 12970, 327-3000

The following companies offer guide and outfitting services and instruction in adventure sports for the Adirondacks.

Adirondack Rock and River Guide Service, Box 219, Keene, 576-2041. Lodging is available for outdoor oriented individuals.

Raquette River Canoe Outfitters, Inc., Box 653, Tupper Lake, 395-3228

Northern Pathfinders Ltd., Box 464, North Creek, 327-3378

The Adirondack Park is a vast area (6 million acres) of publically and privately owned land carefully overseen by the Adirondack Park Agency, whose aim is to protect the area and advise vacationers on wise and full use of available facilities.

The region offers a wealth of recreational opportunities, for the southern and western areas have gentle slopes whereas the northeast features jagged faced, high-peaked mountains. Thus horseback riding, camping, picnicking, hiking, mountaineering, hunting, snowshoeing, and skiing can be practiced at all levels of difficulty. Moreover, sheltered amidst the mountains, a multitude of lakes and streams invite boating of all kinds, swimming, scuba diving, waterskiing, fishing—even icefishing. The air and water everywhere have always been known to be crystal clear and pure. (The fact that acid rain threatens this purity is a major concern upon which many New Yorkers are determined to act.)

Pamphlets, brochures and general information are available at no cost through Adirondack Park Association, Adirondack NY 12808.

The beautiful magazine *ADIRONDACK LIFE* is described in the section on sources of information.

Five Rivers Environmental Education Center, Game Farm Rd, Delmar, 475-0291, is a branch of the NYS Department of Environmental Conservation. The Center, which has been honored with a National Park Service Award, provides an opportunity for people to learn the interdependence of natural phenomena, either on their own as they walk the clearly marked trails using guidebooks or through classes and workshops presented at the site. One trail has been especially adapted to be accessible to the handicapped, and tape recorded descriptions of two trails make it possible for a visually handicapped visitor to tour in the company of a sighted companion. The Center publishes a newsletter, *The Tributary*. One may receive further information or register for the mailing list by using the number or address above. Directions: South on Delaware Ave; right onto Orchard; 1/2 mile to Game Farm Rd on left.

John Boyd Thacher State Park, located 18 miles west of Albany (out New Scotland Ave), offers splendid views of the Hudson-Mohawk Valleys and the peaks of the Adirondack and Green Mountains. Thatcher, as it is called, has fine picnic areas and an olympic swimming pool, but its most popular attraction is the Indian Ladder Geologic Trail, a naturally formed ledge along the Helderberg Escarpment, an area described by geologists and paleontologists as one of the richest fossil-bearing formations in the world. The half mile walk along this trail is truly awesome. The park is open June 16 through Labor Day, 8 am to 10 pm, with the Indian Ladder Trail open 8-8 and the pool open 11-7, weather permitting. In winter, the park is open for ski-touring, snowshoeing, tobogganing and snowmobiling, with heated comfort stations along the trails. Directions: New Scotland Ave (Rte 85) out of Albany to park. From Schenectady, take Rte 146 South to Rte 156 in Altamont. Go up hill, turn left on Rte 157A. Go to end; turn left on Rte 157.

Saratoga Spa State Park, a beautifully landscaped stretch of ground, has outstanding athletic and health facilities. Two golf courses—an 18-hole course and a 9-hole course—two swimming pools and a dozen well- maintained picnic spots are available as are tennis courts, skating rinks and cross country ski trails. Also open to the public are the two bathhouses which offer massage, mineral baths and hot packs. This practice of "bathing," very fashionable in the 20's and 30's, declined for a while but has been regaining popularity in recent years. Those who have taken advantage of this local facility claim that there is no doubt the process makes one feel invigorated and renewed.

Information about the hours and fees for all the park's features is available at Saratoga Spa State Park, P.O. Box W, Saratoga Springs 12866 or at the bathhouses:

Roosevelt Bath Pavilion (open all year) 584-2011
Lincoln Bath Pavilion (open July and August) 584-2010

Directions: Northway (87) to Exit 13N; 9N north to park entrance (on left).

Private Preserves

The Edmund Niles Huyck Preserve and Biological Research Station in Rensselaerville harbors housing and laboratory space for twenty year- round students of the natural sciences and forty summer residents participating in research on the lands and waters which make up the compound. The pre- serve also has an environmental education program for children of pre-kindergarten age through twelve years old. The preserve is open to the public throughout the year for picnicking, fishing, canoeing, and rowboating. Visitors should, however, follow the posted regulations carefully to avoid in- truding on wildlife for whom this is a habitat.

Hikes are scheduled for Sunday afternoons from mid-May to mid- September. In- formation is available from P.O. Box 189 Rensselaerville 12147, 797-3440. Directions: New Scotland Ave (Rte 85) to Rensselaerville; at end of road in the town, turn right; proceed to end of road to sign for Preserve.

The Mohonk Preserve, Mohonk Lake, New Paltz, (914) 255-0919, is open to the public for general recreation—including walking, hiking, horseback riding, bicy- cling, snowshoeing and ski touring. The setting is beautiful. Directions: Thruway to Exit 18; left on Rte 299; 5 miles beyond New Paltz, go right after bridge over Wallkill; bearing left, follow Mountain Rest Rd to Mohonk gate.

The Nature Conservancy's Eastern New York Chapter manages 29 nature pre- serves throughout the eastern New York region. The Conservancy is an international organization dedicated to the preservation of plants, animals and natural communities by protecting the lands and water they need to survive. The public is invited to experience the unique natural habitats of the region by visit- ing the local preserves including the Albany Pine Bush, Mill Creek Marsh on the Hudson River and the Christman Sanctuary in Schenectady County. For further

Every year, our success can be measured in acres saved and species protected. We'll show you what we've done, and how you can make a difference.

GIVE US A CALL AND JOIN THE CHAPTER

Let us welcome you to The Nature Conservancy.

EASTERN NEW YORK CHAPTER
1736 Western Avenue
Albany, New York 12203
(518) 869-0453

information, directions or a copy of the chapter's preserve guide call 869-0453 or write to 1736 Western Avenue, Albany 12203.

Camping

New York State maintains and administers an extraordinary array of campsites. Two agencies supervise their operation: **Department of Environmental Conservation** 50 Wolf Rd Albany 457-2500 oversees camping in the Catskill and Adirondack Forest Preserves; **Office of Parks, Recreation, and Historic Preservation** Agency Bldg 1 Empire State Plaza 474-0456 oversees all other sites. Campsites are available on a first-come-first-served basis. Reservations (which can be made by calling 1-800-456-CAMP with credit cards) are required at some areas. Detailed information is presented in a free brochure, *A Guide to New York State Parks, Recreation and Historic Preservation,* available at either office. Also available are brochures about certain areas or about types of campsites ("Island Camping," for example).

City Parks

The cities and towns of the region maintain dozens of parks and playgrounds which area residents use both for organized activities and personal leisure. Town and city employees organize and supervise programs, lessons, competitions and leagues throughout the year. Information on facilities and schedules is available at the office listed in the blue pages of the telephone book. The principal numbers for the three major cities are as follows:

Albany
General Information 434-4181
Recreation Dept and Scheduling 438-2447
Schenectady . . . . 382-5151 or 382-5152
Troy 270-4600

Albany

In the center of the capital city sits **Washington Park,** a model urban park situated on 90 acres of rolling land designated as parkland by foresighted city planners in 1869. Remnants of the original formal park remain in the bridal paths, the unusual and exotic trees, and the traditional statues. But in the 1990's the park is an up-to-date place with benches, picnic tables, walkways and playgrounds filled with casually dressed urbanites relaxing or participating in the growing number of concerts, festivals and fairs to which the park plays host.

Lincoln Park, the center of which resembles a pair of vast unembellished saucers, is the perfect place for any sort of ball game. The park, located along Morton Ave just below Delaware Ave, also has tennis courts and a swimming pool.

Erastus Corning II Riverfront Preserve runs along the west bank of the Hudson all the way to the city line. It features a pedestrian/bike path, picnic tables, and a series of exercise stations. Specially commissioned sculptures are found throughout the park.

Westland Hills Park, off Colvin Ave between Central and Lincoln Aves, maintains eight diamonds to serve its Little League program with over 2,000 participants. (There are also lighted tennis courts, a supervised junior swimming pool, and a multi-leveled playground.)

Schenectady

The largest of Schenectady's parks is **Central Park,** 500 acres of rolling land in the middle of the city. This park has lots to offer: a rose garden, paddle boats, a duck pond, a train ride, 26 tennis courts, an imaginative playground, and terrain suited for a wide variety of winter and summer sports.

The other principal parks in Schenectady are **Hillhurst, Quackenbush, Rotunda, Steinmetz** and **Woodlawn.**

Troy

Frear Park is Troy's largest park, with ball diamonds, playing fields, picnic areas, and a skating rink. **Knickerbacker Park** and **Prospect Park** are the two other major recreational parks.

Riverfront Park, along the banks of the Hudson, is the site of planned public, cultural and ethnic activities.

Other Recreational Facilities

Jewish Community Centers in Albany 340 Whitehall Rd, 438-6651 and Schenectady 2565 Balltown Rd, 377-8803 offer a wide variety of programs in recreation. Membership is open to the entire community regardless of religious affiliation. Programs range from Yoga and belly-dancing to ballet and basketball. The centers always offer Red Cross swimming programs.

The **Y's** (**YMCA** and **YWCA**) have very active centers in the Capital District, offering good facilities and programs at reasonable prices to anyone who wishes to subscribe. (The Y will never deny access to a program because a person cannot pay the fee.) The numbers for the major centers are:

	YMCA	YWCA
Albany	449-7196	438-6608
Schenectady	374-9136	374-3394
Troy	272-5900	274-7100

The summer camp run by the Schenectady YMCA (Camp Chingachgook, located at Pilot Knob on Lake George) is widely respected.

July 4th, Empire State Plaza, Albany

OTHER THINGS TO DO

This chapter describes activities which have eluded categorization in other chapters. It is organized by time of year, beginning with year-round activities and then turning to seasonal.

YEAR-ROUND

The Air National Guard Facility at the Schenectady County Airport provides an educational and enjoyable tour of the installation, including its maintenance facility, seeing the interior of an aircraft, and a trip to the flight line. For a tour appointment, call 381-7431.

Bridge and Games

Albany Area Chess Club invites everyone to play chess with the forty memberrs of the club each Thursday evening from 7:30 to 11:00 at the Capital District Psychiatric Center, Room 31, New Scotland Ave at South Lake Ave, Albany. Bring your own chess set. Membership is open, with fifteen dollars as the annual dues. For information, call 465-2172.

The Studio of Bridge and Games at 1639 Eastern Parkway, Schenectady, 346-3773. Participants play chess, bridge, adventure games (Dungeons and Dragons, for example) and, of course, duplicate bridge. The studio, directed by Bill and Norma Shelly, organizes tournaments for gamesters of all ages and levels. It is open to the public every afternoon and evening. Table fee.

Duplicate Bridge is sponsored regularly at Point of Woods and St Paul's Church, Albany, 482-3800, and at Regency Park, Albany, 383-8202. Partnerships can be

arranged. A certified instructor specializing in advanced beginners and in intermediate levels is available for your own group of four to eight persons in your
own home or a specified setting. Call 377-7224.

Covered Bridges

Covered bridges are numerous in the outlying area because of the many rivers and
streams surrounding our towns and cities. For those who are interested in design
and construction of wooden and covered bridges the following are interesting to visit:

Buskirk Covered Bridge, old First Northern Turnpike, Argyle, is a 160-foot
Howe Truss over the Hoosic River. On the National Register of Historic Places,
it is reached by Rte 4N to Rte 67E and North on Rte 59.

Eagleville Covered Bridge, Eagleville Rd, Jackson, is a 100-foot double cord,
town lattice truss on the Battenkill. Built around 1858 it is on the National
Register of Historic Places and is reached by I-87N to Exit 14, Rte 29E to Rte 372E
to Rte 313E.

Perrine's Bridge is the oldest public covered bridge in New York State. It crosses
the Walkill River and is open for foot traffic. Rte 9W South to Kingston to Rte 32S
to Rte 213.

Rexleigh Covered Bridge, Rexleigh Rd, South Salem, is a 107-foot Howe Truss
over the Battenkill. On the National Register of Historic Places it may be reached
via I-87N to Exit 14 to Rte 29E to Rte 22N.

Shushan Covered Bridge Museum, Rte 61, Shushan, 854-7220 is a local history
museum and a former one-room schoolhouse with an 1858 bridge over the
Battenkill adjacent. On the National Register of Historic Places, it is open
Memorial Day to Columbus Day. I-87N to Exit 14, Rte 29E to Rte 313E to Rte 61E.

Craft Fairs

Craft fairs are an interesting way to spend a day. Watch and talk with artisans
who produce fine contemporary craft work at reasonable prices or just wander
around the grounds and enjoy tastings from vendors at the outside food court.
Entertainment—including musicians, jugglers, pony rides and informative
booths—are there for your pleasure. Once at the town of the fair, look for the colorful signs and arrows directing you to the parking area. All have admission fees.
Below are four juried shows that are popular with the people of the tri-city area:

Adirondack Green Mountain Craft Fair is held the second weekend in September at the Washington County Fairgrounds, 13 miles East of Exit 14, I-87N, Saratoga Springs on Rte 29 in Greenwich, NY (45 minutes).

Quail Hollow Arts and Crafts Fair is held on Memorial Day and Labor Day weekends at the Ulster County Fairgrounds in New Paltz. I-87S to Exit 18, Rte 44W to Liberty Rd (1 hour, 15 minutes).

Southern Vermont Craft Fair is held in late July at Hildene Estate Meadows, River Rd, Manchester Village, Vermont. Junction of Rtes 7A and 30. (1 hour)

Winterfestival-Lower Ardirondack Regional Arts Council is held in November at the Adirondack Community College Gymnasium. I-87N to Exit 19 to Aviation Rd East, Left on Bay Rd, Glens Falls. (45 minutes)

Dancing

Dancing is enjoyed by a number of varied groups of young and old, women and men. Bring either expertise or the urge to learn, and wear appropriate clothing and shoes to any of the following groups.

Capital District Square and Round Dance Association coordinates the activities of approximately 43 regional clubs which meet regularly from September to May. The Association is responsible for maintaining a schedule of events, providing callers and music, supervising lessons and, in general, promoting the pleasures of modern, square, western and round dancing, and clogging. For information, call 765-4011.

Capital English Country Dancing. A more refined form of Contra- dancing, English country dancing dates from the eighteenth century when it was enjoyed by both court and country people. There is a specific tune for each dance, which is danced to live music with a caller. The group meets monthly at the East Schodack Recreation Hall, East Schodack, and offers workshops in both dancing and in playing the music. Open to the public and beginners are welcome. Loose clothing and soft-soled shoes recommended. There is an admission fee. Call Nancy Yule at 477-5684 for information.

International Folk Dancing is a group which does dances from around the world, but more usually focuses on dances from eastern Europe and the Middle East. The countries most commonly represented are Armenia, Bulgaria, Croatia, Greece, Hungary, Israel, Macedonia, Romania, Russia, Serbia and Turkey. Dances are taught for the first hour of group gatherings and requested dances are done thereafter. The dances are usually line and circle dances with partners not being required. Emphasis is placed on enjoyment, not on attainment of technical proficiency. Soft-soled shoes and a loose belt are required. There is an admission charge. Local groups meet at the following locations: YWCA, Albany, Colvin and Lincoln Aves, Tues 8-11 for beginners and intermediates; call Don Treble at 489-5062 for information. YWCA, Schenectady, at 44 Washington Ave, Wed 7:30-10:30 for beginners and intermediates; call Ron Miller at 356-5544 for information. YWCA, Schenectady, at 44 Washington Ave, Fri 8:15-10:45 for intermediate to advanced; call Silvia Cornell at 785-1812 for information.

New England Contra and Square Dancing is available to the public of all ages and levels of ability at each of the following groups and locations: Hudson-Mohawk Country Dancers meets twice monthly during the year with a beginners workshop for one-half hour before each meeting at the YWCA in Schenectady at 44 Washington Ave; call 438-3035 for information. Eighth Step Contra Dancers meets twice monthly at the Masonic Temple, Rte 9 and 20, East Greenbush; call 438-3035 for information. Old Songs Country Dancing meets twice monthly at the Guilderland Elementary School, Western Ave (Rte 20), Guilderland; call 765-2815 for information.

Old English Morris Dancing is available to everyone, with no age limit, for learning and practice through the group that specializes in this common folk dancing dating from the twelfth century to celebrate springtime and planting. At the Christmas season a traditional horn dance with antlers is performed. The group meets Wednesday evening at Emma Willard School, Pawling Ave, Troy. Admission is free. Call 383-3482 for information.

Scandinavian Couples Dancing is a group which performs folk dances mainly from Norway and Sweden and occasionally from Denmark. Partners are not necessary. The group meets twice monthly on Sunday afternoon at the YWCA in Schenectady at 44 Washington Ave. Beginners are welcome and lessons are taught one-half hour before the regular session begins. Admission is free. Call 377-3915 for information.

Folk Music Concerts and Poetry Readings
Caffe Lena, Inc., 45 Phila St Saratoga, 583-0022, has been the launch site for many renowned performers, many of whom lovingly return on occasion to perform for their appreciative audiences. The program is available at the cafe.

The Eighth Step Coffee House, 14 Willett St, Albany, 434-1703, which claims to be the longest running non-profit coffee house in the United States, is a "Free Stage" performance space which allows local talent to try their skills before a live audience. All members of the community are invited to participate either on stage or in the audience. Regualr season begins each September.

The Half Moon Cafe, 154 Madison Ave Albany, 436-0329, welcomes writers of all media to present their material to a listening audience. Poets and fiction writers read; composers play and sing. Audience discussion is welcome. The cafe also invites local artists to display their works on the wall. The art changes monthly. At the cafe annex (172 Madison Ave) an art center is focused on the politics of peace and justice.

Entertainment Centers

The two **Armories** in the area which host major spectator events—exhibitions, entertainments and sports competitions, for example, are:

Albany
New Scotland Ave 449-1575

Schenectady
Washington Ave 377-8581

Nancy Kuivila
REAL ESTATE, INC.

307 HAMILTON STREET	276 DELAWARE AVENUE
ALBANY, N.Y.	DELMAR, N.Y. 12054
518-465-9761	**518-439-7654**

Empire State Plaza and **Convention Center** host scores of open events each year. These include displays like the college fair, the home show, and the ski show as well as numerous ethnic festivals, road races, fund-raisers and the like. Information on forthcoming events is available through the New York State Office of General Services.

Glens Falls Civic Center provides a stage for such events as hockey league games, rock concerts, the circus, the ice show, and family shows. Information is available at 1-761-3852.

Houston Fieldhouse at RPI provides seating for 5000 to 7000 people for rock concerts, cabaret shows, sporting events and space for such displays as the home show, the boat show, the auto show, the antique show, and the flower show. Call 276-6262.

Knickerbocker Arena, 52 S Pearl St, Albany, 434-1236 is host to sporting events including ice spectaculars, rock concerts, crusades, craft and garden exhibits.

Noontime downtown Albany is a time of vitality. As thousands of people pour from offices, several downtown institutions program educational and cultural activities—from concerts to lectures and slide shows. Publicity for these events appears on bulletin boards throughout downtown and in the entertainment sections of local newspapers: *Preview* section of the Times Union on Thursday; *Stepping Out* section of the Record on Thursday; the arts and entertainment calendar in regular pages on Sunday in the Schenectady Gazette.

Mills

To watch apples being pressed and cider made and bottled is interesting for all family members. In the fall many orchards invite the public to view the process and taste the results. Newspapers announce places and times. One mill in particular is unique:

Eagle Mills Cider Company, Broadalbin 883-5529 processes cider with a water-wheel cider mill circa 1850 which has mechanical hydraulic presses made in 1890. Open July through October it may be reached I-87N to Rte 29W to Rte 30N.

Other mills of interest are:

Log Village Grist Mill, Rte 30, East Hartford, 632-5237, is a working grist mill with the original equipment which was built in 1810. Fresh corn meal is ground and sold as well as freshly pressed cider. Rte 4N to Rte 196E.

Tuthilltown Grist Mill, Albany Post Rd, Gardiner, (914) 225-5695, is the only mill in the United States which makes matzoh flour for Passover. Constructed in 1788 it is on the National Historic Register. Open year round. Rte 32S to New Paltz, South to Gardiner.

Model Railroading

People with passions for railroading are fortunate to have resources in this area for information. Whether a starter or serious modelist, tracks, trains and structures are readily available in hobby shops. Layouts are on display.

Great Train Extravaganza is held early December at the Empire State Plaza Convention Center and displays models, layouts and historical memorabilia. Information and expert advice from fellow railroad afficionados available. Fee.

Mohawk Valley Railroad Co., 2037 Hamburg St, Schenectady, 372-9124 is a train lovers delight. Wander in to try out merchandise, shop for supplies or watch the layouts encircling the store.

Rensselaer Model Railroad Society has displays at Davison Hall on the RPI campus filling three rooms with over 7 miles of detailed constructions of towns, communities and historical sites. Visitors welcome 10 am to 4 pm Fridays and Saturdays. Fee.

Workplace Tours

Costumer, international supplier of theatrical costumes
1020 Barrett St/Schdy
374-7442

View design, cutting, sewing, and finishing
Call for tour appointment
No charge for tour

Freihofer's Bakery
Prospect Rd/Albany
438-6631

Bread Bakery Tour
Daily 9:30 and 11:30
7 year old age limit
Advanced notice required

Garden Way
102nd St and 9th Ave/Troy
~~235-6010~~ *Not There*

Watch manufacturing of
TROY-BILT TILLERS
No children under five

Hudson Mohawk Industrial Gateway
457 Broadway/Troy
274-5267

Arranges tours of area factories for groups

Icarus Furniture 154 4th St/Troy 274-2883	Wood furniture designed and made to order, both religious and household. Call in advance.
Sangamon Mills 58 Columbia St/Cohoes 237-5321	Textile producers Oldest mill in Cohoes Call in advance
Times Union News Plaza/Colonie 454-5694	Monday and Friday to watch presses rolling No one under 11 years old Call in advance

SPRING

Albany Tulip Festival and **Pinksterfest,** annual events commemorating Albany's Dutch heritage and welcoming Spring, are scheduled for the second weekend in May, when thousands of tulips come into blossom in the city's parks. The general schedule is as follows: on Friday morning, the mayor reads an opening proclamation and young Albanians in Dutch costumes scrub State St with traditional broad brooms. On Saturday morning, the Tulip pageant begins, leading up to the crowning of the year's Tulip Queen at about noon in Washington Park. On Saturday afternoon and Sunday, the outdoor fair—Pinksterfest—takes over the Park, with Kinderkermis (the children's carnival) running concurrently in the Park. The celebration also features the Tulip Ball and the Tulip Luncheon, both open to anyone wishing to purchase a ticket. The Mayor's Office for Special Events, 434-2032, oversees the celebration.

Albany Historic House and Garden Tour, held in mid-May, includes plant sales, magicians, gospel singers, entertainment, and exploration of Albany's rich architectural highlights and notable gardens. Free shuttle buses provided by CDTA leave from the Ten Broeck Mansion. Call 436-9826 for information.

Am-Jam, an annual event for motorcycle enthusiasts, is held each Memorial Day weekend at the Cobleskill fairgrounds. There are cycle and novelty games, food vendors, concerts, an antique motorcycle museum, a half-million dollar mobile show featuring chrome products and accessories for cycles. Call 346-0521 for information.

Capital District Garden and Flower Show, an annual event sponsored by the Wildwood Programs, takes place in mid-March in the Knickerbocker Arena, which is converted into a colorful, fragrant, and blooming spectacle by the numerous landscape exhibitors, vendors, supply houses, and educational exhibits.

Other Things To Do

The local newspapers carry announcements of the event, which draws a large number of spectators.

Gardening delights many residents from April through September. Community Gardens, plots of land available for cultivation by residents, are described in the food section of the chapter on shopping. Stores catering to the needs of pleasure gardeners are described in the goods section of the shopping chapter.

The Grecian Cultural Festival is held each year on the third weekend in May at St Sophia's Greek Orthodox Church, 440 Whitehall Rd Albany, 489-4442. Thousands flock to this unique event, savoring the Greek dinners and desserts and enjoying the traditional music and dancing of Greece and the Greek islands. Parishioners display, explain, and sell imported Greek merchandise in booths throughout the parish house.

Maple Sugaring, the laborious process of drawing sap and converting it to syrup and candy, requires extraordinary patience and watchfulness, particularly in the weeks around February 20 to April 15 when the sap is running. Four regional farms welcome curious visitors and, of course, invite them to sample the syrup and to take some home. (Because operations are somewhat dependent on weather conditions, it is best to call ahead to check open hours and to get directions.)

Brannon Enterprises, Inc.
Rte 3, West Chazy 493-7090

Columbia Hill Farm
RD 2, Averill Park 283-2896

Patrick Hill Maple Farm
Potato Farm Rd, HC 69, Morris, NY 13808 . . . . (800) 62MAPLE

Putnam Maple Farm
Beards Hollow Rd, Richmondville 294-7278

Schenectady Museum Festival of Nations, usually held the third weekend in May, is an ethnic festival of entertainment and food with representatives of approximately twenty countries. There is an admission charge. Call 382-7890 for information.

A northeast view from the Capitol

SUMMER

Albany Alive at 5 at the Tri-Centennial Plaza (opposite Kiernan Plaza), Broadway, Albany, is a free multi-cultural and multi-ethnic series of concerts on Thursdays in July from 5-8 pm of all types of music, from nostalgic and cajun to rock and roll.

Alpine Slides, rides that slalom down mountains, usually on the site of ski trails, are maintained at:

> **Bromley Mountain Ski Resort,** Rte 7A, Manchester, Vermont, (802) 824-5522 NYS Rte 7E to Vermont Rte 7N to Rte 7A.

> **Jiminy Peak,** Hancock, Massachusetts I-90E to Exit 7, East on Rte 43 to Hancock, right at Jimminy Peak sign to Brodie Mountain Rd 783-5431.

> **Pico Alpine Slide** Killington, Vermont, (802) 775-4345 I-87N to Rte 149 (Exit 20), East to Rte 4E.

The Altamont Fair usurps the picturesque Helderberg village of Altamont each August. It combines a genuine country fair (including serious farm competitions—animal husbandry contests, cooking and sewing displays, and art shows) with a midway, live entertainment, an antique auto show, a circus museum, a carriage museum, and a fire equipment museum. The result of this variety is that the fair is one of the best there is.

Batteau Project, held at Schenectady's Riverside Park on a summer weekend, includes watching costumed boat builders recreate an 18th century river batteau commissioned by Philip Schuyler in 1792 and a reenactment of the 1792 Mohawk River trip. There are period encampments, an oxen parade, and children's activities. Free. For information, call 382-5147.

Butterfly Museum, Rte 67, East Durham, 634-7759 offers a large collection of species from throughout the world. Also shown in this private collection are shells and a variety of insects. Open June through Labor Day. Take Rte 32S to Freehold, turn right to Rte 67.

The Capital District Scottish Games usually held in August at the Altamont Fairgrounds, 785-5951, is a Celtic festival featuring bagpipe music, Irish and Scottish dancers, athletic competitions, food, music, and fun. Fee.

Catskill Game Farm is a wonderful place for a family to spend a day. The founders, whose principal concern was the conservation of rare and vanishing animal species, designed a suitable habitat for each, hoping they would live and breed. The result is an expansive wooded shelter through which visitors may walk and observe a great variety of interesting animals, sheltered but not really confined. Favorites for children are the nursery where newborn animals are kept, the petting and feeding area where deer, goats, and llamas roam uncaged, and a rather spectacular playground. A single admission fee covers most of the activities offered, though additional charges are imposed for mechanical amusements at the playground. Refreshments are sold at concessions, and picnic tables are available for those who bring their own food. Directions: Thruway to Exit 21; Rte 23 West to Rte 32 South. Route is well marked.

The Clearwater docked in Rensselaer

Clearwater is the sloop which sails the Hudson River piloted by environmentalists committed to heightening citizen awareness of the importance of keeping the river free of industrial and urban pollution. The ship's arrival in port is usually announced in area newspapers.

Adults and school children board the Clearwater to explore the natural history and ecology of the region, to help hoist the sails and steer the boat, and examine fish and water samples for a first-hand view of what is happening in the waterways around them. For information, write to Clearwater, Inc., 112 Market Pl, Poughkeepsie, 12601.

Empire State Regatta is a two-day rowing event on the Hudson River held on the first full weekend in June at the Corning Preserve. Sponsored by the City of Albany and private corporations, its team participants come from far and wide in the United Sates and Canada. It attracts thousands who enjoy the sport, the food and entertainment, and the spectacular fireworks on Saturday evening. Free. For information, call 434-2032.

Fireworks of the first magnitude are set off on the Fourth of July and other celebratory occasions at the Empire State Plaza. It's a perfect stage: the tower windows reflect the dazzle, and the architectural hollows echo the collective sighs of the delighted spectators. Moreover, the platform comfortably accommodates great crowds, assuring all an unobstructed view. Price Chopper has been the host at Fourth of July celebrations in recent years.

Frontier Town, North Hudson, is America's oldest western theme park. It features the life and legends of our great frontier, including rodeos, powwows, stagecoaches, farmer's museum, and a forge plate for the warship Monitor. Directions: I-87N to Exit 29, turn right and follow signs. Open from spring to fall. For information, call 532-7181.

Great Escape Fun Park, Rte 9 Lake George, is a wonderful family amusement park. Well-kept gardens and immaculately maintained walks thread their way through carefully run, imaginatively designed rides geared for all levels of fun-seekers—from daredevils to rail clingers—such as, the Steamin Demon Roller Coaster and the Desperado Plunge Flume Ride. Different sections of the park also offer entertainment and refreshments; picnic tables are open to those who bring their own food. The admission fee includes all rides and all shows. Information is available at 792-6568. Open: Memorial Day to Labor Day 9:30-6 daily. Directions: I-87N to Exit 19; follow signs.

Heldeberg Workshop, Picard Rd, Voorheesville, 765-2777, was organized over thirty years ago by four mothers to give school aged children a summer enrichment program aimed at both indoor and outdoor activities and classes in numerous subjects not offered in the public schools.

Hoffman's Playland, Rte 9 Latham, is a small, clean, well-run amusement park with rides, miniature golf, a driving range, and snacks of various kinds. Tickets purchased by the book offer substantial savings.

Indian Ladder Farms, Rte 156 Voorheesville, lures natives to an annual summer-autumn orgy of fruit-picking and general overindulgence in the fragrance of fresh baked pies, cookies, and cider donuts. Apples being processed for cider can be watched through a large picture window. Fresh cider is available year round. Open all year, except major holidays in winter, Mon-Sat 9-5, Sun 10-5. Information is available at 765-2956.

Nature Walks in any of Schenectady County's five Nature Preserves—Schenectady County Forest Preserve in Duanesburg, Indian Kill Nature Preserve in Glenville, Plotter Kill Nature Preserve in Rotterdam, Amy Lemaire Woods in the City of Schenectady, and the Schenectady Museum and Planetarium Nature Preserve in Niskayuna—are possible any day. Information is available in two booklets, *Natural Areas of Schenctady County* and *Natural Areas of Albany County,* published by the Environmental Clearinghouse of Schenectady, 2851 Aqueduct Rd, Niskayuna. Call 370-4125.

Northeast Air Show is Schenectady County Airport's tribute to the art of flying. The show includes a ground display of civilian and military aircraft as well as in-flight demonstrations. The event has grown steadily over the years. Information circulars are published in April and distributed throughout the Capital District.

RCCA: The Arts Center Riverfront Arts Fest is held on the third weekend in June in Riverfront Park in Troy. Selected works of area craftspersons stand in competition in a juried show on display throughout the weekend. Ethnic food booths, arts activities for children, diverse entertainers—from tumblers and clowns to serious musicians—attract an audience of over 40,000 people over the two days. A particular attraction is the street painting on River St. The works of winning artists from the weekend are shown in subsequent weeks at the headquarters of The Arts Center. Information is available at 189 2nd St, Troy, 273-0552.

Riverside Park, in Agawam, Massachusetts, is an enormous supermarket of an amusement park. The 150 acre site presents rides, shows, games, food, merchandise, and attractions of all kinds (from arcades to stock car races, merry-go-rounds to hamburger stands). But the unchallenged stars of this thrill-seekers' paradise are the roller coasters: the Cyclone boasts the steepest climb and drop of any in the United States; the antique wooden Thunderball creaks and squeals in concert with its passengers; the new Black Widow loop defies not only death but description. Admission to this fun-park, which first opened its doors in 1939, can be purchased in various combinations. Information is available at (413) 786-9300. Directions: Thruway to Mass Pike Exit 4; Rte 5 South (5.8 mi) to Rte 57; Rte 57 to Rte 159 South (Main St, Agawam); 2.9 miles to park.

The Victorian Picnic is an annual event at Oakwood Cemetery in Troy, sponsored by the Mohawk-Hudson Industrial Gateway and the Troy Cemetery Association. The event's purpose is to relive a pleasant Victorian summer afternoon. It includes a picnic supper, lawn croquet, coach rides through the grounds, and competition for the best Victorian costume. For information, call 274-5267.

Tuesday in the Park is an annual event in Schenectady's Central Park with increasing activities and growing attendance each year. It is an urban fair with entertainment, food, rides, and children's activities concluding with fireworks. For information, 382-5147.

Waterford Flight is a set of lift locks—the highest in the world—that raise boats from the Hudson River to the Mohawk River above the Cohoes Falls. Each of the five locks lifts the craft 33 to 35 feet. Each boat therefore climbs a staggering 168.8 feet. The trail is well marked and facilities are maintained by the Department of Parks and Recreation. A brochure with more information is available through the Waterford Historical Museum (open Saturday and Sunday afternoons) or the New York State Department of Transportation, Region I office, 474-6715. Directions: in the town of Waterford take Flight Rd off of Fonda Rd.

Water Slide World near Lake George Village is a water-oriented fun park with acres of water fun for all ages. It boasts the only "wave pool" in New York in addition to lots of twisting, turning, and straight slides. There is a small, toddler-sized water park with slides and a water fall. Take I-87N to Exit 21 to Rte 9 one-half mile south of Lake George Village. Open June through Labor Day, 10 am to 6 pm. Information, 668-4407.

Winterhawk Bluegrass Festival, Rothvoss Farm, Rte 22, eight miles south of Hillsdale has for over ten years electrified audiences with flying fiddle bows and fast finger guitar plucking for four music filled, foot stomping days, usually the third weekend of July. Performers are multi-talented world-famous singers, pickers and songwriters. For information and schedule call 479-7216. Admission charge.

Zoom Flume Amusement Park, Shady Glen Rd off Rte 145, East Durham, 239-4559 is a water park for the whole family. It offers water slides, water fall, arcade, and bumper boats. Open daily Memorial Day through Labor Day. Fee.

Cruises
Lake and River Cruises

On The Hudson River

Captain JP Cruise Line in Troy provides sightseeing and dinner boat tours on the Hudson in an air conditioned and heated paddlewheeler which holds 600 passengers. Various tours last from two hours to four hours; also available is a two-day river cruise. The boat is also available for charter for private parties. Captain JP is located behind City Hall in Troy at Water Front Park. The office is at 278 River St, 12180. For information, call 270-1901.

Dutch Apple Cruises Inc., 1666 Julianne Dr, Castleton, 463-0220, cruises the Hudson River from Albany to Castleton four times daily. There are also three cruises a week that pass through the federal lock and dam and the Erie Canal Park. The boats are anchored at the Snow Dock at the foot of Broadway and Quay St, in Albany, near the U Haul building.

The Spirit of St Joseph, 40 Riverside Ave, Rensselaer, 449-2664 is a three-deck paddlewheeler docked at the Port of Rensselaer which can accomodate 400 passengers on its regularly scheduled and varied cruises, including dinner cruises, senior citizen lunch cruises, evening jazz and Dixieland cruises, a Thursday evening grand Italian buffet cruise, and Friday and Saturday night dinner cruises.

On The Mohawk River

Collar City Charters, 427 River St, Troy, 272-5341, offers a forty-one foot steel hull boat, the Lockmaster, for hire for touring the New York State Canal System. The boat is completely outfitted for sleeping, cooking, and dining. A comprehensive three-hour course of instruction and fuel for a week-long cruise of the Hudson and Mohawk valleys are included in the rental arrangements.

Erie Canal Cruises on the Mohawk River, including a day cruise at 1:30 and a dinner cruise at 6:30 daily except Monday, are provided by Riverboat Cruises, Inc., One Terminal Rd, Clifton Park 12065, aboard the Nightingale III, which accomodates 90 passengers. The three-hour cruises, including a sightseeing narration, usually pass through one of the fascinating Erie Canal locks in the daytime. Advance reservations are recommended and are required for the dinner cruises. Groups may charter the entire boat. All trips leave from the Northeast end of Rte 9 bridge at Crescent; the ticket office is at the dock. For information, call 273-8878.

On Lake George

For information on cruise times for all Lake George cruises below, visit or call Lake George Steamboat Co., Steel Pier Beach Rd, Lake George Village, 668-5777.

Lac Du Saint Sacrement, the newest and largest of the Lake George cruise ships, offers a variety of cruises, including lunch and dinner cruises, a Friday specialty cruise (with a different theme each week), and Saturday moonlight cruises with lively entertainment.

Mohican makes a complete tour of the 32-mile length of Lake George, leaving at 9 am, arriving at Ticonderoga at 11:15, and returning to Lake George Village at 1:30. There is also a two and a quarter hour afternoon cruise of the southern half of Lake George—the Paradise Bay Cruise—which departs at 2:30.

Steamboat Minne-Ha-Ha, an authentic steamboat built in 1969, plies Lake George merrily playing her steam-powered calliope on her seven one-hour shore-line cruises and her two evening Dixieland and jazz cruises daily from June through September 2.

On Lake Sacandaga
Great Sacandaga Steamship Company Sam's Harbor Marine, Rte 30 Woods Hollow Rd, Broadalbin, (800) 836-0276 offers cruises on the 29-mile-long Great Sacandaga Lake, with views of portions of the 125 miles of shore line. May through October.

FALL

Apple Picking has become an annual tradition for many Capital District families. Most area orchards invite patrons to climb the trees themselves in search of the perfect fruit. As a result, residents have become quite knowledgeable in the subtleties of species; they argue the virtue of their favorite variety and discuss vehemently the best weeks to pick each. From mid- September on, local newspapers carry orchard announcements of what trees are ready for picking.

Come Sunday, a festival celebrating the contributions of Black Americans to our culture is held early in September in Washington Park, Albany, and is free to the public. The event is produced by the Albany-Schenectady League of Arts, the Washington Park Conservancy and the Mayor's Office of Special Events.

Foliage Tours, though not generally organized, are part of the fall ritual in the Capital District. This has become true in large part because the area is the perfect center for touring: glorious colors appear in every direction over a period of five weeks or more. As autumn approaches, media report the progress of color. Although exact dates depend somewhat on the summer rainfall, the "North Country" generally peaks in the last week of September, the Capital District— including the Helderbergs—by Columbus Day, and the Catskills during the last

Fo' Castle County Store, Burnt Hills

two weeks of October. A foliage report and a brochure are available at the Department of Economic Development, 1 Commerce Plaza, Albany, or call 1-800-CALLNYS. One of the region's most spectacular tours is the three-state triangle—Capital District to Bennington VT to Williamstown MA and back.

Hay Rides and Sleigh Rides are a way for groups to get some fall and winter fun going. Call ahead for information and directions to the following providers: Rolling Meadows Farm, White Rd, Ballston Spa, 885-1655, and Viewmere Farm, Rte 40, Schaghticoke, 753-4630.

Iroquois Indian Festival, an annual event celebrating the creativity of the Iroquois Indians, is held on the Saturday and Sunday of Labor Day weekend. The festival features lacrosse games between the Iroquois Nationals and white teams; Iroquois speakers on contemporary problems; stories written about or by Iroquois; films on Iroquois life; handicrafts; children's games; and foods and recipes. For information, call the Iroquois Indian Museum, Caverns Rd, Howes Cave, 296-8949. The museum is about one hour west of Albany.

Lark Fest, Lark St Albany, has become Upstate's largest street festival. From 9 to 5 on a September Saturday, Lark St from Central to Madison becomes an urban fair grounds. Lark St merchants display their wares, in friendly competition with invited street vendors, fast food impressarios, and performing musicians for the attention of the thousands of visitors. For details, call 463-7182.

The Medieval Fair, usually held the third weekend in October, is arranged by the Cathedral of All Saints in Albany. Parishioners remove the seats and convert the nave into what the medieval cathedral in fact was—a center for art, music, entertainment, and commerce as well as the focus of religious solemnity. The variety of its offerings—which include caligraphy, puppetry, tumbling, juggling, music, and medieval food—attracts a wide range of people. For information, call 465-1342.

Rensselaer County Regional Chamber of Commerce Harvest Festival, a two-day community celebration of autumn, is one of the region's newer attractions. It includes arts and crafts displays, food booths, apple and pumpkin picking, old-fashioned music, and numerous children's activities. For dates and information, call 274-7020.

The Walkabout is an annual house and garden tour conducted each September by the Schenectady County Historical Society and the Stockade Association. Participants pay a fee and receive a well illustrated map and brochure to guide them in a walking tour of various homes, churches, and buildings in the historic district of the Stockade. Information is available at the Schenectady County Historical Society, 32 Washington Ave Schenectady, 374-0263.

WINTER

The Annual Christmas Greens Show at the Rensselaer County Historical Society, 57-59 Second St Troy, 272-7232, offers an opportunity to tour the lovely Hart-Cluett Mansion and view beautifully rendered Christmas decorations.

The Festival of Trees at The Albany Institute of History and Art, 125 Washington Ave, Albany, 463-4478, presents scores of trees, each sponsored and decorated by a community group or business. Many things make this show appealing, not the least of which is the variety—the blend of sleek, trendy, witty, innovative, simple and traditional decorations combining to make a wonderful show.

First Night in Albany, taking its cue from a similar successful enterprise in Boston, is a multi-venue celebration of the arts held each New Year's Eve. It begins with a parade at 6 pm and is followed by various performances continuously from 7-11:30 pm in over fifty locations by more than 250 performers. Free shuttle buses are available for "button" wearers for all locations. There are street vendors and snacks at some locations. Ben and Jerry's serves 2000 ice cream sundaes. Programs are available prior to the event. Buttons are sold at a discount in area locations before Dec 29; children under five are free. For information, Mayor's Office of Special Events, 434-2032.

Historic Cherry Hill, 523 1/2 South Pearl St, Albany, 434-4791, invites the public each December to celebrate the holiday season with a visit to the mansion located in the south end of Albany. Built in 1787 for Philip and Maria Van Rensselaer, the house was lived in continuously for five generations of one family, until 1963. The special open house, offered on the first or second Sunday of December, features period music, refreshments made from Van Rensselaer family recipes, thematic displays throughout the house, and a large decorated Christmas tree in the formal parlor. Fee.

The Schenectady Christmas Parade, sponsored by the Schenectady Chamber of Commerce and held annually on the Friday evening after Thanksgiving, is the largest nightime parade in the Northeast. Moving along State St is a line of marching bands, floats, and clowns that enchants the crowd of children and adults.

The Schenectady Colonial Festival, held in February, celebrates the city's colonial heritage with worship services, a costume ball, re-enactments of colonial life, horse and dog cart rides, snowman contests, and several school programs. For information, call (800) 962-8007.

Schenectady's Wintertainment, held in February, is an evening of music, dance, puppets, theatrical performances, and a laser show. There is no charge. For information, call (800) 962-8007.

Snow Expo, the oldest continuous Snow Expo in the United States, includes a swap shop, ski movies, and over 150 exhibitions sponsored by manufacturers, retailers, and ski centers. The Expo is usually held the first weekend in November at the Empire State Convention Center in Albany, 783-1333. Fee.

Tree Cutting at Christmas. Tagging and cutting one's own Christmas tree is an activity that heralds the season for many in the area. The following places for this area are open from Thanksgiving to Christmas: Bob's Christmas Trees, 1227 West Galway Rd, Galway, 882-9455; Fred Oettinger, Knox Cave Rd, Knox, 872-1331; George VanElten, Knox, 872-1897.

Victorian Stroll is a downtown Troy Victorian shopping stroll, where the sights, sounds, and scents of the holiday season come to life in stores and restaurants. There are sidewalk carolers, strolling minstrels, jugglers, and dancers to add to the festivity. A free shuttle service and a vintage horse-drawn carriage ride (with charge) depart from City Hall. For information, call 272-8308.

National Baseball Hall of Fame and Museum, Cooperstown

NOT FAR AWAY

The Capital District is within easy reach of many beautiful towns, exciting cities, interesting sites, and lively amusement centers. This chapter describes principal attractions at a distance of one half hour or more from the tri-cities. It is divided into four parts on the basis of general direction. In each instance, estimated driving times are given. Times are measured from the center of Albany. All places represented in the chapter were found to be well worth the journey required.

NORTH OF THE CAPITAL DISTRICT

Round Lake

Round Lake Village, formerly a Methodist camp meeting "tent" community for the largest camp meetings in the United States retains—thanks to the efforts of the Round Lake Historical Society—much of its large concentration of Victorian architecutre organized in the original wheel design for the streets. The village is listed on the National Register of Historic Places. Because of the preservation, the distinctive painting of the buildings, and the quaintness of the grounds, the village has become a good place for a walking tour. There are also concerts in the auditorium, which houses the notable 1847 Tracker pipe organ, including jazz, country music, and an acoustic series. Directions: I-87N to exit 11, go 1/2 mile east to the village; or take Rte 9 to Round Lake, 1/2 mile to the west.

Saratoga

In August, Saratoga Springs is a fascinating place to be. The world's most spectacular thoroughbreds gather for a brief season and lure with them a dazzling assemblage of some of the world's most colorful individuals—third generation multi-millionaires, world champion jockeys, internationally respected trainers, and glittering entertainment personalities. Mansions which sit empty for eleven months shimmer well into the night; stables desolate from September to July bustle from before dawn to dusk; the performing arts center, dormant from September to June, fills with music as the summer sun goes down. In town, the hotels and restaurants honor reservations made months in advance and the Fasig-Tipton Pavilion quietly responds to bids in the hundreds of thousands of dollars.

When the horses leave and the musicians pack up, Saratoga changes. It becomes again a quiet, charming city. In both of its states, Saratoga is a pleasant place to be. Directions: I-87 North to Exit 13N. (Forty minutes.)

The **Urban Cultural Park,** Broadway and Congress St, Saratoga Springs, 587-3241, is located in the former **Drink Hall**. This beautiful beaux-arts building is reminiscent of many European structures with its long wings and stately columns. Among the displays is a four-sided tableau depicting the city's history of recreation, architecture, transportation and its people. Also, a gazebo traces the evolution of the mineral springs describing each of the three varieties of water. Murals show well-dressed visitors partaking of the minerals to aid in alleviating gastric disorders. The building served as the terminal for the Hudson Valley Railway Station from 1915 to 1941 and many of the old trolley benches carved of chestnut line the walls.

Saratoga Circuit Tours, Inc. 417 Broadway, Saratoga Springs, 587-3656, offers a two-hour tour departing from the Urban Cultural Park opposite the entrance to Congress Park. Step-on guides are available for group tours year round. Information available at the tour office.

Saratoga Springs Preservation Foundation, 6 Lake Ave Saratoga Springs, 587-5030, offers tours of architecture, parks, sculpture, and burial grounds. Tours are by appointment except for the annual fall house tour and the annual candlelight house tour.

Congress Park and the Canfield Casino. In the center of Saratoga Springs sits a thirty-three acre park which houses handsome sculptural pieces, landscaped ponds, mineral springs, and the **Canfield Casino,** an elegant nineteenth century gambling hall. The casino, which features domed windows, and stained glass panels, is owned by the city of Saratoga Springs and may be rented. On the second and third floors the Historical Society of Saratoga Springs runs a museum of local history.

Gideon Putnam Hotel is a charming old resort nestled amidst tall pines on the grounds of the Saratoga Spa State Park. It is a center of activity during August when the flat track is in action. The general public is welcome in the dining room and the gift shop which displays an interesting selection of antique jewelry. Reservations are suggested in high season, 584-3000. Bikes are available for rental at the Gideon Putnam in July and August, 9 am-6 pm weather permitting. The terrain throughout the park is level and the surroundings are beautiful so it is the perfect place for casual peddling or serious racing. Directions: Take I-87 North to Exit 13N. Take Rte 9 North. Follow signs. (Thirty minutes.)

The Baths in Saratoga Spa State Park, 584-2011, welcome men and women to take the baths at the Lincoln Spa, open in the summer only, and the Roosevelt Spa open all year. This consists of relaxing in a deep tub filled with warm effervescent water and then, wrapped in an oversized towel, moving to a cot for a massage and rest. The personnel at the baths are congenial and gracious. Everyone who tries this luxury reports feeling greatly restored and refreshed. The fee for the bath is reasonable. Information is available at 584-2010 or 584-2011. Directions: I-87N to Exit 13N; Rte 9 North to entrance.

National Museum of Dance, South Broadway is described in the Chapter on Arts.

National Museum of Racing, Union Ave, is described in the chapter on Museums.

Saratoga Harness Hall of Fame is described in the chapter on Museums.

Saratoga Spa State Park is described in the chapter on Sports and Recreation.

Yaddo is a Victorian estate in Saratoga Springs set aside by Spenser Trask as a retreat for invited artists, writers and composers. Among those whom Yaddo has served over the years are such luminaries as Robert Lowell, Flannery O'Connor, Aaron Copland, Jessamyn West, William Carlos Williams, Carson McCullers and Saul Bellow. The house is not open to the public, but it is possible to drive through and visit the grounds. Directions: take I-87N to Exit 14. Go west on Union St. Watch for sign on left after crossing over I-87.

Stillwater

Saratoga National Historic Park, Rtes 4 and 32 between Stillwater and Schuylerville, 664-9821, is an historic area marking the site of the critical encounter of the Revolution, the Battle of Saratoga. A visitor center provides information about the historical moment and guidance for a complete driving tour of the battlefield. Free. The park is open from Apr 1-Nov 30 from 9-5; July-Aug 9-6. The center is open daily except Thanksgiving, Christmas and New Year. Directions: Take I-87N to Exit 12. Follow clearly marked signs to park. (Forty minutes.)

Nearby is **Schuyler House,** beautiful home of General Philip Schuyler and Elizabeth Schuyler. Free. Open mid-June to Labor Day, 10-5.

Wilton

Grant Cottage, Rte 9 eight miles north of Saratoga Springs, 587-8277, was the home of President Ulysses Grant and family when he was writing his memoirs and the place he died in July 1885. Now a State Historic Site, period furniture, letters, and personal possessions are on display. Open from Memorial Day to Labor Day. There is a fee. (Forty-five minutes.)

Glens Falls

The Hyde Collection, 161 Warren St, 792-1761 was founded by Charlotte Pruyn Hyde in 1952 as an art museum for the greater Glens Falls region. Hyde House, the Florentine style villa of Mrs. Hyde, houses most of the original collection of European Old Master and American works of art and European antiques. The new Education Wing displays temporary exhibits and works of art recently acquired by the museum. Numerous educational activities and concerts are offered throughout the year. Tours of the museum are given daily from 1-3. Museum shop. Admission. Open Tues-Sun 10-5. Directions: I-87 North to Exit 18. Take Broad St to the center of town. Bear right on Warren St. (One hour.)

Lake George

Lake George is a sensationally beautiful natural lake on which many local residents rent or own summer homes. The village at the foot of the lake has become a center for summer entertainment. Some of the attractions offered are described in the chapter "Other Things to Do." The public beach along the foot of the lake gives a lovely view of the water and mountains. Sailing on the lake can be exciting and challenging, and the width of the lake makes it a wonderful place for waterskiing. Directions: Take I-87 North to Exit 21. Follow Rte 9 North. (One hour.)

Marcella Sembrick Opera Museum, Lakeshore Drive, Rte 9N, Bolton Landing, is a treasury of opera memorabilia. Located in the summer studio used by the famous soprano, the museum displays letters, photographs, and awards of Ms. Sembrick and other noted opera stars. Free. Open July 1-Labor Day daily 10-12:30; 2-5:30. 1-644-9839. Directions: Take I-87 North to Exit 22. Follow 9N towards Bolton Landing. (One hour and fifteen minutes.)

Cambridge

New Skete Monasteries are houses of religious orders of monks and nuns originally affiliated with the Russian Orthodox Church. The monasteries support their chosen life of prayer by practicing various arts and making the fruits of their labors available to the public. The monks, 677-3928, train dogs, craft icons, and operate a butcher shop and bakery. The nuns, 677-3810, make icons, sew liturgical vestments, and prepare cheesecakes and fruitcakes. The Companions of New Skete, 677-8863, are married monastics who produce calligraphy cards and dog beds. All foodstuffs are available at each monastery and their shops are open to the public. Directions: Rte 7 East to Rte 22 North. (About one hour and fifteen minutes.)

Ticonderoga

Fort Ticonderoga, 585-2821, is a splendid historic site. The stone fortress situated on a hill at the juncture of Lake George and Lake Champlain provides not only a spectacular panorama, but also a glimpse of what it must have been like both to attack and to defend a fort. The holdings of the military museum complement the fort's impressive structure, as do well-staged cannon drills, musketry shows, and fife and drum presentations. Guided tours are available. Open mid-May to mid-Oct. Admission. Directions: Take I-87N to Exit 28; turn right; follow signs. (Two hours.)

Adirondack Mountains

Adirondack Museum, Blue Mountain Lake, is located in the center of the 6,000,000 acre Adirondack Park. It tells through displays how man initially used the mountains to live simply and make a living from the animals and natural resources he found there, how he was joined by others seeking recreation, and how others came who sought commercial gain. Exhibits focus on themes of logging, boating, road and rail transportation, mining, outdoor recreation, schooling and rustic furniture. Admission. Gift shop and cafeteria. Open Memorial Day through Oct 15, 9:30-5:30. 1-352-7311. Directions: Take I-87N to Exit 23. Take Rte 28 to Rte 28N. (Two hours.)

SOUTH OF THE CAPITAL DISTRICT

Vineyards and Wineries dot the Hudson Valley Region. Information on wine production in the region is available at the Hudson Regional Wine Council, 42 Catherine St, Poughkeepsie 12601, (914) 452-4910. The vineyards listed below generally offer tours and wine tasting. Some are open only in summer but others are open year round; some charge a fee. Because schedules change, it is best to call or write the vineyard for hours open. A free regional "Winery Tours" guide is available at Cascade Mountain Winery.

Brotherhood Winery
35 North St, Washingtonville, (914) 496-3661

Adirondack Museum, Blue Mountain Lake

Cascade Mountain Winery
Flint Hill Rd, Amenia, (914) 373-9021

Clinton Vineyard
Schultzville Rd, Clinton Corners, (914) 266-5372

El Paso Winery
Rte 9W, Ulster Park, (914) 331-8642

Millbrook Vineyards
Wing Rd, Millbrook, (914) 677-8383

Regent Champagne Cellars
200 Blue Point Rd Rte 9W, Highland, (914) 691-7296

Royal Kedem Winery
P.O. Box 811 Dock Rd, Milton, (914) 795-2240

Valley Vineyards
Oregon Trail Rd, Walker Valley, (914) 744-3449

West Side of the Hudson
Coxsackie

Bronck House Museum, is a cluster of buildings and fields in which the settlement of the area is commemorated. The oldest structure is the 1663 stone house built by Pieter Bronck to establish the claim on the enormous stretch of land. The surrounding buildings and cemeteries show what life was like in this home lived in by eight generations of Broncks. Admission. Open: June through Labor Day, Tues-Sat 10-5; Sun 2-6. 731-8862. Directions: Take N.Y.S. Thruway to Exit 21B. Take 9W south 3 3/4 miles to Pieter Bronck Rd on right at red barn. (Forty minutes.)

Catskill

Thomas Cole House, 218 Spring St, 943-6553 is the historically preserved house of the founder of the Hudson River School of painting, which included such master landscapists as Frederic Church, Alexander Wyant and George Inness. Open July through Labor Day, Wed-Sun. Fee. Directions: NYS Thruway to Exit 21 to Rte 9W. (Forty-five minutes.)

Prattsville

Pratt Museum, Main St (Rte 23), Prattsville, 299-3395, is the Victorian-era homestead of successful businessman Zadock Pratt who was a member of Congress in the 1830's and helped launch the Smithsonian Museum and the intercontinental railway. The home displays a local hero and community builder's achievements and frequently hosts special events throughout the summer months. Wed-Sun 1-5 pm through Columbus Day. Donation. Directions: NYS Thruway South to Exit 21. Rte 23 West. (One hour and a half.)

Woodstock

Woodstock is a lovely little Catskill town southwest of Saugerties. The wooded setting, the privacy, and the presence of a longstanding summer arts colony have made Woodstock a place where musicians, dancers, writers, sculptors, painters—artists of all forms—feel comfortable living and working. The main street of the town houses shops in which their work can be viewed and purchased. Directions: Take N.Y.S. Thruway Exit 20. Go west on Rte 212. (One hour.)

Information on exhibits of artwork throughout the region is available at the Woodstock Artists Association, 28 Tinker St, (914) 679-2940. This organization also has its own gallery.

Tubing on the Esopus is a frolicking family entertainment practiced on the free-flowing Esopus Creek off Rte 28 north of Woodstock, (914) 679-2079. **F.S. Tube and Raft Rental,** 4 Church St, Phoencia (914) 688-5553, has one and two-seat tubes available May through Sept.

Byrdcliffe is the summer arts and crafts colony established in 1902 by Ralph Radcliffe Whitehead. Over the years, it has supported the work of hundreds of creative persons, some of them of renown—Charlotte Perkins Gilman, Harry Hopkins, John Dewey, Thomas Mann, Wallace Stevens, and Eva Watson-Schultz, for example. Today, supervised by The Woodstock Guild, Byrdcliffe continues its mission of providing a quiet, stimulating place for artists and craftspersons to work during summer. Visitors are welcome to tour the facility. A map and further information is available through The Woodstock Guild, 34 Tinker St, Woodstock NY 12498.

The Woodstock Guild also promotes the **Byrdcliffe Theater,** which presents theatrical entertainment in the summer, much of it of an experimental nature; the **Kleinert Arts Center,** which displays fine arts and crafts in ongoing exhibits during the summer; and the **Byrdcliffe Barn,** which offers a candlelight and champagne classical piano series in July and August. Information is available at the Guild Office.

Maverick Concert Hall, Box 102, Woodstock, (914) 679-7558, built in 1916, offers Sunday Chamber music with local and internationally known musicians in the summer.

Opus 40, 7480 Fite Rd, Saugerties, is difficult to explain. The lifetime accomplishment of stone sculptor Harvey Fite, it is best described as an enormous spacial decoration composed of huge pieces of stone drawn from a neighboring quarry and shaped into a garden. Smooth ramps lead to platforms, walls, benches— spaces enhanced by contemporary sculptural pieces. Because Fite was conscious of the relationship of his work to the surroundings, there are beautiful vistas everywhere. The impact is overpowering. Information about accommodations for visitors is available at (914) 246-3400.

Kingston

Senate House, 312 Fair St, was the first meeting place of the government of New York in July 1776. The rooms have been carefully preserved and restored to give an accurate impression of what life was like in colonial times. Free. Open: end of Apr through Oct Wed-Sat 10-5; Sun 1-5. (914) 338-2786. Directions: Take N.Y.S. Thruway south to Exit 19. At circle take exit to Washington Ave. At second light turn left onto N. Front St Take third right onto Fair St. (One hour.)

New Paltz

Stone Houses, Huguenot St, is a group of 18th century stone homes and a church built by a group of Huguenot settlers from Northern France. The buildings are charmingly clustered into a little community surrounded by fine old trees and gardens. Admission. Houses open June through Sept, Wed-Sat 10-4; Sun 1-4 except July and Aug 10-4. (914) 255-1660. Directions: Take N.Y.S. Thruway south to Exit 18. Take Rte 299 West through New Paltz. Just before bridge turn right on Huguenot St. (One hour and twenty-minutes.)

Lake Mohonk Mountain House is a resort hotel located on a small lake atop a mountain near New Paltz. The hotel, a Victorian wonder with turrets, porches and gingerbread, is extraordinary in its preservation of a gracious style long abandoned by most commercial hostelries. Well- maintained gardens and walking paths are open to day visitors as is the dining room. Reservations are required for the dining room. This resort has great appeal for those of all ages interested in physical activity in a healthy environment. (914) 255-1000. Directions: Take N.Y.S. Thruway south to Exit 18. Turn left on Rte 299. Five miles beyond New Paltz, after crossing bridge turn right. Bear left and follow Mountain Rest Rd to Mohonk Gate. (One hour and forty-five minutes.)

West Point

The United States Military Academy is a great place to visit. The **Visitor's Center,** (914) 561-2671, located just outside the gates in Highland Falls is the best place to start. There are bilingual tours daily. The Center provides interesting background—the history of West Point, stories about famous graduates, replicas of the academy's past, and an explanation of the nature of the college as it currently exists.

Once within the military compound, the visitor may walk through the grounds, tour the museum, visit the Cadet Chapel and the Catholic Chapel, and enjoy the scenery. Some of the buildings of the college are open to visitors. It is of course best to plan a visit to coincide with a parade or a sporting contest. The corps of cadets parade during the school year on a schedule available at the Public Affairs Office (914) 938-3507. The schedule of sporting events open to the public is released by the Sports Information Office (914) 938-3303 or 938-3512.

Food is available on the post at the Hotel Thayer. (On weekends the restaurant is very crowded and there may be a long wait.) Many visitors bring their own food and either picnic or tailgate in areas designated for public use. (Parking restrictions and all motor vehicle laws are strictly enforced.) Visitors in the company of a cadet who has made arrangements in advance may dine in the Mess Hall, and cadets may accompany a guest to Eisenhower Hall for light refreshments. The Officers Club on base is restricted to officers and their guests.

A fine gift shop is located in the Visitors Center. Directions: Take N.Y.S. Thruway south to Exit 17. Turn left on 17K into Newburgh. Turn right on 9W and then follow signs. (Two hours.)

Mountainville

The Storm King Art Center, in Mountainville outside of Cornwall, (914) 534-3115, is a 400 acre sculpture park and museum, much of it of monumental scale. Selective exhibits of sculpture are shown in an annual exhibit in the French Normandy style house. Among the artists of the over 160 pieces at the Center are Isamu Noguchi, Louise Nevelson, Richard Serra, and David Smith. Open daily Apr through Nov 11, 11-5:30. Suggested donation. Directions: N.Y.S. Thruway to Exit 17. Left on Rte 17K to center of Newburgh. Right onto Rte 32 South. Go six miles, through Vails Gate, and down a hill. Right on Orrs Mill Rd. Go 1/2 mile. Left onto Old Pleasant Hill Rd. Entrance 1/2 mile on left. (Two hours and a half.)

East Side of the Hudson
Malden Bridge

Malden Bridge Arts Center, Hoose Rd, 766-3616 centers around the summer art studio of local artist Betty Warren. It consists of three units: the home of The Malden Bridge Art League; the Malden Bridge School of Art, which offers summer workshops in drawing and painting; the Bridge Gallery, which hosts two exhibits in the summer, one by a professional artist, the other of works of artists in the Malden Bridge Art League. Call for hours. Directions: Take I-90 East to Exit 12. Turn right onto Rte 9. Go approximately one mile. Turn left on to Rte 32. Go 5 miles. Turn left onto Rte 66. Take first left turn. (One-half hour.)

Old Chatham

The Shaker Museum, has a collection of artifacts of the Shaker community based in this area in the 18th and 19th centuries. Furniture, baskets, and working tools are arranged in the buildings to recreate the lifestyle of simple dignity espoused by the Shakers. Admission. Open: May 1-Oct 31 from 10 am-5 pm. Library open year round for research. 1-794-9100. Directions: Take I-90 East to exit 11E. Go right on Rte 20. Turn right on Rte 66. Go through Malden Bridge and follow signs to Shaker Museum. (Forty minutes.)

Kinderhook

Kinderhook was the birth place of Martin Van Buren, the eighth president of the United States. There are several architecturally important houses to visit:

Ichabod Crane School House, Rte 9H in Kinderhook, 758-9265, is an historic preservation of the formerly typical one-room school house. Open May through Oct. Free. (Thirty minutes.)

James Vanderpool House, a federal-period house operated by the Columbia County Historical Society, is furnished with early nineteenth-century furniture and decorative arts. Admission. Open Memorial Day to Labor Day. Tues-Sat 11-5; Sun 1-5. 758-9265. Directions: Take I-90 East to Exit B1. Take Rte 9 South. (One-half hour.)

Lindenwald, the Martin Van Buren National Historic Site and the President's retirement home in 1839, was a federal style house which was extensively modified to resemble the Van Buren's Victorian taste. The National Park Service, which administers the site, has restored the home to its appearance prior to the President's death in 1862. Open May through Oct. Admission. 758-9689. Directions: Take I-90 East to Exit B1. Take Rte 9 South to 9H South. House is two miles south of village. (One-half hour.)

Van Allen House operated by the Columbia County Historical Society, is an eighteenth-century farmhouse built by Luykas Van Allen, a farmer and merchant, in 1737. It is furnished in the period. Admission. Open Memorial Day to Labor Day, Tues-Sat 11-5; Sun 1-5. 758-9265. Directions: Take I-90 East to Exit B1. Take Rte 9 South to 9H South. (One-half hour.)

Hudson

Hudson, originally settled by whaling families from Nantucket and New England, has a rich supply of about twenty antique shops, primarily stretching along Warren St.

American Museum of Fire Fighting, Harry Howard Ave, located at Firemen's Home in Hudson, is a fascinating display of instruments of fire fighting from the primitive buckets and horse drawn pumps to the contemporary swiveling snorkel. Included in the collection are parade models used by volunteer companies for purposes of pageantry rather than fire extinction. As a result, one need not be a fire fighting buff to enjoy this museum, for the array is dazzling. It is a wonderful museum for families. Free. Open Apr 1 through Nov, except Mon, from 9:30-4:30. 828-7695. Directions: Take N.Y.S. Thruway south to Exit 21. Go east on Rte 23 across Rip Van Winkle Bridge. Once in Hudson, follow signs to Firemen's Home. (Fifty minutes.)

Olana is not easy to define, for it is of interest to anyone interested in art, gardens or architecture, for anyone seeking a spectacular view of the Hudson River, or anyone wanting to picnic, hike, ski, skate or sled. Olana was the home of the American artist Frederick Edwin Church, a 19th century landscape artist of the Hudson River School and a world traveler. The structure and decor of the house, the thoughtfully planned grounds, and the objects on display in the house reflect his eclectic taste and philosophy. From the windows, especially as the sun is setting, the visitor can see landscapes which inspired Church's paintings.

Administered by the NYS Office of Parks, Recreation, and Historic Preservation. Olana is open Memorial Day through October. Wed-Sat 12-4; Sun 1-4. Grounds open year round till dusk. 828-0135. Admission fee. Directions: Take N.Y.S. Thruway south to Exit 21. Go east on Rte 23 across Rip Van Winkle Bridge. Turn south on 9G. (Forty-five minutes.)

Germantown

Clermont, is the estate of the Livingston family, many of whom played signifi-cant political roles in the birth and development of the United States and the state of New York. The core of the house dates to 1777; subsequent additions reflect the architectural and decorative tastes of varing ages.

The grounds surrounding the house offer nature walks, picnic areas and facilities for hiking, snowshoeing and cross-country skiing. Excellent literature describing the history of the house and family are available.

Clermont is now a historic site and state park. The house is open Memorial Day to the last Sunday in October. Call for seasonal hours. Grounds are open 6 am-dark all year. 537-4240. Directions: Take N.Y.S. Thruway south to Exit 21. Take Rte 23 East to Rte 9G South. (One hour.)

Annandale-on-Hudson

Historic Hudson Valley, 150 White Plains Rd, Tarrytown, (914) 631-8200 coordi-nates the touring activities of selected properties along the Hudson River south of Albany to New York City. Included are Montgomery Place in Annandale-on-Hudson, Van Cortlandt Manor in Croton-on-Hudson, Philipsburg Manor in North Tarrytown, Union Church of Pocantico Hills, and Sunnyside in Tarrytown. **Montgomery Place,** a 400 acre property which gives a glimpse of estate life and a firsthand look at restoration in progress, is closest to the Capital District. Montgomery Place is open Apr-Oct, 10-5 daily; weekends only 10-5 in March, Nov-Dec; closed Jan-Feb. There is an admission charge. Call for hours at other properties. Memberships in Friends of Historic Hudson Valley are available.

Rhinebeck

The principal **Anemone** growers on the East Coast are located in Rhinebeck. Dazzling colors line the greenhouses, and great bouquets are available at wholesale prices. Ralph Pitcher's nursery is open from 7-5:30 seven days a week. (914) 876-3974. Directions: Take N.Y.S. Thruway south to Exit 19. Go east over Kingston Rhinecliff Bridge to Rte 9G. Turn right. Take first left onto Middle Rd turning at sign for hybrid and cut flowers. Watch for red barn and greenhouses. (One hour and fifteen minutes.)

Old Rhinebeck Aerodrome is a museum and arena for aircraft. In the hangar the visitor can see planes from the World War I era and earlier, and from the stands the visitor can witness air shows featuring stunt flights, synchronized displays, and antique and customized planes in motion. The aerodrome is open May 15 through October seven days a week from 10 am to 5 pm. Aerial shows Sat-Sun at 2:30, June 15-Oct 15. (914) 758-8610. Directions: Take N.Y.S. Thruway south to Exit 19. Go east over Kingston-Rhinecliff Bridge to Rte 9G. Turn right onto 9G and follow signs. (One hour and fifteen minutes.)

Millbrook

Innisfree Garden, (914) 677-8000, is a man-made natural wonder, a cup garden designed and build by Walter Beck over a period of 22 years from 1930-1952. Beck literally rearranged the landscape—moving rocks, streams and waterfalls, constructing terraces, slopes and walls, decorating space with plants and vines. At this mammoth site, Beck improved on nature but eschewed artifice. Open: May through Oct with no admission fee Wed-Fri, two dollar admission on Sat-Sun for those twelve years and older. (One hour and thirty minutes.)

Hyde Park

Hyde Park, a National Historic Site, is a park, museum, library and national monument maintained on the site of the childhood home of Franklin Delano Roosevelt. The house, maintained as it was in 1945, is a charming and warm home filled with historic memorabilia and signs of human vitality. The museum houses a diverse collection of fascinating items ranging from FDR's boyhood pony cart to documents which shaped national and international events. Eleanor's years as wife of the President and as world figure in her own right are also documented. The chronological display offers a wonderful opportunity for visitors to learn—or relearn—what happened in the world between 1932- 1945, and in the case of Eleanor's humanitarian activities, between 1932- 1962. Admission fee to the house and museum. The house is open 9-5 every day except Thanksgiving, Christmas and New Year's. The tours on tape are particularly fine at Hyde Park. (914) 229-9115. Directions: N.Y.S. Thruway south to Exit 18. Go east on Rte 299 to Rte 9W. Go south on 9W to Mid-Hudson Bridge. Cross Bridge. Go north on Rte 9N. (Two hours.)

"Springwood," FDR's Home in Hyde Park

Val-Kill, Hyde Park, was Eleanor Roosevelt's personal retreat from 1927 through
1946. Here, eminent guests—Haile Selassie, Nikita Krushchev, John Kennedy,
and Jawaharal Nehru, for example—sought her counsel. Here, too, she began an
experiment in business for local and unemployed youth. The house is open daily,
May-Oct, 9-5; weekends in Nov-Dec, Mar-Apr, 9-5; closed Jan-Feb. Reached by
private vehicle from Hyde Park Museum. Information is available through the
Park Service (914) 229-9115. Directions: See Hyde Park.

Vanderbilt Mansion is an enormous mansion built by the American millionaire,
Frederick William Vanderbilt, son of Commodore Cornelius Vanderbilt, to provide a place to entertain and house many guests in lavish style at one time—as
was the practice of many nouveau riche industrialists at the end of the 19th
century. The landscaping and the view of the Hudson from the lawns are spectacular. Open daily 9-5 Apr-Oct; closed Tues-Wed, Nov-Mar. The grounds are open
until dusk. (914) 229-2501. Directions: Follow directions for Hyde Park and continue on Rte 9N. (Two hours and fifteen minutes.)

Garrison

Boscobel, is a beautiful mansion set on the highlands of the Hudson across from
West Point. The house itself is handsome, the interior is furnished with Federal
furniture and china, glass, and silver imported from Europe, and the view from the
lawns and gardens is spectacular. Admission. Open: Apr-Oct, Wed-Mon 9:30-5. (914)
265-3638. Directions: N.Y.S. Thruway south to 84 East to 9D South. (Two hours.)

Purchase

Donald M. Kendal Sculpture Gardens at Pepsi Co, (914) 253-2900, is a display
of over forty modern and contemporary sculptures by world famous artists in
gardens designed by the internationally famous garden designer Russell Page. A
walking tour guide brochure is available. Directions: Take N.Y.S. Thruway south.
Go east on Rte 287 to exit 8E. go straight forward to second left turn onto Anderson Hill Rd for a few miles. The Gardens are on the right, across from SUNY
Purchase. Open 9-5 daily. Free. (Two and a half hours.)

New York City

New York, the metropolis that hums day and night, is a second home to many
residents of the Capital District. An easy three hours away by car, even closer by
bus (Trailways runs frequent trips daily) or by train (Amtrak travels at 110 mph
along a beautiful stretch of track on the east bank of the Hudson River) the cultural, commercial and social opportunities of New York are second to none. Once
in the city the visitor has access to the efficient, relatively inexpensive mass tran-

sit system. Maps of bus routes and subways are available through *I Love New York,* Commerce Plaza Albany, (800) CALL NYS.

This office also will send free maps of the city and brochures on shopping, touring, dining, and enjoying the night life. Bookstores and libraries in the Capital District carry comprehensive guides to the city.

Information is also available through The New York Convention and Visitors Bureau (212) 397-8222. (Three hours by car.)

Places to Visit
Air Craft Carrier Intrepid
Bronx Zoo
Central Park and Zoo
Ellis Island Immigration Museum
Empire State Building
Guinness Hall of World Records
Hayden Planetarium
Lower East Side Tenement Museum
New York Botanical Gardens (Bronx)
Enid A. Haupt Conservatory
New York Stock Exchange and Commodities Exchange
Rockefeller Center
South St Seaport
Statue of Liberty
Trump Tower
United Nations Building
World Trade Center

Libraries
New York Public Library, Main Branch

Museums
American Museum of Natural History
Cloisters
Cooper-Hewitt Museum
Frick Museum
Guggenheim Museum
Pierpont Morgan Library
Metropolitan Museum of Art
Museum of the City of New York
Museum of Modern Art
Museum of Holography
Whitney Museum

Notable Houses of Worship
Cathedral of St. John the Divine
St. Bartholemew's Church
St. Patrick's Cathedral
Temple Emmanuel
Trinity Church

Rides
Carriage Ride (Central Park)
Sightseeing Boats (Dayline)
Staten Island Ferry

Walks
Fifth Ave (90th St to 34th St)
Madison Ave (95th St-South)
Chinatown/Little Italy
Greenwich Village/SoHo/TriBeca
Wall Street

Plays
New York is still the national capital for dramatic arts. Theaters vary somewhat on show times, but the traditional hours still dominate; that is, Matinees Wed. and Sat. at 2:00; evening performances Mon-Sat at 8. Half-price tickets are available day of performance at Times Square Ticket Center, Broadway at 47th St Many Broadway theatres will accept ticket orders on major credit cards by telephone. Charter buses offer theatre excursions. These are advertised locally.

Entertainment: The world reknowned Art Deco theater, **Radio City Music Hall,** features family shows of many varieties.

Washington, DC
Washington, though not nearby, is popular with area residents as a place to visit, particularly in spring and early summer. The Travel section of the *Sunday New York Times* frequently advertises outstanding weekend specials in Washington hotels.

Residents who plan a trip to the Capital may get special visitor passes to the White House and the galleries in the houses of Congress plus helpful tips on visiting the city by calling the office of their local Congressional Representative. (Numbers are in the blue pages of the telephone directory.)

EAST OF THE CAPITAL DISTRICT

Vermont

Bennington

Bennington is a charming New England town with many things for the visitor to see and do. The approach to Bennington is itself splendid. Rte 7 comes to a rise at the border between New York and Vermont, and all the beauty of rural Vermont is on display. Although the area is lovely throughout the year, it is particularly spectacular in the autumn. Directions: Take 787 North to Rte 7 East to Bennington. (One hour.)

In addition to scenic beauty Bennington offers historic sites, museums, and stores, presented here more or less in order for the visitor approaching from the Capital District.

Old First Church, (802) 447-1223 is a beautiful, graceful church, with its eloquence of line and simplicity of decor. Built in 1805, it still functions as an active center of worship. For this reason, visiting hours are somewhat dependent upon the needs of the congregation. However, even from the outside the church is a pleasure to see.

Beside and behind the church, enclosed in a splendid white fence, is Old Burying Ground, the cemetery in which rest the founders of the town, many soldiers from the American Revolution, as well as Robert Frost, the poet. The tomb markers, many of Puritan style, are of interest to students of art, history and religion.

Monument Avenue, the street which extends up from the church, is lined with magnificent colonial homes and beautiful trees.

Bennington Battle Monument is an obelisk commemorating the defeat of British Troops by the Green Mountain Boys. There is an historically accurate, full color diorama depicting the battle. A tourist office located at the base of the monument provides information and access to the tower which visitors may climb. Open Apr through May. Admission.

Bennington Museum, (802) 447-1571, is a regional museum which features early American furniture, glass, paintings, and sculpture, a collection of Bennington pottery, and the works of Grandma Moses, the notable American primitive painter. Additionally, a collection of some of her personal belongings and other memorabilia is on display in a small schoolhouse. Admission. Open Jan 2 to Dec 23. Closed Thanksgiving.

Potters' Yard is a collection of shops all worthy of a visit. Of particular note is **Bennington Potters,** 324 County St, (802) 447-7531, which has both a display room-sales room and a grist mill where factory seconds and overuns of this fine pottery are sold. Also for sale are interesting candles, placemats, napkins, prints, cookware and wools. Tours of the factory are available by reservation for buses. **The Brasserie** in the Potters' Yard serves pleasant meals both inside and on the patio. Open: Mon-Sat 11:30-5, Sun 10:30-5. Information is available at (802) 447-7922.

Park McCullough House, Park and West Sts, North Bennington, (802) 442-5441, is an 1865 Victorian mansion with handsome wood paneling, Italian marble mantles, original furniture, and portraits of two former governors who lived in the house. Open May through Oct. Fee. Directions: From Bennington take VT Rte 7 North to Rte 67A. In North Bennington turn up hill to West St. Gate is at top of hill. (One and one half hours.)

Images from the Past, West Main St, (802) 442-3204, provides a glimpse of history and a nostalgic memory trip with its display of available prints, cards, and early photos. Open May through Oct for pre-arranged group tours of Historic Bennington with a slide orientation and a guide. Fee.

Joseph Cerniglia Winery, 37 West Rd Rte 9, (802) 442-3531, offers free tours and tasting of its critically acclaimed eleven varieties of Vermont wines. Open daily 10-5.

Bennington's Oldcastle Theater Company, a twenty-year-old professional theater company in residence at Southern Vermont College in June through December, presents musicals, mysteries, comedies, and youth theater. For information and a brochure, call (802) 447-0564.

Manchester

Manchester is another beautiful old Vermont town with many interesting places to shop and to eat. The shops are well worth visiting for pleasure and/or buying. Directions: Take 787 to Rte 7 East to Bennington. Take VT Rte 7 North. (One hour and forty-five minutes.)

Hildene, the summer home of Robert Todd Lincoln, son of Abraham Lincoln, was occupied by descendants until 1975. The house contains a pipe organ and is furnished with family possessions. The formal gardens have been restored. Admission. Open mid-May-Oct, 9:30-4:30. (802) 362-1788. Directions: Follow directions to Manchester. House is on Rte 7A, 2 miles south of the junction of Rte 7A and 11/30, in Manchester.

Shelburne

Shelburne Farms, Harbor Rd Shelburne, (802) 985-8686, is a non-profit orgar
tion whose purpose is to teach and demonstrate the stewardship of natural ar
agricultural resources. Listed on the National Register of Historic Places, it ha
Visitor Center and Farm Store, from which tours leave on open-air wagons w:
stops at the gardens, the dairy barn, and the Shelburne House. A walking trai
the farm animal area winds through fields and woodlands with a spectacular
view of Lake Champlain and the Adirondacks. Directions: I-87N to Exit 21 to
149E to Rte 4N to VT Rte 30N to Rte 7N. (Two hours and forty-five minutes.)

Shelburne Museum, Rte 7 Shelburne, (802) 985-3346, houses nationally celebrated collections of American folk art, artifacts, and architecture. On its
forty-five acres are historic buildings, period homes, and perennial gardens.
An 1840 General Store and a one-room schoolhouse are featured attractions. ,
orientation film acquaints visitors with the many attractions of the extensive
seum. Open daily, 9-5, from mid May through mid Oct. Free. Directions:
I-87N to exit 21 to Rte 149E to Rte 4N to Vt Rte 30N to Rte 7N. (Two hours an
forty-five minutes.)

Massachusetts
The Berkshires

The Berkshires is a region in Western Massachusetts united as much by its cc
mon pursuits as by its geography. Chosen almost simultaneously by the 19th
century artistic colony and the affluent as a center for their summer lives, the
has remained to this day a focal point of literature, music, dance, and the exp
sive arts. Many of the mansions built as "summer cottages" in the opulent ei
the end of the last century have become schools, monasteries, convents and :
Writers, composers, and choreographers as well as performing artists contin
flock to the area, especially in July and August.

General tours of the area are interesting, but some places in and around
Stockbridge and Lenox serve as focal points.

Discover the Berkshires is a helpful guidebook to the Berkshire area. It include
of the Bed and Breakfast Associations in the Berkshires, and information on
recreational, cultural, and seasonal activities of the four seasons of the year.
mation on the Berkshires also may be obtained by calling or writing the Ber
Hills Visitors Bureau, Berkshire Common, Plaza Level, Pittsfield, MA 01201
(413) 443-9186.

Berkshire Opera Company, Rte 7, Lenox, (413) 243-1343, a professional op
group with young performers from across the country, performs famous op

"A Girl with a Fan" by Pierre Auguste Renoir, Clark Art Institute, Williamstown

in English in the 500-seat indoor amphitheater on the grounds of the Cranwell estate in the summer.

The Fall Foliage Festival in North Adams, a week-long event usually held in the last week of September, culminates in a large parade celebrating the season and the harvest. For information, write or call the Northern Berkshire Chamber of Commerce, 69 Main St, North Adams, MA 01247, (413) 663-3735.

The Fourth of July Parade held annually in Pittsfield claims to be the largest in the United States. The festivities begin at 10 am and are televised nationally. Good vantage points are gotten early around the Park Square and the Berkshire County Courthouse. For information, call or write Berkshire Hills Visitors Bureau, Berkshire Common, Plaza Level, Pittsfield MA 01201, (413) 443-9186 or (413) 499-3861.

Williamstown

Williamstown is an interesting place to visit for several reasons, beauty being the first. Williamstown is so like the college town of fiction—a small New England town with splendid old trees, wide streets, beautiful colonial homes, impressive fraternity houses, small tweedy shops, well-dressed students, and ever-so-slightly rumpled professors—that it seems more like a Hollywood set than a real town.

In addition to serving as idyllic home for **Williams College,** an excellent undergraduate college of liberal arts, Williamstown is the home of the **Clark Art Institute,** an outstanding museum of fine arts featuring a collection of French Impressionist paintings including more than thirty Renoirs, American works, noteworthy works by European masters, and beautiful porcelains and silver. No admission. The Institute was established by Robert Sterling Clark, an heir to the Singer sewing machine fortune, and his wife Francine. The Institute is open Tues-Sun, 10-5. (413) 458-9545.

The Williams College Museum of Art mounts excellent exhibits. Because it serves a multi-purpose art department, the displays cover a full range of art forms and historical periods. In addition to its permanent collection, there are changing exhibits with an emphasis on American, Modern, Contemporary, and Non-western arts. No admission. Museum is open Mon-Sat 10-5; Sun 1-5. (413) 597-2429.

Directions: Take Rte 787 North to Rte 7 through Troy to Rte 2. Follow Rte 2 to Williamstown. (One hour.)

Stockbridge

Stockbridge is a charming town in the valley. Information about its history, its points of interest and its most famed citizen, Norman Rockwell, are readily available in restaurants and stores or at the Visitor Information Booth opposite the Red Lion Inn. Directions: Take I-90 East to N.Y.S. Thruway to Mass. Pike. Take Exit 2. Go south on Rte 102 to Stockbridge. (One hour.)

The Red Lion Inn, Main St, Stockbridge, has served travelers since 1773 when it was a stagecoach stop. The inn serves fine meals. Many travelers plan their day in the Berkshires around a stop at this historic spot. The Inn is described further in the chapter on Lodging and the chapter on Restaurants.

Berkshire Botanical Garden, Rte 102 and Rte 183, Stockbridge, (413) 298-3926, is a non-profit horticultural center established "to educate its members and the public in the art and enjoyment of growing things." On display are types of garden settings, formal plantings, vegetable plots, rock gardens, and greenhouses, including a solar greenhouse. An annual harvest festival is held the first Saturday in October. Open mid-May to mid-Oct. The greenhouses are open all year. Fee.

Chesterwood, (413) 298-3579, the home and studio of sculptor Daniel Chester French, is a fascinating place, for on display is the plaster cast French used to model the statue of the seated Lincoln now located within the Lincoln Memorial in Washington. Admission. Open May 1st-Oct 31, 10-5. Directions: From Stockbridge take Rte 102 West two miles to Rte 183. Turn left onto Rte 183; go one mile to the Chesterwood sign at Mohawk Lake Rd; turn right and follow signs for one half mile. Chesterwood is on the right.

Naumkeg, Stockbridge, (413) 298-3239, is the gabled mansion designed by the famous architect Stanford White in 1885 for Joseph Choate, the Ambassador to England and noted attorney. There is an admission charge. Open late June-Labor Day: Tues-Sun and Mon holidays; Memorial Day-late June, Labor Day-Columbus Day: Sat- Sun and Mon Holidays. Hours: 10-4:15. The gardens, designed by Fletcher Steele, are open daily, all season, 10-5. Directions: take I-90 and/or N.Y.S. Thruway to Mass Turnpike; take exit 2 off the Mass Turnpike; take Rte 102 West towards Stockbridge Center; from the intersection of Rte 102 and Rte 7 at the Red Lion Inn take Pine St north; bear left on Prospect Hill Rd for one-half mile. Entrance on the left.

Norman Rockwell Museum, Main St Stockbridge MA 01262, (413) 298-3822, displays 50 original pieces by the famed Stockbridge resident, acknowledged Dean of poster art. The collection of paintings, drawings, and sketches, which changes each year, must be seen in the company of a guide. A gift shop sells books and prints. Open: daily There is an admission fee. A new five million dollar museum, which will provide more space for exhibits and additional programs, is expected to be completed in the late fall of 1993 on a forty-acre site three miles west of the present museum.

Hancock

Hancock Shaker Village, Rte 20, Pittsfield, (413) 443-0188, is a restored Shaker community showing the material and ideological contributions of the Shakers to American society. The site includes eighteenth and nineteenth-century Shaker buildings, herb and heirloom vegetable gardens, and craft demonstrations. This is a working farm with historic breeds of livestock. Candlelight Shaker dinners with a program are offered Saturday evenings July-October by reservation. Open May 1-Oct 31, 9:30-5:30 for self-guided tours, April-November, 10-3 guided tours on the hour and December 1-March 30 guided tours by appointment. Admission. Directions: Take I-90 East to Rte 20. Go east, cross the Mass line and continue to Pittsfield. (One hour.)

Lenox

Lenox is a beautiful town of interest because its setting is so picturesque and because it is the site of Tanglewood, the keystone of music in the Berkshires. Directions: Take I-90 East to N.Y.S. Thruway Exit B3. Follow signs to Massachusetts Rte 102. Take 102 to Rte 183 North. Tanglewood is 4-5 miles up road. (One hour and fifteen minutes.)

The Mount, was the summer home of Edith Wharton, the author of *Ethan Frome, The Age of Innocence, The House of Mirth,* and others. It is currently being restored to serve as an historical site and is the residence for a theater company, Shakespeare and Company. (The company is described in the chapter "The Arts.") The owners of the house, the Edith Wharton Restoration Company, Inc., offer tours of the 29 room mansion. Admission. Directions: Take I-90 East to N.Y.S. Thruway to Mass Pike. Take Exit 2. Follow Rte 20W to Rte 7 South to junction of Rtes 7 and 7A—Plunkett Rd. (One hour and ten minutes.)

Tanglewood, the summer home of the Boston Symphony, was the brainchild of three persons of imagination and will—Dr. Henry Hadley, Gertrude Robinson Smith and Serge Koussivitsky. They envisioned a center where young musicians could come to learn from masters and where the public could enjoy the fruits of their collaboration in the fresh summer mountain air. The center, located on an estate donated to the symphony, includes the music shed for performances and other buildings for study and practice. Information about concerts is included in the section on music.

Pittsfield

Arrowhead, (413) 442-1793, was the home of Herman Melville during his most prolific years as a writer. Here he wrote *Moby Dick* and *The Piazza Tales*. The house has been refurnished to represent its appearance at the time Melville was living and working under its roof. Admission. Open: Memorial Day through Oct. Open Nov through Memorial Day for group tours Directions: Take I-90 East to N.Y.S. Thruway and Mass. Pike to Exit 2. Take Rte 20 North to Pittsfield. Right onto Holmes Rd. Entrance is ahead on left. (One hour and ten minutes.)

Berkshire Museum, 39 South St, (413) 443-7171, founded in 1903 by a descendant of the founders of Crane & Co., is three museums in one, with collections in art, natural science, and history, many of which relate to Berkshire County's cultural and natural past and present. There is an admission charge; children under twelve are free. Open year round, Tues-Sat 10-5, Sun, 1-5; open Mondays in July and Aug from 10-5.

Springfield

The Basketball Hall of Fame, 1150 W. Columbus Ave, Springfield, (413) 781-6500, is both a museum and a Hall of Fame. The displays trace the history of the sport from its birth at Springfield in 1891 to the present. Additions to the museum include a high school room honoring coaches and stars of the sport at that level and exhibits of great women players. Admission. Open: daily Sept-June 10-5; July-Aug 10-6. (Closed Thanksgiving, Christmas, New Years.) (413) 781-6500. Directions: Take I-90 East to N.Y.S. Thruway to Mass. Pike to Exit 6 to Rte 291 South. Watch for signs. (One hour and forty-five minutes.)

Sturbridge

Old Sturbridge Village, Rte 20 Sturbridge, (508) 347-3362, an outdoor museum designed to recreate life in a 19th century New England town, is an interesting and entertaining spot for families to spend a day. Visitors can watch demonstrations of crafts and arts and participate in some of the events. Informative brochures outlining special occasions and giving details about hours and fees are available by mail or phone. The brochures stress that comfortable warm clothing is recommended. Admission. Open: Apr 1 to Nov 30, 9-5 daily; winter 10-4 Tues-Sun. Directions: Take I-90 East to N.Y.S. Thruway to Mass. Pike to Exit 9. Follow Rte 20 West one mile. (Two hours.)

Boston

Boston is only three hours away—an easy ride along the New York State Thruway and the Massachusetts Turnpike. Commercial bus lines run the route daily, and charter companies—Wade Tours, and Yankee Trails—offer occasional excursions to the city. The Travel section of the Sunday *New York Times* frequently carries ads for weekend packages at Boston hotels at considerably reduced prices. Additional information is listed in Boston's premier newspaper, *The Boston Globe*, available at the main branches of the public libraries and at the cosmopolitan news-stands listed in the information and shopping chapters of this book.

Boston has lots to offer: excellent museums, interesting historic sites, unique entertainment centers, handsome campuses, good public transportation—and, of course, the Red Sox, the Celtics, the Bruins and the New England Patriots. (Three hours drive.)

The Official Guide to Greater Boston, a small booklet published by the Greater Boston Convention and Tourist Bureau Inc., is excellent. It briefly describes each point of interest, giving open hours and admission prices, and suggests hotels and restaurants. It is available for a small fee from the Bureau's two offices—at the Prudential Plaza, 800 Boylston St (617) 536-4100, and at the Boston Common Information Center, 146 Tremont St. Both are open daily, 9-5. These offices also sell a clear map of the city, *The Official Boston Map and Freedom Trail Guide*.

What follows is a list of recommended things to do, places to see, and sources of information.

Recommended Walks
Boston is a city of neighborhoods, a city most rewarding to the visitor willing to walk a bit. Much of Boston developed with an unique blend of residential and small commercial architecture; the result is that the city appears divided into distinctive, self-contained pieces, manageable for residents and tourists. It is easy to get from one part of town to another by foot, or, if tired, by hopping on the "T", Boston's rapid transit system. The "T" connects all major downtown points of interest, as well as areas beyond the city's central district. Below is a list of the many places to stroll.

Beacon Hill
Boston Common and Boston Gardens
Copley Square and Newbury St
Freedom Trail (16 Historic Sites)
Government Center

Places to Visit
Boston Public Library
Christian Science Center
Faneuil Hall and Quincy Market
Harvard Square and Harvard University
John Hancock Observatory
John F. Kennedy Library

New England Aquarium
Skywalk (Prudential Center)
Subway
U.S.S. Constitution

Museums
Boston Tea Party Ship and Museum
Childrens Museum
Computer Museum
Harvard Museum
Museum of Fine Arts
Museum of Science

Music and Ballet
Bank of Boston Celebrity Series
Boston Ballet, 19 Clarendon St
Boston Pops Orchestra, Symphony Hall
Boston Symphony Orchestra, Symphony Hall

Sports
Boston is a college town—with thousands of students bringing vitality to both sides of the Charles River. Their highly competitive teams draw loyal supporters from the city at large as well as from the campuses. In addition to the usual centerpieces, football and basketball, Boston enthusiastically supports a longstanding tradition of rowing on the Charles.

Bostonians also fiercely cheer their four professional clubs.

Boston Bruins (hockey)
Boston Celtics (basketball)
Boston Red Sox (baseball)
New England Patriots (football)

Connecticut
Bristol

American Clock and Watch Museum, 100 Maple St off Rte 6, (203) 583-6070, exhibits over 3000 timepieces—many made in Connecticut—in an 1801 house. Open March through Nov. Admission fee. Directions: Take I-90 East to Exit 2 to Rte 85 South to Rte 6 East. (Two hours.)

New England Carousel Museum, 95 Riverside Ave, (203) 585-5411, is the first and only museum of its kind on the east coast. The finest pieces of antique carousel art are displayed in a restored turn-of-the-century factory. Open daily. Admission fee. Directions; Take I-90 est to exit 2 to Rte 8 South to Rte 6 East. (Two hours.)

Coventry

Caprilands Herb Farms, 534 Silver St, Coventry, (203) 742-7244, has over eight acres of grounds including thirty-two herb gardens, each with a different theme. A luncheon program—by reservation only—includes lectures on the growth and use of herbs and a full-course luncheon made with herbs and plants grown on the premises. Also on the grounds are a guest cottage, a greenhouse, and book and herb shops. A catalog of herbs is available without charge. Open daily 9-5. No fee for grounds and shops. There is a luncheon fee. Directions: take I-90 East to I-91 South to Rte 44 East to Rte 31 East. (Two hours.)

Nathan Hale Homestead, South St off Rte 44, (Coventry) (203) 742-6917, is the 1776 home of Connecticut's state hero. Filled with memorabilia, the house and the surrounding farm reflect the lifestyle of his prosperous farming family. Open daily mid May through mid Oct. Admission fee. Directions: Take I-90 East to I-91 South to Rte 44 East to Rte 31 East. (Two hours and fifteen minutes.)

Hartford

Nook Farm is the carefully maintained home of Mark Twain during the years he was writing *The Adventures of Tom Sawyer, The Adventures of Huckleberry Finn, The Prince and the Pauper,* and *A Connecticut Yankee in King Arthur's Court.* The mid-Victorian home includes a girls' nursery, a billiard room, and a library, all of which are furnished with original pieces or replicas. Admission. Tours take 45 minutes. Open: June-Aug, daily 10-4:30; Sept-May, Tues-Sat. 10-4:30, Sun 1-4. (203) 525-9317. Directions: Take I-90 East to N.Y.S. Thruway and Mass. Pike. Take Exit 4 for I-91 South to I-84W. Take Exit 46. Go east on Sisson Ave, then right onto Farmington Ave. (Two hours.)

Old State House, 800 Main St, Hartford, (203) 522-6766, designed by Charles Bulfinch in 1796, is the oldest State House in the nation. The original portrait of George Washington by Gilbert Stuart hangs in this building. Open: Mon-Sat 10-5, Sun 12-5. Free. Directions: I-90 East to I-91 South to South Main St exit. (Two hours.)

Wadsworth Atheneum, 600 Main St, Hartford, (203) 724-7911, the nation's oldest continuously operating public art musuem, houses more than 45,000 works of art. Open: Tues-Sun 11-5. Fee. Directions: I-90 East to I-90 South to South Main St exit.

Litchfield

Tapping Reeve House and Law School, South St, Rte 63, Litchfield, (203) 567-4501, established in 1773, is the first law school in North America. Graduates include John C. Calhoun, Aaron Burr, and over 130 members of Congress. Reeve

House, furnished in keeping with the period, is open mid-Apr to mid-Nov, Tues-Sat. Admission fee. Directions: take I-90 East to Exit 2; Rte 8 South to Rte 118W to Rte 63. (Two hours.)

White Flower Farm is a botanical haven. The grounds are laid out in beautiful planned gardens so that the visitor may learn at first hand the principles of good garden design.

All of the varieties for sale are unique or at least unusual. A beautiful, informative catalog is published four times a year; mail orders are welcome. (203) 567-8789. Directions: Take I-90 East to Exit 2; Rte 8 South to Rte 118W to Rte 63S. (Two hours and fifteen minutes.)

Woodbury

Mill House Antiques, Rte 6, has a wide variety of fine quality furniture and accessories collected from country estates in England, Scotland, and Wales. Open Wed-Mon 9-5. (203) 263-3446. Directions: Take N.Y.S. Thruway to Taconic Parkway south to I-84 East to Exit 15. Take Rte 6 North for seven miles. (Two hours and a half.)

WEST OF THE CAPITAL DISTRICT

Amsterdam

Guy Park, 366 West Main Ave, Amsterdam, 842-7550, is an historic 18th century home situated on lock 11 of the Barge Canal. It was built in 1766 by regional hero Sir William Johnson as a wedding present for his daughter Mary and his nephew Guy Johnson. Free. Open: mid-May through Oct. Directions: Take N.Y.S. Thruway west to Exit 27. Go north on Rte 30. Left on Main St (Rte 5); left on Evelyn St. (Forty minutes.)

Fonda

Mohawk-Caughnawaga Museum, Rte 5, 1/4 mile west of Fonda, 853-3646, is adjacent to the **National Shrine of Kateri Tekawitha,** the famous local Catholic martyr. The museum focuses on the life of the Indians resident in the Mohawk Valley since pre-history. Situated near the excavation site of a seventeenth century Indian village, the museum contains many artifacts from the archeological dig. Nearby are extensive nature trails and picnic areas. Mid-May to mid-October, daily 9 am-4pm. Donation. Directions: NYS Thruway to Exit 28, Rte 5W. (Forty minutes.)

Esperance

The George Landis Arboretum is both an exhibition center and an experimental outpost. Its 100 acres of land hold over two thousand species of plantings, many of them exotic trees, flowers and bushes from far lands. The Arboretum staff tend their gardens carefully, measuring what conditions are required for each planting to survive in this climate. They also cooperate with other botanical gardens and arboreta in international seed exchanges and maintain a library of botanical holdings. Visitors are welcome to tour the grounds or attend formal programs. Information is available at the Arboretum, Esperance 12006, (518) 875-6935. Directions: Rte 20 to Esperance; right onto Rte 44 (Charleston St); at sharp bend in Rte 44, straight onto Lape Rd. (Forty minutes.)

Howes Cave

Howe Caverns on Rte 7 between Central Bridge and Cobleskill, 296-8990 is a series of carefully lighted, interestingly presented underground caves and subterranean waterways. The one hour twenty minute tour and underground boat ride leaves at frequent intervals. Visitors should bring a sweater or jacket as the temperature in the caves is 52 degrees. Open 9-6 year round except Christmas, Thanksgiving and New Year's Day. Admission. Directions: Take Rte 20 West to Rte 7. Follow signs to Howe Caverns. (Forty-five minutes.)

Iroquois Indian Museum, Caverns Rd Box 7, 296-8949, in 1992 added a new Iroquois long house to the eleven year old institution which focuses both on the Iroquois of the present and the past. On the forty-five acres there is a children's museum, an outdoor amphitheater for craft demonstrations, dance and other performances, and a nature park for the study of plants and animals from an Iroquois perspective. There is a fee. Open daily all year, 10-5:30. Directions: I-90 West to exit 25A to I-88; take Cobleskill-Middleburg exit; east on Rte 7 left onto Caverns Rd. Museum is at foot of Howe Caverns hill. (Forty-five minutes.)

Johnstown

Johnson Hall, Hall Ave, Johnstown, is the estate of William Johnson, a fascinating and significant figure in 18th Century American History. A small building to the side of the main house displays interesting memorabilia of the man and his era. Free. Open Wed-Sun 9-5. (518) 762-8712. Directions: Take N.Y.S. Thruway west to Exit 28. Turn left on Riverside Drive. Take right across Mohawk Bridge into Fonda. Go left on Rte 5 then right on 30A to Johnstown. Go left on E. Main St (Rte 29W). Go right on N. Williams St and right on Hall Ave. (Fifty minutes.)

Rensselaerville

Rensselaerville is an appealing village filled with beautifully crafted 19th century homes and the carefully preserved remnants of active though modest industry. It was in fact the original location of the Huyck Felt Mills. Within the boundaries of the village are the Huyck Preserve, a site for the study of natural habitats, and the Rensselaerville Institute, a facility which supports study of humanity's use of technology. Directions: Take Rte 85 (New Scotland Ave) to Rensselaerville. (Fifty minutes.) The Rensselaerville Institute is described further in the chapter on Education.

Cooperstown

Cooperstown is a picturesque but vital town filled with points of interest for the visitor. Directions: Take N.Y.S. Thruway west to Exit 25A to I-88 West; take Emmons Exit. Take Rte 28N to Rte 80N. (One hour and a half.)

The Farmer's Museum, Lake Rd Rte 80, depicts in believable fashion the life of early rural settlers in N.Y. State. Men and women on the staff use authentic tools to perform manual arts at which all colonists were skilled. Admission. Open: daily May-Oct, 9-6. Call for Nov-Apr schedule. (607) 547-2533.

Fenimore House, Lake Rd Rte 80, is a museum containing American folk art, painting and articles related to James Fenimore Cooper. Admission. Open: daily May-Oct, 9-6. Call for Nov-Apr schedule. (607) 547-2533.

Hyde Hall, (607) 547-5098 or 8462, is a neo-classic country mansion built by George Hyde Clark in the early 1800s that remained as the family home until the early 1960s. The house was designed by the noted Albany architect Phillip Hooker. Tours are held at 1, 2, 3, and 4 pm on weekends and holidays, and by request on week days. There is an admission charge. Directions: Take the N.Y.S. Thruway to exit 25A to I-88; take I-88 to exit 24 at Duanesburg. Take Rte 20 West for thirty-seven miles to East Springfield; turn left on county road 31 and go three miles south to Mill Rd; turn right to Hyde Hall. (One hour.)

National Baseball Hall of Fame and Museum contains mementos of great moments in the sport generally believed to have been born in this little town. Great excitement fills Cooperstown on the day new members are inducted and on the day of the annual Old Timer's Game, early in August. Tickets are sold well in advance of this last event. Admission. Open year round. Closed Thanksgiving, Christmas, and New Years Day. (607) 547-9988.

Otesaga Hotel is a fine old resort that stands at the foot of Lake Otsego. The golf course is excellent. Buffet luncheon is served on the terrace during the summer. (607) 547-9931. The hotel is described further in the chapter on Lodging.

Cooper Inn, an elegant house in the village, offers accommodations to travelers. Guests may use other facilities of the Otesaga Hotel. (607) 547-9931. The Inn is described further in the chapter on Lodging.

Syracuse

Burnet Park Zoo, just off Wilbur Ave, (315) 435-8516, established in 1914 and reconstructed in 1986, now uses its thirty-six acres to create an environment as close as possible to the natural habitat of the living creatures in its exhibitions designed around seven different theme areas, both indoor and out. Open every day except Christmas and New Years, 10-4:30; handicapped accessible. There is a shop and a restaurant. Directions: N.Y.S. Thruway west to Exit 39, to I-690 East and follow Zoo signs. (Two hours.)

Utica

The Munson Williams Proctor Institute, 310 Genesee St, has three parts: a Museum of Art, a School of Arts, and a Division of Performing Arts. The Museum collection, housed in a building designed by architect Philip Johnson, includes works by major artists—Cole, Pollock, Arp, Picasso, Kandinsky, Mondrian, Klee, Calder, and Moore—as well as many fine works by lesser known figures. Changing exhibits of paintings, sculpture, graphic art, and photographs are drawn from the Museum's collection and from circulating exhibitions from other museums. At nearby Fountain Elms, an 1850 Italianate house, the Museum's collection of early American furniture and decorative arts is displayed. The Museum is open Tues-Sat 10-5; Sun 1-5.

The School of Art offers a college-level program, leading to a degree in fine arts, offered in cooperation with area colleges. Courses are available in painting, drawing, sculpture, metal arts, pottery, ceramics, graphic arts, photography, figure drawing, quilting, and dance. The School also offers non-credit courses in the same areas for adults and children in the community.

The Performing Arts Division offers world class performing arts throughout the year, including the Great Artists Series at the Stanley Performing Arts Center, The Guest Artists Series, Centerstage, Focus on Performing Arts, For Kids Only, a film series, and concerts in the court.

During July, the Institute offers a six-day arts festival featuring an outdoor art show and an open air performing arts performance. Free. Directions: N.Y.S.

Thruway to exit 31; follow signs to downtown Utica to Genesee St south. (One hour and a half.)

F.X. Matt Brewing Company—Tour Center, Court and Varick Sts provides a guided one hour tour through the halls and rooms where Matts Premium, Utica and Maximus Super are brewed. This is followed by a tour of the bottling facility, a trolley ride, and a stop at the 1888 Tavern. Here, in an atmosphere characteristic of the era when this family-operated brewery was founded, the participant may enjoy a complimentary mug of Matts Premium Beer (or root beer for those who prefer). Free. Open year round, (315) 732-0022.

Directions: N.Y.S. Thruway to exit 31. Follow signs for downtown Utica. Proceed to Court St. Turn right. Three blocks down on right side. (One hour and a half.)

New York State Education Building

PRIMARY AND SECONDARY SCHOOLS

Public Schools

All three cities and all the suburban regions of the five county area have comprehensive educational systems K-12. They work together to provide active, highly competitive intermural athletic leagues and to share resources. Information regarding programs and special services is available through the local school district.

There are two Magnet Schools within the City School District of Albany: the Thomas O'Brien School of Science and Technology, which admits for full day pre-K through grade 6, and offers, among other courses, science and computer laboratory classes as well as weekly instruction by a NYS Museum specialist; the Albany School of Humanities, which admits for full day K through grade 6, and offers, among other courses, classes in dance, art, Spanish, and other culturally-oriented focuses. Applications for these schools may be obtained from the School District offices, 462-7100. Students are accepted by lottery, with an emphasis placed on racial balance.

Non-Public Schools

In addition to public schools, area residents may choose from a group of schools with widely differing objectives and correspondingly diverse approaches. Because the nature of education is dependent on individual values, the descriptions presented here are limited to comments offered by administrators of the schools or by official catalogue copy. These descriptions should help the reader draw some sense of the school, and telephone numbers for further information have been provided. The grade levels encompassed by the schools differ, as the descriptions are presented alphabetically.

All schools in this section, even those with religious affiliation, accept students regardless of race, color or creed.

The Academy of the Holy Names, 1065 New Scotland Rd, Albany, 438-6553 and 489-2559. The Lower and Middle School is a private day school for girls (pre-K for four-year olds is co-ed). The goal of the school is to "place the student in learning situations where satisfaction and self-development come through continuous, sequential progress and success." Classes are small and the curriculum is structured to permit progress at individual rates. The Upper School (grades 9-12) is a college preparatory school for girls. The Sisters of the Holy Names supervise the programs on all levels.

Albany Academy, Academy Rd, Albany, 465-1461. Established in 1813 with the goal of training boys for positions of leadership and achievement, the Academy members many prominent Albanians among its graduates. Athletics are stressed as is academic progress within small classes. A full-day pre-school and kindergar-

ten is offered by the Academy in addition to Grades 1-12. Cross enrollment with Albany Academy for Girls is available for grades 9 through 12.

Albany Academy for Girls, 140 Academy Rd Albany, 463-2201. Founded in 1814, it was one of the first schools ever devoted exclusively to the education of young women. It offers a challenging college preparatory program. Housed in a splendid facility, it features small classes and warm concern for the individual. The school offers full-day pre-K through grade 12. Cross enrollment with Albany Academy is available for grades 9 through 12.

The Brown School, (Nursery School is located at 1184 Rugby Rd, Schenectady, 346-6139; K through 5 is located on Eleanor St, Schenectady, 370-0366) was founded in 1893 to offer "quality education in an informal, relaxed atmosphere." Enrollment is limited to ten students per grade, and the curriculum is "extremely flexible to allow each child to advance at his own rate." The school enrolls a large percentage of international students.

The Children's School at Emma Willard is located on the Emma Willard School campus. It provides a program for students three years of age through grade 3. The program is designed to provide a developmentally appropriate program for the young child, taking into account individual differences and learning styles. It is an arts based program with a policy of thematic instruction which integrates curricular areas. The aim of the Children's School is to offer academic perceptions of themselves as learners. For information, call 274-3476.

Christian Brothers Academy, 1 De LaSalle Rd, Albany, 462-5447. CBA is a private Roman Catholic military college preparatory school for boys grades 6 through 12 run by the Brothers of the Christian Schools. Fifty percent of faculty are Brothers; the remaining members are lay teachers.

The Doane-Stuart School, Albany, 465-5222. This is a coeducational, independent, ecumenical school created through a merger of two old Albany schools—the Roman Catholic Kenwood Academy, a member of the network of Sacred Heart schools, and the Episcopal St. Agnes School. It offers an ecumenical Christian religious program. The primary school (pre-K through 8th grade) provides individualized instruction and emphasizes the arts and humanities, with individual acceleration possible. The secondary level offers college preparatory programs for resident and day students, grades 9-12.

Emma Willard School, 285 Pawling Ave, Troy, 274-4440, was founded in 1814 by pioneer educator Emma Hart Willard for the higher education of young women. It serves boarding and day students for grade 9 through 12 and for the post-graduate year. Academic excellence has been a tradition at Emma Willard. The college preparatory program is complemented by independent study in the community, a visual and performing arts program, leadership training, and competitive inter-scholastic athletics. The 92 acre campus features English Tudor Gothic architecture.

The Free School, 8 Elm St, Albany, 434-3072, established in 1920, is the oldest al-ternative free school in Albany county. Serving pre-school to junior high school students, the school, with nine full-time teachers, provides for approximately fifty students a closely-knit educational atmosphere which stresses developing a sense of self in meeting the challenges of the world. There is a sliding scale tu-ition. Applications are open to all.

The Hebrew Academy of the Capital District, 54 Sand Creek Rd, Albany, 482-0464. This is a co-educational school (grades K through 8) founded to provide close study of the Judaic and secular studies for young people and prepare them to pursue both at more advanced levels. The orientation of the small classes is the approach to all subjects with an awareness of their meaning in the context of both Jewish and Western democratic traditions.

La Salle Institute, 174 Williams Rd, Troy, 283-2500. This is a Catholic college pre-paratory school for boys grades 6 through 12 conducted by the Christian Brothers. Enrollment is about 500 students. LaSalle has an accredited Jr. ROTC program for grades 9-12. College credit courses are available through an arrange-ment with neighboring Hudson Valley Community College.

Loudonville Christian School, 374 Loudon Rd, Loudonville, 434-6051. This school was founded in 1960 by a group of parents concerned with the Christian education of children. It is a coeducational school with classes from pre-school through grade eight. The class schedule provides time for Chapel, devotions, and prayer. The curriculum of the school includes a course in Biblical studies and em-phasizes that "secular"courses are taught from the standpoint of a Biblical view of God, man and the world. Also included in the curriculum is New York State Regents in Math and Science. The school also takes pride in its programs in art, music and physical education.

Robert C. Parker School, 141 Main Ave, Wynantskill, 286-3449. This co-educa-tional school, started in the fall of 1991 as an outgrowth of The Emma Willard Children's School, focuses on self-paced learning and on individual challenge and achievement within a cooperative learning environment. At its start it had grades four through six. Plans call for adding grade seven in 1992 and grade eight in 1993.

St. Gregory's School, Old Niskayuna Rd Loudonville, 785-6621. This is a school run by Roman Catholic laymen to offer accelerated courses for boys grades 1-8. The pre-school and kindergarten programs, enroll girls as well as boys. Grades one through eight aim at preparing students for advanced entry into the most competitive secondary schools in the country. Science is taught from the first grade; French from the third grade; and Latin and computer science from the fifth grade.

Parochial and Diocesan Schools

The Capital District has a system of primary schools (K-8) supported by the Roman Catholic Diocese. Most are affiliated with and in part financed by local parishes. The students pay a tuition based both on ability to contribute and on the number of children of a given family enrolled at the school. The Diocese also operates four high schools—**Bishop Maginn High School** in Albany, **Catholic Central High School** in Troy, **Notre Dame-Bishop Gibbons** in Schenectady, and **Saratoga Central Catholic High School** in Saratoga Springs.

No student is denied entrance to any of the schools on the basis of religion or financial status. The number to call for information regarding Diocesan Schools is 453-6666.

INSTITUTIONS OF HIGHER EDUCATION

The 16 colleges and universities in the Capital District have formed a consortium designed to share resources and cooperate in making educational opportunities more accessible to all students. Students enrolled at any one of the colleges, through a cross-registration, may enroll in any course not available on the home campus. The consortium is called the Hudson Mohawk Association of Colleges and Universities, 91 Fiddler's Ln Latham, 785-3219.

Nomenclature

The structure of the educational system in New York State is quite straightforward, but the choice of names for the units has led to confusion.

The University of the State of New York is the term applied to the entire educational system within the state—private and public—from nursery school through the most advanced graduate degree. This body, presided over by the Board of Regents, grants and revokes licenses and oversees the work of the Department of Education of the State of New York, which plays a more practical role in the governance of education.

State University of New York (SUNY) is the coordinating center of the public institutions of higher learning in the state. This includes 4 university centers, 13 colleges of arts and sciences, 6 colleges and centers for the health sciences, 6 agricultural and technical colleges, 8 specialized colleges and 29 community colleges—64 campuses in all. These offices—called SUNY Central—provide administrative support for the single units and facilitate expanded cooperation between the various campuses.

University at Albany (SUNY) is the university center, the autonomous branch of the SUNY system, which has academic buildings and dormitories on its old and new campuses located in Albany.

Two-Year Colleges

Bryant and Stratton Business Institute, 1259 Central Ave, Albany, 437-1802, owned and operated by descendants of the Bryant and Stratton family, offers day and evening courses in business, computer science, secretarial skills, travel and tourism.

Hudson Valley Community College, Vandenburgh Ave, Troy, 283-1100, sponsored by the County of Rensselaer under the program of the State University of New York, is a large multipurpose institution which serves a wide variety of needs. It provides AA and AS degrees for those bound for four year colleges, AAS and AOS degrees for those directly entering business, industry or trades, and courses and certificates for residents who need to acquire a specific skill or learn some specific information. A direct result of the recognition in the early 60's that education should not be available only for the intellectually elite, Hudson Valley states that, "The underachiever, the disadvantaged, as well as the ambitious, the financially able—these and others from the community—come to Hudson Valley to receive educational opportunities they might not otherwise attain."

Maria College, 700 New Scotland Ave, Albany, 438-3111, is a private, independent, co-educational, two-year college sponsored by the Sisters of Mercy. It serves three different groups of students: those who intend to transfer to four year colleges; those who seek career training; and those who seek enrichment and personal development. Maria, tailoring its programs to meet the needs of students, offers two options in addition to the traditional daily schedule—an evening degree, and the Weekend College. These allow working adults to integrate their studies with their other responsibilites but also to complete their degrees on schedule. The college consciously

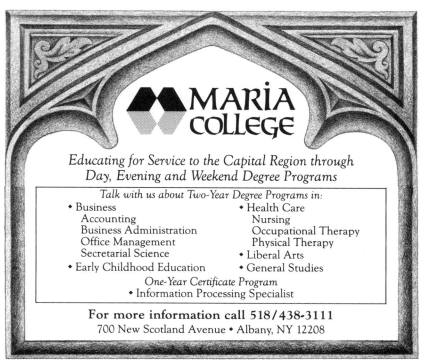

MARIA COLLEGE

Educating for Service to the Capital Region through Day, Evening and Weekend Degree Programs

Talk with us about Two-Year Degree Programs in:
- Business
  Accounting
  Business Administration
  Office Management
  Secretarial Science
- Early Childhood Education

- Health Care
  Nursing
  Occupational Therapy
  Physical Therapy
- Liberal Arts
- General Studies

One-Year Certificate Program
- Information Processing Specialist

For more information call 518/438-3111
700 New Scotland Avenue • Albany, NY 12208

retains its small size to insure that the personal quality which has become its trademark continues

Mildred Elley Business School, 227 Quail St, Albany, 472-9227, is a small co-ed institution offering two-year programs in business management, court reporting, hospitality management, and executive secretary skills; and one-year programs in computer accounting, word processing, and paralegal studies. Day and evening classes.

Sage Junior College of Albany, one of the Sage Colleges, 140 New Scotland Ave, Albany, 445-1711 was established as a co-educational college in 1957. Today, Sage JCA has an outstanding reputation for preparing students for transfer to four year colleges or for direct career entry. Sage JCA offers more than 30 associates degrees in a wide range of fields, including the fine arts, business communications, paralegal and child care management, serving more than 700 students from throughout the Northeast and 10 foreign countries.

Schenectady County Community College, Washington Ave, Schenectady, 346-6211, offers 34 career, transfer and certificate programs. In addition to two-year programs leading to the A.A., A.S., A.A.S., and A.O.S. degrees, and to one-year certificates, the college also serves business and industry through individually designed training programs of varying time frames and through non-credit offerings in vocational and avocational areas. SCCC is fully accredited by the Middle States Association of College and Schools, and is one of the only 17 two-year colleges in the nation to hold the prestigious National Schools of Music accreditation. SCCC, which enrolls almost 4000 full and part-time students, provides access to all through low tuition, day, evening and weekend classes, counseling and developmental coursework, and special support services for returning adults, minority and disabled students.

Spencer Business And Technical Institute, 200 State St, Schenectady, 374-7619, founded in 1893 and locally owned and operated, offers programs in such areas as fashion merchandising, electronics, accounting, court reporting, travel and tourism, secretarial skills, and private security. Courses of study run from 6 to 21 months.

Hospital-Based Nursing Schools

In addition to nursing degrees offered at two and four year colleges in the area, there are three programs situated in hospitals. These are **Ellis Hospital School of Nursing,** 382-4471; **Memorial Hospital School of Nursing,** 471-3260; **Samaritan Hospital School of Nursing,** 271-3285.

Four-Year Colleges and Graduate Schools

The College of St. Rose, 432 Western Ave, Albany, 454-5111, is a private, co-educational liberal arts college with 3800 students from 16 states and 35 foreign countries. The College takes pride in the personal quality created by the intimacy of the campus and the smallness of the student body. In addition to the liberal arts undergraduate program, the College presents Masters Degree programs in a variety of areas. It is particularly known for its offerings in Special Education, Communication Disorders, and Music. An adult **Weekend Advantage Program,** held every other weekend, has a range of courses including business, computer science, education, and English. The credit from these weekend courses may be applied toward any of the college's 33 undergraduate degrees. The college has an Adult Continuing Education Division with a strong following. Bachelor's degrees or certification can be earned through evening study.

The Nelson A. Rockefeller School of Public Affairs and Policy, 135 Western Ave, Albany, 442-5289 was established in 1981 by the State University of New York and includes the following: The School of Public Affairs, The School of Criminal Justice, The School of Social Welfare and The School of Information Science and Policy. Over 100 scholars and 50 researchers provide education through 11 graduate programs to over 1300 graduate students. Undergraduates are accepted at the School of Criminal Justice.

Rensselaer Polytechnic Institute, Troy, 266-6000, is a co-educational, non-sectarian, private university, known as RPI or Rensselaer. It offers 117 under graduate and graduate degree programs in five schools—Architecture, Engineering, Humanities-Social Sciences, Management and Science—as well as in several interdisciplinary areas. Approximately 6000 students attend this well established university long known for the rigor of its standards and the excellence of its programs, especially those in engineering and the sciences.

Russell Sage College, Troy, 270-2000, one of the Sage Colleges, was founded in 1916 with what was a revolutionary purpose: to educate women to participate fully in the life and work of society. Today the College, recognizing the changing contexts of women's lives, carries that purpose forward while remaining committed to the integration of liberal arts and career-focused study. Its one thousand students select from a variety of fields and can share the academic and social life of nearby RPI.

Sage Evening College, 140 New Scotland Ave, Albany, 445-1717, one of the Sage Colleges, was founded in 1949 to offer degree and professional development programs to women and men; it also offers contract courses, seminars, and workshops for government employees and various employers. The faculty of the

College is drawn from faculty of Russell Sage College, Sage Junior College, and a core of adjunct faculty from business, government, and human services institutions in the area.

Sage Graduate School, Troy, 270-2264, one of the Sage Colleges, offered its first Masters degree in 1950. Since then the School has initiated a number of innovative and flexible programs to meet the needs of students preparing for professional roles. There are now over 1200 students enrolled in the variety of academic fields the School offers.

Siena College, Loudonville, 783-2307, is a private, coeducational, Catholic liberal arts college under the auspices of the Franciscan Order. Founded in 1937 as a small men's school, the college now enrolls 2500 undergraduates. In addition to its academic offerings, Siena takes pride in its athletic program and its series of guest lectures and personal appearances.

Skidmore College, Saratoga Springs, 584-5000, is an independent liberal arts college with an enrollment of approximately 2150 men and women. With its relatively small size and with a student-faculty ratio of 11 to 1, Skidmore is a closely-knit community of students and teachers. Originally a college for women, Skidmore became coed in 1971. Skidmore takes pride in its Liberal Studies curriculum, which was implemented in 1985 after several years of faculty research and planning. In the early 60's the college abandoned its downtown campus and moved to an entirely new campus of 850 wooded acres at the northwest edge of Saratoga Springs. In 1970 Skidmore received approval to form a Phi Beta Kappa chapter, and established its University Without Walls, one of the earliest non-traditional degree programs in the country.

Union College, Schenectady, 370-6000, describes itself as an "independent, primarily undergraduate, residential college for men and women of high academic promise and strong personal motivation." Established in 1795, Union was the first college chartered by the Regents of the State of New York. It claims to have the oldest designed campus in the United States. Until 1970 it admitted men only; today this seasoned institution enjoys a long-standing reputation of academic excellence and student and alumni loyalty. The excellent cultural enrichment program is often open to the public.

University at Albany (SUNY), 1400 Washington Ave Albany, 442-3300, founded in 1844, is the oldest unit of the state university system and one of its four university centers. The largest educational institution in the area, it enrolls 12,000 undergraduate students each year in 45 major fields as well as 5,000 graduate students in 47 fields. Admission to all these programs is highly competitive.

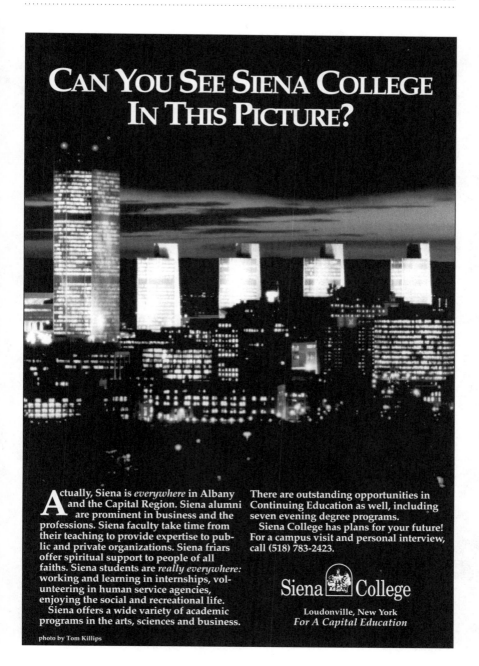

CAN YOU SEE SIENA COLLEGE IN THIS PICTURE?

Actually, Siena is *everywhere* in Albany and the Capital Region. Siena alumni are prominent in business and the professions. Siena faculty take time from their teaching to provide expertise to public and private organizations. Siena friars offer spiritual support to people of all faiths. Siena students are *really everywhere:* working and learning in internships, volunteering in human service agencies, enjoying the social and recreational life.

Siena offers a wide variety of academic programs in the arts, sciences and business.

photo by Tom Killips

There are outstanding opportunities in Continuing Education as well, including seven evening degree programs.

Siena College has plans for your future! For a campus visit and personal interview, call (518) 783-2423.

Siena College

Loudonville, New York
For A Capital Education

Although the University is supported by the allocation of funds by the legislature, students also pay tuition according to a scale adjusted to year of study and state of residence.

Campus tours are conducted regularly throughout the year so that the public can become aware of the University's facilities and of the resources it provides to the community.

The University Art Gallery, with exhibits of local, national, and international artists, is open each Tuesday through Friday, free to the public.

The University offers credit courses to area residents through its Continuing Education Program. Information is available at 442-5140.

Professional Schools

Union University consists of five units: Union College, three professional schools—Albany College of Pharmacy, Albany Law School, and Albany Medical College—and the Dudley Observatory.

Albany College of Pharmacy, 106 New Scotland Ave, Albany, 445-7211, offers a rigorous five year program leading to a bachelor of science in pharmacy as well as an accelerated program toward a bachelor of science in pharmacy with a master of science in health systems management from Union College, and an excellent four year program leading to a bachelor of science in medical technology, which may be obtained on a part-time, flexible basis. Numbered among its alumni are many of the practicing health professionals in the area. Graduates work in hospitals, clinics, laboratories and retail pharmacies, enter other areas of science or business, or go on to graduate school in dentistry, medicine or law.

Albany Law School, 80 New Scotland Ave, Albany, 445-2311, is one of the oldest law schools in the United States. It offers a three year program leading to the J.D. degree and cooperates with several Capital District colleges to grant six year combined degrees in law and management or law and business administration.

Albany Medical College, New Scotland Ave, Albany, 445-3125, was founded in 1839. It prepares physicians to serve in all forms of practice, using the facilities of the 674 bed Albany Medical Center Hospital, the 469 bed Stratton Veterans Administration Medical Center and the other affiliated hospitals in the Capital District to provide wide-ranging, in-depth clinical instruction.

CONTINUING EDUCATION

Continuing education is an important component in the offerings of many secondary, undergraduate, and professional institutions in the area. Some of the schools described in the earlier sections offer programs designed to help graduates keep their information up-to-date or to develop a new field of interest. Details and schedules are available through the main numbers. In addition, the following groups organize educational opportunities for adults.

Capital District Center of SUNY, Empire State College, 845 Central Ave, Albany, 485-5964, a part of the state university system, is an alternate approach to higher education. Adult students engage in contract learning with mentors. Associate, Bachelors, and Masters degrees are offered.

Institute for Arts and Education, University at Albany, 107 Ten Broeck Dutch Quad, Albany, 442-4240, coordinates an arts related program with teachers on how to relate the arts to curriculum and a program on how to expand knowledge of the arts of adults. Courses usually are offered on Saturdays.

The Knowledge Network, 311 Hamilton St, Albany, 465-0055, is the largest continuing education program in the Capital District. Established in 1981, the company publishes a monthly catalog with more than 100 courses in such areas as computers, cooking, business, careers, photography, self-hypnosis, stress management, writing, sports and forgein languages.

The Knowledge Network has a practical approach: recruit talented practitioners and make their services accessible at reasonable times, places, and cost. Courses are usually held in one evening session.

Project Learn, Albany Medical Center Bolton Hall 201 New Scotland Ave, Albany, 445-4067 is a collaborative venture in nursing education (the first of its kind in New York State) between the Albany Medical Center and the Regents College Degree Program of the University of the State of New York. It is designed to help working, self-directed nurse learners attain their career potentials and thus enhance the quality of health care services in the community. Since its start in 1987, the program has enrolled approximately 400 students in programs leading to the Bachelor of Science in Nursing degree or the Associate degree in Nursing. Nurses in the program have the advantage of on-site advisement in the Albany Medical Center.

Regents College, University of the State of New York 1450 Western Ave, Albany, 474-3703, was established in 1970 to make education accessible for motivated students throughout the country to earn one of the eighteen associate or baccalaurate degrees offered, while working or tending to family or other responsibilities. These resourceful learners work with advisors to complete courses in business, liberal arts, nursing, or technology, and earn credits through a variety of methods, including traditional college courses, proficiency examinations, special assessment, military education, and evaluation of business and industrial training. The oldest and largest assessment and evaluation institution in the United States, the college strives to expand individual horizons and career options. A faculty from numerous universities and colleges develops the curriculum, defines standards, and verifies degree completion.

OTHER EDUCATIONAL VENTURES

In addition to the educational programs listed in the chapter on the arts there are the following educational ventures in the tri-city area aimed at enhancing the mind and well-being.

Elderhostel, a unique college program for those 60 years of age or older, has been hosted by Russell Sage College for several years. Over 500 colleges and universities in the US, Canada, and Europe enroll senior citizens for week-long programs in July through October. Participants live in dormitories, enroll in courses, and share facilities with other students and participate in a variety of social activities. Designed to meet the needs of older persons who wish to develop new interests and to stimulate intellectual curiosity, Elderhostel combines the tradition of European-style hosteling and education. For information, Sage Evening College Office of Conferences and Health Science Continung Education, 270-2395.

The Nelson A. Rockefeller Institute of Government, 411 State St, Albany, 443-5522, was established in 1981 as a vehicle through which New York's academic community and governmental community could serve one another. Faculty from the 64 campuses of the State University work with citizens and officials on important issues of public affairs and policy. The Institute accomplishes its work through sponsoring fellowships, internships, and conferences and by supporting publications.

Rensselaer Newman Foundation Chapel and Cultural Center at RPI, 2125 Burdett Ave, Troy, 274-7793, hosts lectures, films, conversations, discussions, art exhibits and other cultural events throughout the year. Situated in a flexible contemporary building, the center specifically serves the RPI community but welcomes participation by the general populace.

Rensselaerville Institute, known until 1983 as the Institute on Man and Science, is an independent, non-profit educational center which focuses on self-help as a solution to community decline and as innovation for meeting change and solving problems. It is currently working with New York State as well as other states on approaches to water and waste problems. The Institute's Innovation Group enables individuals or organizations to lead change by example, with gains in productivity, morale, customer service and a focus on results. As part of this work, the Institute publishes "Innovating", a quarterly publication with national circulation. On its 100 acre campus, the Institute sponsors educational programs for area schools and presents summer public programs of visual and performing artists. It also serves as a conference center for groups needing a retreat setting for educational meetings. The Institute is located in Rensselaerville, a town on the National Register of Historic Places, 25 miles southwest of Albany on Rte 85, telephone 797-3783.

Sagamore Institute, Sagamore Lodge and Conference Center, Raquette Lake, (315) 354-5311, is a non-profit educational organization which conducts workshops, conferences, institutes, and programs for a variety of youth and adult groups, using the Lodge originally built as the Vanderbilt Retreat. This historic "Adirondack Great Camp," intended as a site for simple but extensive entertaining, has 46 bedrooms, 26 stone fireplaces, and recreational facilities for all seasons. It stands by the shore of a mile-long lake.

LECTURES & DISCUSSIONS

Albany Public Library, 161 Washington Ave, 449-3380, provides a varied program of book reviews and guest lectures free of charge. Monthly calendars of events are available at all branches of the library.

Albany Round Table is an independent association of individuals and representatives of organizations who meet monthly for lunch October to May, generally every second Wednesday on activities affecting the life of the city center. The Round Table gatherings include guest speakers and a community forum on topical issues. Information on meetings is available at P.O. Box 7101, Albany 12224. For reservation call 434-4457.

New York State Writers Institute was established in 1984 to acknowledge the importance of writers and writing for the well-being of society. The Institute has two major objectives: first, it creates opportunities for aspiring writers to meet with experienced writers; second, it makes it possible for the general public to hear eminent writers (Saul Bellow, Toni Morrison, and John Updike, for example) read their work and discuss their perception of the role of writing and the writer. The Institute, conceived by William Kennedy, is centered at the University at Albany, 442-5620.

Troy Public Library, 2nd and Ferry St, 274-7071, hosts the library's Business Breakfast Series on the second Wednesday of the month in fall and spring at 7:45 am on topics relating to small businesses, real estate, and marketing and personnel strategies. A free continental breakfast is served.

New York State Education Building

Troy Public Library

PUBLIC LIBRARIES

The Public Libraries in Albany, Schenectady, and Troy are more than repositories of books and papers; they are vibrant cultural forces in the community. Each has a collection of materials on local history and well-trained, knowledgeable staff. They all offer special programs that appeal to various groups in the community—from preschoolers to octogenarians, from the erudite to the learning disabled. All their services are free of charge.

The libraries invite citizens to be Friends of the Library by making a small donation each year. Members receive a monthly calendar of events and notices of special programs. The branches and telephone numbers are listed below:

Albany
Main, 161 Washington Ave 449-3380
Delaware, 485 Delaware Ave 463-0254
New Scotland, 369 New Scotland Ave 482-6661
John A. Howe, Schuyler and Broad St 472-9485
Pine Hills, 517 Western Ave 482-7911

Schenectady
Main Library, Liberty & Clinton 382-3511
Duane Branch, 1331 State St 382-3504
Glenville, 20 Glenridge Rd 382-3306
Hamilton Hill, 700 Cray St 382-3581
Niskayuna, Story Ave & VanAntwerp Rd 382-3566
Mt. Pleasant, 1026 Crane St 382-3505
Quaker St, Bull St & Rte 7 895-2719

Scotia Branch, 14 Mohawk Ave 382-3506
Rotterdam, 2558 Guilderland Ave 382-3507
Woodlawn, 2 Sanford St 382-3508

Troy
Main Library, 100 Second St 274-7071
Lansingburgh, 114th St & 4th Ave 235-5310
Sycaway, Hoosick & Lee 274-1822

SPECIALIZED LIBRARIES

The McKinney Library, in the Rice Building at the Albany Institute of History
and Art, 125 Washington Ave, Albany, 463-4478, is in possession of an important
collection of diaries, letters, manuscripts, maps, broadsides, historic photographs,
and ephemera of Albany's past. Open: Tues-Fri 9-3.

The New York State Library, 474-7646, located in the Cultural Education Center
of the Empire State Plaza, is a research library serving the government and the
people of New York State. The collection of 4.5 million items, including rare
books and manuscripts, is available for use within the building. Direct borrowing
privileges are granted to permanent state employees, attorneys and physicians.
All other patrons may use material or may borrow material on interlibrary loan.

The Library has an online catalog. Staff are available to explain its use. Librarians
from various subject backgrounds staff the Reference Desk. Behind the desk is located the Electronic Reference Station were various electronic indexes are
centralized.

The library also provides other important services: statewide interlibrary loan,
database service, legislative and governmental service, and special facilities for
the blind and visually handicapped. Also located in the building are the archives
of New York State Government. Open: Mon-Fri 9-5.

ACADEMIC LIBRARIES

All of the colleges in the Capital District have libraries designed primarily to
serve the needs of their own students and faculty.

Residents not attached to a campus may apply to the loan desk at the library to
learn what privileges are offered to the general public. Most of the libraries are
willing to assist visitors and residents in any way they can. Expert librarians will
answer questions in person or on the telephone.

The libraries vary in the breadth and depth of their holdings. The University at Albany (SUNY) library is the largest and most comprehensive; other campus libraries excel in fields in which their curriculums concentrate. Descriptions of these specializations can be found in the chapter on Education.

PROFESSIONAL LIBRARIES

The three professional colleges in the area have specialized collections available to their own faculty and students as well as to practitioners of the profession.

Schaffer Law Library at the Albany Law School, 445-2340, is open to the general public Mon-Sat 9-5, Sun 10-5. Call for further information.

The Albany College of Pharmacy Library, 445-7217, has summer hours and winter hours. Summer: Mon-Fri 8-4; winter: Mon-Thurs 8-11, Fri 8-4:30, Sat 12-5, Sun 1-11.

Schaffer Library of Health Sciences of Albany Medical College, 445-5586, is open Mon-Thurs 8 am-Midnight, Fri 8 am-9 pm, Sat 10-10, Sun 12-12.

McKinney Library, Albany Institute of History and Art

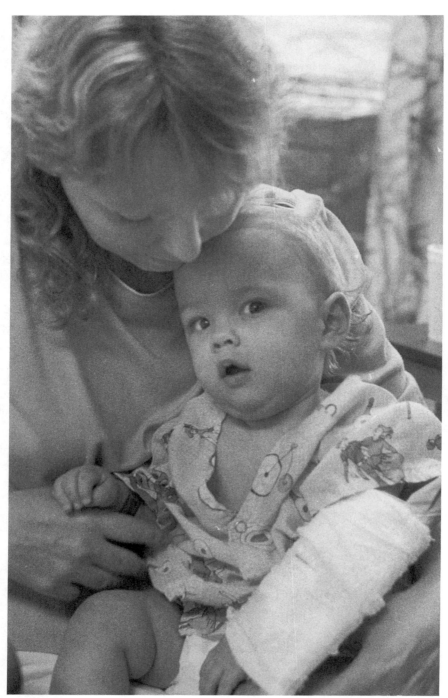

Ellis Hospital

HEALTHCARE
& RELATED SERVICES

The Capital District has an astonishing abundance of institutions and agencies dedicated to assisting people in need. It would not be possible to describe adequately all of the facilities and services to which residents of the region have access. What follows is, rather, a presentation of portraits of all the major hospitals and clinics and a description of a representative sample of some of the most active social service agencies in the region.

EMERGENCY NUMBERS

	Albany	Schenectady	Troy
Fire	463-1234	374-3311	272-3400
Police	463-4141	374-7744	270-4411
Rape Crisis	445-7547	346-2266	271-3257

Child Abuse 800-342-3720
Crisis Intervention
   Capital District Psychiatric Center 447-9650
   Drug Abuse Hotline 1-800-522-5353
   Poison Control Hotline 1-800-336-6997

HOSPITALS

Albany
The Albany Medical Center, New Scotland Ave Albany, a major academic medical institution serving a 20-county region of northeastern New York and western

New England, is made up of two entities, the Albany Medical College and the Albany Medical Center Hospital. They provide the most advanced forms of patient care, teaching and research.

The Albany Medical College is a part of Union University. It was founded in 1839 and is the only medical school between New York City and Montreal. The student population approximates 500 and there are more than 325 faculty members. Sponsored research programs account for approximately one third of the college's operating budget.

The Albany Medical Center Hospital is a 674-bed teaching hospital. It operates numerous specialty clinics and is the largest provider of open heart surgery, kidney transplants, and intensive care of trauma victims in this area. It was named in 1982 as New York State's first designated Regional Trauma Center.

General Information	445-3125
Patient Information	445-3791
Emergency Room	445-3131
Physician Referral	445-3616
Hearing Rehabilitation Center	445-4535

Child's Hospital, 25 Hackett Blvd Albany, is a small medical facility which functions under the auspices of the Episcopal Diocese of Albany. Although founded in 1874 as a hospital for children, it has emerged as a center for special surgery for both children and adults. The emphasis is on elective and outpatient surgery, with most work done in the areas of ophthalmology, enterology, and oral and plastic surgery.

General Information	462-4211

Memorial Hospital, Northern Blvd Albany is a 212-bed facility which offers care for surgical and medical patients. The hospital also staffs a general clinic, and has a diabetes treatment center.

General Information	471-3221
Emergency Room	471-3111
Clinic	471-3171
TTY (for hearing impaired)	447-3526

St. Peter's Hospital, 315 S. Manning Blvd Albany, was established in 1869 by the Sisters of Mercy. This 447-bed teaching hospital has a variety of special features including: St. Peter's Hospice; St. Peter's Alcohol Rehabilitation Center; Family Health Center; Mobile Meals; Emergency Care; and Home Care.

General Information	454-1550

Emergency Department 454-1324
Family Health Center 463-1169

Stratton Veterans Affairs Medical Center Hospital, Holland Ave Albany, with
469 beds, is the only veterans hospital in the area. It provides medical and surgical services for short term and long term care of veterans of the armed forces.

General Information 462-3311

Schenectady

Bellevue Women's Hospital, 2210 Troy Rd Schenectady, is a 40-bed women's
hospital which specializes in obstetrics, neonatology, gynecology, urology, peri-
natology, genetics, and infertility. The hospital serves an 18 county area, with half
its patients coming from outside Schenectady County.

General Information 346-9400
Community Education 346-9410

Ellis Hospital, 1101 Nott St Schenectady, is a 378-bed teaching hospital serving
Schenectady and surrounding counties. It is known for its comprehensive program in intensive care, oncology, neurology, and cardiovascular concerns, and for
its recently appointed cardiac surgery unit. An 82 bed nursing home is adjacent
to the hospital.

General Information 382-4124
Emergency Room 382-4121

St. Clare's Hospital, 600 McClellan St Schenectady, is a 296-bed multi-purpose
hospital supervised by the Sisters of the Poor of St. Francis. This relatively new
hospital opened its doors in 1949. In addition to its medical and surgical care of
inpatients and outpatients, St. Clare's offers a Family Health Center and a Family
Practice Residency Program aimed at providing both comprehensive family
health maintenance and general medical care.

General Information 382-2000

Sunnyview Rehabilitation Hospital, 1270 Belmont Ave Schenectady, services
patients with stroke, spinal cord and brain injuries, chronic pain, and
neuromuscular diseases. A fully accredited hospital with 101 inpatient beds and a
large outpatient clientele, it serves both children and adults. Sunnyview has its
own physicians and therapists to whom area professionals may refer patients.

General Information 382-4500

Troy

Leonard Hospital, New Turnpike Rd Troy, is a 143-bed community hospital serving Troy, Mechanicville, Clifton Park-Half Moon, and Waterford. In addition to general medical-surgical care and outpatient services, Leonard offers a unique 28-day inpatient Alcoholism Rehabilitation Program and a hospital-based Home Health Care Agency.

General Information 235-0310
Emergency Room 235-6717

St. Mary's Hospital, Oakwood and Massachusetts Aves Troy, is a 200-bed community hospital supervised by the Daughters of Charity of St. Vincent de Paul. It is a general hospital with inpatient and outpatient services. It also operates a health center for children and adolescents.

General Information 272-5000
Poison Information 272-5792

Samaritan Hospital, 2215 Burdett Ave Troy, is a 272-bed medical-surgical facility with such speciality services as cancer treatment, mental health unit, alcohol/drug detoxification, and corporate health services. The Louis and Hortense Rubin Dialysis Center is the only chronic dialysis facility in the Capital District. The Samaritan also sponsors prompt care facilities in Cohoes and Schodack.

General Information 271-3300
Emergency Room 371-3424

CLINICS

In addition to the clinics associated with area hospitals, the region has independent clinics which serve the general community.

The Albany County Department of Health, S. Ferry St Albany, provides comprehensive public health service including home nursing, x-ray, dental, and physical therapy. It operates programs on health education and offers a multiphasic screening program (comprehensive medical testing with the results being sent to the patient's personal physician) for a very low fee. The facility is open M-F 9-5. Information about the services and hours of the various clinics is available at the numbers listed below:

Chest 447-4594
Dental 447-4587
Obstetrics 447-4589

Pediatric	447-4589
Albany	447-4580
Ravena	756-6914
Cohoes	235-4044
Sexually transmitted diseases	447-4596

Albany County Mental Health Clinic, 175 Green St Albany, is a community outpatient psychiatric facility. It is open Mon-Fri 9-5. Adult clinic: 447-4555. Childrens clinic: 447-4550.

Rensselaer County Department of Health, 1600 7th Ave Troy, is a public health agency serving the entire county. It operates four clinics—Immunization, Child Health Conference, Chest Consultation, and Venereal Disease. It offers skilled nursing services plus physical therapy, and speech therapy. Anyone seeking information may call one of the three offices:

Troy	270-2660
Rensselaer	462-4256
Hoosick Falls	686-7310

Schenectady County Public Health Services, 1 Broadway Center Schenectady is a public health and home health agency offering skilled nursing, physical therapy, speech therapy, occupational therapy, social work services, and home health aide services. It also supervises four clinics—Well Child, Adult Health, Comprehensive Health Screening, and Diabetes.

General Information 372-8296

Whitney M. Young, Jr. Health Center, Inc., Lark and Arbor Drs in Albany, a health facility providing outpatient medical, dental, psychological, educational and rehabilitational services to adults and children. Methods of payment to this independent facility include a sliding scale fee, independent insurance, Medicaid, and Medicare. The staff also assist clients in obtaining financial support from the County Department of Social Services.

General Information 465-4771

SPECIAL CARE FACILITIES

Capital District Psychiatric Center, often called CDPC, offers inpatient and outpatient care for psychiatric patients from the entire area. It is located in a dramatic modern complex adjacent to the Albany Medical Center on New Scotland Ave in Albany.

General Information 447-9611
Crisis Intervention 447-9650

Center for the Disabled, 314 Manning Blvd Albany, has a twofold purpose—to
create community awareness of the needs and promise of the disabled and to
provide a comprehensive range of services to people of all ages who are developmentally disabled, including senior citizens functionally impaired and
individuals with head injuries. The programs include center residences, a center
school, day treatment, physical and occupational therapy, vocational development, speech therapy, home services, and out- client services. Currently the
center serves approximately 8000 clients from twelve counties, with satellite clinics in Clifton Park, Troy, and Hudson.

General Information 489-8336
Community Relations 437-0294

Farrano House, 27 North Main Ave, Albany, sponsored by Community Mater-
nity Services under the direction of the Catholic Diocese of Albany, was founded
in 1987 by Father Michael Farrano to address the needs of children affected with
the HIV virus. It has since evolved into a group home for up to six children and
serves as a daycare respite for children with special needs as well as for those
with the HIV virus.

General Information 437-0567

Hope House, Inc., main offices at 68 Tivoli St, Albany 12207, begun in 1966 by a
young Roman Catholic priest, Howard Hubbard (now Bishop of Albany), was
the first response to the need for drug treatment in Northeastern New York. The
residency program provides comprehensive services for youth and adults experiencing difficulty with alcohol and chemicals. A variety of programs includes
adult and juvenile counseling centers, and a medically supervised outpatient
clinic. In July and August, trained tennis coaches direct and teach tennis and
drug education free of charge to children six to eighteen years of age.

General Information 465-7879

Hospice Care is a service which exists to assist terminally ill patients and their
families. A staff of nurses, physicians, therapists, social workers, and trained volunteers work together to provide care for outpatients (80% of the hospice
caseload) and inpatients. Currently three hospice care programs serve the area:

General Information
  Hospice at St. Peter's 454-1686
  Hospice of Schenectady 377-8846
  Hospice of Rensselaer 271-1901

Mercy House, 12 St. Joseph's Terr, Albany, is a shelter for women in crisis with children. Here the staff, under the direction of Catholic Charities provides three meals, room, and is an advocacy for counseling to women who seek assistance.

General Information 434-3531

Oswald D. Heck/Eleanor Roosevelt Disabilities Services Office, Balltown and Consaul Rds in Schenectady, serves the mentally retarded and developmentally disabled in the six-county area in a variety of ways. It offers assessment and program development for individual clients, and works in the community to improve the quality of opportunities in education, health care, and social and psychological adjustment available for those under its care. In addition, the Center provides residential units for approximately 250 severely multi- handicapped people of all ages. All services fall under the supervision of the State of New York Office of Mental Retardation and Developmental Disabilities.

General Information 370-7370

Parson's Child and Family Center, 60 Academy Rd Albany, offers a wide variety of services for special children and their families. Included are two Special Education programs, one for children who exhibit autistic-like or atypical behavior, another for those who are not able to adjust to the community school. There are also two 24-hour care programs, one for emotionally disturbed, developmentally disabled, and surrendered children and youth for whom community living is not an option, the other for adolescents who are willing and able to live in a supervised group home in the community. It also offers a clinic for counseling family and children and an outreach program for children and families in the home.

General Information 426-2600

Ronald McDonald House, 139 S Lake Ave Albany, is part of a nationwide network of homes established with the help of the fast food chain foundation to serve as home-away-from-home for families of seriously ill children who are being cared for in major medical centers. The facility is staffed by two full and one part-time persons and operated with the help of many volunteers. It is funded by gifts in kind and monies raised within and without the Capital District. In this handsome house, families may sleep, cook, relax, and, if they wish, share their experiences with other families of ill children. Cost is nominal.

General Information 438-2655

St. Anne Institute, 160 N. Main Ave Albany, 489-7411, provides shelter, counseling, and education for children in crisis. The oldest service is its residential treatment and prevention program for girls from twelve to eighteen years old whom social agencies or the courts believe to be in need of supervision and counseling. In addition to these children, who come from throughout New York State, St. Anne's welcomes about 25-30 girls from surrounding counties into a day program of teaching and counseling. There is a campus school which is fully accredited and certified as a special school.

St. Anne's also sponsors a sex abuse prevention program for males and females, and an extensive program for family members for sex counseling.

St. Catherine's Center for Children, 40 North Main Ave Albany, 453-6700 originally established in 1886 as a home for young, orphaned children, has evolved into a multi-service agency focusing on problems of child abuse and neglect, emotional disturbance, and homelessness. It offers a day treatment program, a residential and prevention program, and a homeless family program. A not-for-profit human service agency and an affiliate of Catholic Charities, St. Catherine's is a member of the United Way of Northeastern New York Inc. All of its programs are licensed and certified by the New York State Departments of Education, Social Services, and the Office of Mental Health.

St. Margaret's Center for Children, 27 Hackett Blvd Albany, is a total nursing care facility for infants and children who are so ill or so developmentally disabled as to require skilled nursing care. As one of only two institutions in the State of New York dedicated to the care of these children, it receives patients referred from throughout the state. Sitting quietly on a hill behind Child's Hospital, St. Margaret's has served special children since its founding in 1883 as part of the Episcopal Diocese of Albany.

General Information 465-2461

St. Peter's Addiction Recovery Center, known by its acronym, **SPARC,** serves the entire area in the treatment of alcoholism and some forms of drug addiction. It operates a male community residence for patients seeking a full time recovery program as well as day treatment through an outpatient clinic. It receives patients referred through the courts and other social agencies as well as self-defined patients. It also offers programs dealing with alcoholism prevention. The Center is located at 2232 Western Ave, Guilderland.

General Information 452-6700
Admission 452-6714

Wildwood, a familiar word in the area, is the name used to describe programs run by the Capital District Chapter of the New York State Association for the Learning Disabled. The program has benefited more than 3000 families in its twenty-four year history. Today Wildwood provides quality educational, vocational, social, recreational/respite, residential, and therapeutic programs for more than 550 neurologically impaired, learning-disabled, or autistic children, adults and their families from a thirteen county area.

Wildwood School 356-6331
Administrative Offices 356-6410

SOCIAL SERVICES

Sources of Information

As noted in the beginning of this chapter, the Capital District has an astounding number of health care and social agencies to serve the needs of its people. In 1978, through a cooperative effort of coordinating bodies, a directory was published listing and describing over 650 social service units. This **Six County Human Services Directory,** is indexed by type of service as well as by alphabetical order. Copies are available for purchase at **The Council of Community Services of Northeast New York,** 901 Madison Ave in Albany, 489-4791, or 272 River St, Troy, 272-1000, or for use without charge at the branches of the public libraries.

Catholic Charities of the Diocese of Albany, a vital part of the regional community in social services of all kinds, has compiled a **Directory of Human Services of the Roman Catholic Diocese of Albany**. It is available through the central office at 40 North Main Ave, Albany, 453-6650.

Humor Institute, 110 Spring St Saratoga, 587-8770, operates a non-profit mail order and walk-in bookstore featuring books related to human relations for teachers, counselors, and group leaders. Also included for sale are books on health care, business, and education.

Some Social Agencies

This chapter does not pretend to be a comprehensive description of social services available to residents of the Capital District: that in itself would require several volumes. It does seem valuable, however, in addition to giving readers access to available directories, to present portraits of representative agencies as a way of demonstrating the remarkable variety of services available and of indicating the considerable number of people whose lives are devoted to easing human difficulties. Here, then, is a representative sample of social agencies.

Catholic Charities is a corporate name for a wide-ranging network of social agencies and residential facilities which serve over 100,000 persons each year. The central office, which coordinates the activities of the hundreds of health and human services personnel throughout the region, is located at 40 North Main Ave, Albany, 453-6650.

Center for Family and Youth, 135 Ontario St, Albany, established in 1969 (originally as Project Strive), is a comprehensive child and family services agency providing supportive services for "at risk" youths and families from the Capital District. In addition to its daily therapeutic after school and evening programs, the Center also provides residential services to adolescent and young adults through the Lewis A. Swyer Shelter for Youth and provides opportunities through its Youth Industries Program.

General Information 462-4745

Equinox Inc. 214 Lark St Albany, began in 1969 as a crisis intervention service and is now a counseling agency with a variety of programs. The counseling service offers out-patient support primarily concerning substance abuse plus a fifteen bed program for those requiring temporary shelter. The youth shelter provides temporary quarters and counseling for runaway or homeless youth. One of the newer programs is a Youth Shelter designed to teach independent living for children who cannot go back home. The main goal is to reunite families through counseling. Equinox is also known for the annual Thanksgiving dinner it provides for anyone in the Capital District free of charge. The dinner is supported by generous donations of goods, food, and volunteer time.

General Information 434-6135
Domestic Violence Shelter 432-7865

Displaced Homemaker Center, 315 Hamilton St, Albany, 434-3103 assists individuals who, as homemakers not employed outside the home, have been economically dependent and have lost or are in danger of losing financial support. The program offers free job search techniques, resume preparation, computer literacy instruction, support group sessions, and internships. Classes run continuously from September through May. The center is funded by the New York State Department of Labor and administered by the New York State AFL-CIO. **The Schenectady/Fulmont Displaced Homemaker Program** serves Schenectady, Saratoga, Washington, Warren, Fulton, and Montgomery counties. Its offices are located at 148 Clinton St Schenectady, 374-9181, and at Fulton-Montgomery Community College, Johnston, 762-4651, ext 348.

Homeless and Travelers Aid Society of the Capital District, Inc, 200 Green St, Albany, is a twenty-four hour referral and short term counseling agency serving homeless persons, persons at risk of becoming homeless, and stranded travellers in Albany, Rensselaer, Saratoga, and Schenectady counties. Homeless and Travelers Aid case workers provide assessment, crisis counseling, referral to shelters, short-term case management and some forms of assistance with transportation.

General Information 463-2124

Human Rights Commission is a community agency dedicated to the idea that all citizens should live in harmony and that the rights of individuals of all ethnic and all religious groups are inviolable. It serves on three levels: processing complaints of discrimination; assisting in counseling and placement to insure fair housing; intervening in group conflicts to prevent violation of individual rights and disruption of the community.

Information:
Albany 434-5184
Schenectady 382-3290
Troy 270-4520

Infoline is a free confidential information and referral service staffed by persons equipped to offer information or referral on the following topics: adoption, aging, alcoholism, clothing, cultural opportunities, personal counseling, day care, education, employment, environmental concerns, family planning, financial problems, food, handicaps, health, housing, legal problems, recreation, transportation, and volunteer opportunities. In Schenectady it is supported by the Human Services Planning Council and is the clearing house for Schenectady County self-help groups.

Infoline
Schenectady Area 374-2244

Jewish Family Services, 930 Madison Ave Albany, 482-8856, and 246 Union St, Schenectady, 372-3716, is a non-sectarian counseling and referral agency for families and individuals. Its professionals offer assistance in such areas as emotional adjustment, strained family relationships, marital problems, depression, unemployment, and childhood-adolescent issues. A special program provides supportive services for Jewish aged. Visits are by appointment.

Meals for the Homebound Over 60 are provided under several programs functioning throughout the Capital District. In each case hot meals are delivered to the subscriber's home. Although there is no specific fee charged, there is a suggested donation requested. Information is available at the following four centers:

Meals on Wheels, Inc.
20 Rensselaer St, Albany 465-6465

Mobile Meals Program
St. Peter's Hospital, Albany 454-1536

Nutrition Program for the Elderly of Schenectady County
Glendale Home 384-3682

Home Delivered Meals Program
County Office Building, Troy 270-2739

Northeast Parent and Child Society, 120 Park Ave Schenectady, serves the abused and the troubled child and his or her family. It was formed in 1983 through the consolidation of Parkhurst Parent and Child Center and Children's Home of Schenectady with the goal of providing a variety of therapeutic, educational, and residential services. The services break into three categories: prevention programs designed to prevent out-of-home placement while youngsters and families work out difficulties; a special school designed to reach children whose learning disabilities or emotional handicaps limit their ability to perform in a public school setting; residential programs designed to shelter children temporarily or to teach those who will never be able to return home how to live independently.

General Information 346-1284

Planned Parenthood provides professional medical counseling, medically supervised contraception, infertility counseling, abortion and adoption referrals, pregnancy tests, and general consultation and education about family planning and sexual responsibility. Information is available at the three area offices:

259 Lark St Albany 434-2182
414 Union St Schenectady 374-5353
5 Broadway Troy 274-5640

Project Hope is an outpatient counseling program begun in 1976 under the auspices of Hope House for children twelve to fifteen years old and their families who are experiencing difficulty with schools, community, law, or family life. Individual and group counseling is held twice weekly after school. Family counseling is also available in the client's home on a weekly basis. Project Hope also offers a prevention program for developing more effective skills for maintaining the child in his or her home and school district environment. There are three active Project Hope locations in the area: route 9W, Selkirk, 767-2445, serving Bethlehem,

Coeymans, Westerlo, and Rensselaerville; Guilderland, 861-5175, serving Guilderland, New Scotland, Voorheesville, Berne, and Knox; Albany (for girls 12-15 years old), 465-7378, serving Albany, Watervliet, Colonie, Green Island, and Cohoes.

Schenectady County Action Program (SCAP) provides a variety of services ranging from Head Start and Welfare Counseling to Weatherization of Homes.

General Information 374-9425

Sunnyside Center, 9th at Engles, Troy, has as its major focus the prevention of and intervention in delinquency. This United Way/Catholic Charities sponsored agency operates a youth program for 5-16 year olds, offering them recreation and group counseling, as well as individual tutoring and homework assistance. Young people may learn cooking, dancing, ceramics, and arts and crafts after school. There is also a day-care center for children three to five years of age in preparation for kindergarten. During the summer children may also engage in swimming and recreation.

General Information 274-5986

Trinity Institution began in 1918 with the purpose of meeting the needs of the poor in Albany's South End, the city's port of entry for immigrants. It sought to help by improving the neighborhood as a setting for family life. Since that time, the area has built up a core of permanent residents through which flows a constant stream of newcomers; Trinity reaches out to both. Throughout the years, the Institution, a non-sectarian, multi- purpose social service agency, has modified its programs to serve its clientele regardless of race, color, creed, age, sex, or country of origin. Many of Trinity's programs are directed to the development of children and youth, with family counseling and intervention as well as with recreation. The Institution is located at 15 Trinity Pl, Albany.

General Information 449-5155

Unity House, 401 Monroe St, Troy, was initiated in 1971 as a small program to supply basic support to families in low income neighborhoods. Since then, with the support of its founding agency, Catholic Charities, as well as funding from private and public sources, it has grown to have six programs—a day care center for developmentally delayed children, an office of mental health with a three-step residency transition program, a Families in Crisis program with a 24 hour Hotline, a street ministry, a social club, a transportation program, and a group home for the elderly.

General Information 274-2607
Families in Crisis Hot Line 272-2370

Visiting Nurse Association, with centers in Albany, Schenectady, and Troy, is much more than its name implies. Originally established to provide skilled nursing care to the sick, the aged and the poor, VNA now brings nursing, physical therapy, occupational therapy, speech therapy, nutritional guidance, medical social services, and nursing aide services to the homes of all people referred to them, regardless of age or income. Information is available at the three offices:

35 Colvin Ave Albany 489-2681
1520 Maxon Rd Schdy 382-7932
2212 Burdett Ave Troy 274-6200

Volunteer Services, which are crucial to the functioning of so many social service agencies, are coordinated by three groups in the Capital District. These agencies match the skills and interests of the volunteer to the needs of the community. Anyone wishing to volunteer, even a small amount of time, can call the offices below for advice and placement:

Volunteer Center of Albany
340 First St, Albany 434-2061

Voluntary Action Center
152 Barrett St, Schdy 374-2244

Volunteer Bureau of the Troy Area
272 River St, Troy 274-7234

Playground, Empire State Plaza

St. George's Cemetery, Schenectady

THE PAST

The earliest known residents of the Capital District were the Mahican Indians. They lived a simple existence along the banks of the Hudson River. Their chief sat at the peace sachem at Schodack, and Albany served as the great Fire Place of the Mahican where the tribe would gather for social and ceremonial events.

Their neighbors were the Iroquois, a powerful confederation of five nations— Mohawks, Senecas, Onondagas, Oneidas and Cayugas. One hundred years before the coming of white settlers, the Iroquois made war on the Mahicans in hopes of gaining possession of the Hudson Valley. They gradually succeeded, and in 1626, even the Mahicans who had resisted were driven off into the Berkshires—forever.

In 1609, into this region sailed a small ship, the Half Moon, under the command of Henry Hudson. The ship stayed four days (September 19-23) so that the crew could observe the land and test the waters for further navigability. Hudson returned to the Netherlands and gave a favorable report, but nothing developed further for many years. Then in 1624, the Dutch West India Company, anxious to establish a fur trading center, decided to found a permanent settlement in the area. Eighteen families, French-speaking Walloons from the South Netherlands, came up the river and built a fort and houses at what is now the foot of Madison Ave and Broadway in Albany. This was Fort Orange. The Indians chose to befriend these settlers who were thus free to move about the land without fear of harassment.

The settlement prospered but it did not grow. The Dutch government wanted to strengthen its claim on the area. To encourage immigration, particularly of persons who would develop the land by farming, the Netherlands established a patroon system in 1628 which gave large tracts of land to anyone who would settle 50 adults on the land within 50 years. In this way Kiliaen Van Rensselaer acquired 1250 square miles of land surrounding the Hudson-Mohawk River Valley. The settlers who came for Van Rensselaer at that time—really as indentured servants, for the patroon owner had feudal power over the land—were Swedes, Norwegians, Scots, Irish, Danes and Germans. These settlers quite naturally wanted to get in on the prosperity of the fur trade, so they clustered their homes around Fort Orange. Squabbles arose and Peter Stuyvesant was summoned from New Amsterdam (New York) to bring peace. He recognized that for the patroon system to work, the new settlers had to be encouraged more actively to develop the land. He thus defined an area around Fort Orange proper as the Place of the Beaver (Beverwyck) and banned patroon settlers from that region. Thus agriculture joined trading as a major activity. The Iroquois, though engaged in their own constant war with the Algonquins, the tribe who had once occupied the region but who had been displaced to Canada and constantly sought to reclaim the land, maintained friendly relations with the European settlers. Indeed they taught the newcomers their considerable skill in farming, tanning, road building, and medicinal herbs.

Across the river, near the confluence of the Hudson and Mohawk Rivers, a Dutch settler named Jean Barensten Wemp in 1659 bought a large tract of land from the Indians. He died shortly thereafter and the land passed to the Vanderheydens and Lansings. This settlement, which was eventually to become Troy, remained a quiet agricultural community for a while.

To the West, meanwhile, in 1651 Arendt Van Curler, also from Holland, purchased 128 square miles from the Mohawks and with fifteen other families established a patroon. They nestled together in houses built beside the confluence of the Mohawk River and the Binne Kill. To define their area and defend themselves against their enemies, the French, the families erected a stockade fence around their homes. There they dwelled in peace and prosperity, farming the land and living simply until 1690. In that year King William's War broke out and on February 8-9 the entire settlement was burned and most residents were either killed or taken captive. The few survivors planned to abandon their land, but several Mohawk Indians, led by one named Lawrence, persuaded them to stay and helped them rebuild on the same land, the area today called the Stockade.

Except for this violent intrusion, the area remained peaceful. Slow growth and moderate prosperity marked all three communities. In spite of the fact that the Dutch surrendered the colony to England in 1664, few English settlers moved north from New Amsterdam (New York City). Thus the power structure remained essentially the same, and strong Dutch influence persisted.

Wars, perhaps more than anything else, brought changes for the three cities. Located at the crossroads of rivers and mountain ranges, the area was the inevitable place of embarkation and debarkation of troops. King Williams' War (1689-1697),

Queen Anne's War (1702-1713), King George's War (1744-1748), and the French and Indian War, the conflict which pitted the British and Iroquois against the French and Algonquins (1754- 1763), were all fought around or near the cities. Then, of course, came the American Revolution.

Since one third of the Revolution was fought in New York, all of these people lived in quite constant fear of attacks by the British Navy, the British Army, Indians still friendly to the British, or Loyalists.

Albany's position in the struggle was pivotal. The British held New York City. The Americans held West Point. Together they crippled vital shipping. The British knew that if they could capture Albany they could easily seize West Point by simultaneous attack from the north and the south and could thus control all movement from Canada to New York City. But they could not take Albany. In 1777 the British Army's campaign was rebuffed at Saratoga. This battle is called the turning point of the Revolution because sagging American morale was dramatically lifted, because the French consequently agreed to fight on the side of the colonists, and because the British thereafter abandoned all hope of capturing Albany.

After the battle of Saratoga, life was less turbulent. In 1779 colonists fought against the Indians and the British to the west and in 1780-81 there were small retaliatory attacks right in the city of Albany, but thereafter little battling took place in the region.

Wall Mural, South Troy

Ironically, in those years of military tempest and political turmoil, there came a group of people whose way was of peace. In 1774 Ann Lee left England to settle in the New World with followers in the United Society of Believers in the Second Coming of Christ, the Shakers. They settled in Watervliet in 1776 and later established communal societies, the first at New Lebanon in 1787. Agriculturalists and craftsmen, they left a definite mark on the area, in spite of their small numbers and quiet ways.

So too did the other people who began to come in greater numbers. In 1710 there was a major influx of Palatine Germans. After the Revolution, the prospect of land and the lure of adventure brought about major movements of colonists, particularly from Connecticut and Massachusetts. Geography brought them through the region; some stayed. Then came the waves of European immigration in the 19th century. Notable were the Irish who came first in the 1820's to work on the Erie Canal and later—one million of them between 1847-1869 to New York City—to escape the Great Famine and its tragic aftermath. In 1907 large numbers of Sicilians came in the last major ethnic immigration to the region.

The 19th century brought the railroads and the potential for growth. Once the rail link between Albany and Schenectady was laid, the cities began to grow toward one another. The 19th century also brought industry. Troy's location near natural sources of power (the Wynantskill and the Poestenkill) and beside a major natural artery of transportation (the Hudson) made it and its neighbors, Cohoes and Watervliet, the perfect sites for plants and factories. Schenectady's situation at the Mohawk River and Erie Canal made it ideal for manufacture, and Albany's location made it a logical center for transshipment. It was, for example, a crucial link in the movement of lumber from the Adirondacks.

In 1828 a retired minister in Troy began to market collars made by local women in their homes. With the subsequent invention of the sewing machine, this "piecework" grew into a major industry which moved from the home into the factory. At the peak of the collar and cuff trade, more than twenty collar manufacturers were based in Troy.

The same years witnessed the growth of many major industries. Factories turned out many diverse products, the most famous being those derived from the iron and textile industries. The Burden Iron Works boasted of producing fifty-one million horseshoes in one year, and the metal plates for the Civil War ship the Monitor were made in the mills of Troy.

The year 1828 was also dynamic across the river in Waterford. In that year, the King's Water Power Canal was constructed according to designs by John Fuller King. This provided for the construction of two dams across the Mohawk River and a half mile canal running parallel to the river. Factories were then built along the canal, and each industry was given its own gate and sluiceway to draw and control water power. Thus knitting mills, dye works, flour mills, paper companies, machine works, twine factories, and saw mills grew up and flourished along the canal.

In Cohoes the textile industry flourished. Mills were built beside the Falls, and factories and mill houses sprouted up all along the roads leading from the Falls. Cohoes became a community based on the textile mills.

Papermaking was also a natural. With natural sources of power and an abundance of lumber being moved through the area, paper-making plants prospered. So too did the brewing industry. The high quality of the water flowing into the area made it the ideal choice for beermaking.

In 1851 Schenectady Locomotive Works (later called American Locomotive Company) began to build engines to haul trains for railroads all over the world. Then in 1892, the General Electric Company was formed by merging the Edison General Electric Company and the Thomson-Houston Company. Schenectady became a thriving center of commerce, industry and science and was called "The City that Lights and Hauls the World." This growth continued through both world wars as the city's factories were used in the production of heavy military equipment and trains for transport. In nearby Watervliet the arsenal worked night and day to turn out artillery and anti-aircraft guns.

Time has modified the focal points in the development of all these cities. With a suddenness that matched the drama of its rise, the industrial center of Troy declined. To this day conflicting reasons are advanced to explain the withdrawal of industry from the city. Some claim that persistent labor troubles drove industry to areas where labor was cheap and docile. Others say that the monopolistic attitude of industrial magnates concentrated the power dangerously in the hands of a few, kept other industry out of the region and paved the way to disaster when "the few" left. Others claim that with the development of inexpensive fuel-driven factory equipment Troy lost its competitive edge and industries began to move closer to the raw materials they had been transporting for processing in Troy. Whatever the reasons, the results were clear. Factories closed. Jobs became scarce. Capital dried up. The city suffered a serious and sudden economic decline from which it still struggles to recover. The new George M. Low Center for Industrial Innovation and the Rensselaer Technology Park in North Greenbush were designed to help provide the stimuli needed to promote new growth in the area.

There is no mystery about the death of the brewing industry. Prohibition dealt it a fatal blow.

The post World War II shift from canals and railroads to highways and air transport brought a major industrial crisis to Schenectady. American Locomotive

Company (ALCO) fought to stay alive, but in 1970 it ceased to operate. (General Electric, however, continues major design and manufacture operations in the city.)

The growth in state and regional government, the expanded demand for higher education, and the increased call for medical care have caused a movement away from the factory into the office. Today 27% of the population works for government, with the second largest cohort, 26%, working in service industries— primarily health care, social services, and education. In 1991, the proportion of persons engaged in manufacture had fallen to 10.5%. Not surprisingly, given the strong base in both lumber and paper, the highest percent of these jobs were in printing and publishing, followed by lumber and wood products.

The region boasts a disproportionate percentage of the population with PhDs and a higher general level of educational achievement than New York State or the United States. The average income, as reported in the 1991 profile by the Capital District Regional Planning Commission, is $23,250.

Population trends in the Capital District are typical of trends in urban areas throughout the United States. The post-World War II surge (1941-1960 showed growth of 21%) began to level off in the 60s, and the growth in the 80s was 7.7%. Predictably, the growth is uneven, central cities lost residents while suburbs gained; and Saratoga County experienced record growth while Schenectady county declined.

As of 1990, 44% of the population lived in cities, 47% in suburbs, and 9% in rural areas. People have also changed their choice of home. The two-family home, once a mainstay in the region, has fallen in favor, now constituting only 15% of homes. A growing number of people choose the private home (61%), but there has also been an increase in the number of multiple dwellings, up to 24%.

This history, of necessity brief, is intended to give an overview of the region in the four centuries of recorded history. In the following chapter is a list of books, papers, and pamphlets which provide more detailed description and analysis of people and events. Area libraries and museums have carefuly preserved much of the printed record, and their librarians are anxious to help people unearth ancestry, track down elusive historical figures, or pinpoint an event. They know well the contents of city directories, birth, death, and marriage announcements, and church and cemetery records. They also preserve local newspapers on microfilm.

Schenectady Stockade

Empire State Plaza

GENERAL INTEREST

Remembrance of Patria:
Dutch Arts and Culture in Colonial America 1609-1776
Roderic H. Blackburn and Ruth Piwonka. Albany Institute of History and Art, 1988. Richly illustrated analysis of Dutch culture and art in America before the Revolution.

A Profile of Change in the Capital District.
Capital District Regional Planning Commission, July 1991. Demographic data concerning population, housing, employment, and transportation.

Albany County
Albany: Capital City on the Hudson
Jack McEneny. Windsor Publications, 1981. Contains excellent chronology, brief sketches of major commercial firms, and beautiful photographs.

Albany Chronicles
Cuyler Reynolds. Albany, 1909. Incomparable compendium of details of daily life in the city from the landing of the *Half Moon* until 1909.

Albany—Dutch, English, and American
Codman Hislop. Angus Press, 1936. Comprehensive history of emergence and development of city of Albany.

Albany Medical College and Albany Hospital—A History: 1839-1982
Dr. Richard T. Beebe. 1982. History of the hospital and its surrounding community by an eminent practicioner for over 50 years.

Albany: Three Centuries a County
C.R. Roseberry. Albany County Tricentennial Commission, 1983. Brief histories of each of the towns, villages, and cities in Albany County.

An Albany Girlhood
Huybertie Pruyn Hamlin, edited by Alice P. Kenney. Washington Park Press Ltd., 1990. Autobiographical details of life on Elk St, 1873-1898, by member of the city's eminent Pruyn family.

Bicentennial History of Albany
George Roger Howell and Jonathan Tenney, 1886.

Capitol Story
C.R. Roseberry. Albany, 1982. Clearly written, handsomely illustrated history of the Capitol building.

Experiencing Albany: Perspectives on a Grand City's Past
Edited by Anne Roberts and Judith A. VanDyk. Nelson A. Rockefeller Institute of Government, 1986. Lectures by leading educators about events and places in Albany.

Flashback: A Fresh Look at Albany's Past
C.R. Roseberry, edited by Susanne Dumbleton. Washington Park Press Ltd., 1986. Essays on seminal events and figures of national prominence in the region.

Guide to Historical Resources in Albany County, New York Repositories
Cornell University, 1984. Very helpful list of unpublished sources of information.

Historic Albany: Its Churches and Synagogues
Edited by Anne Roberts and Marcia Cockrell. Nelson A. Rockefeller Institute of Government, 1987.

The History of the City of Albany
Arthur James Weise. Albany, 1884. Comprehensive scholarly history.

The Hudson River Valley: From Saratoga Springs to New York City, A History and Guide, 1992-93 Edition
Tim Mulligan. Helpful, up-to-date guidebook.

The Making of *Ironweed*
Penguin, 1988. Photographs of the filming of the William Kennedy novel in Albany, Troy, and surrounding communities. Photographs by Claudio Edinger. Introduction by Kennedy.

Murder at Cherry Hill
Louis C. Jones. Historic Cherry Hill, 1982. Gripping tale of love, intrigue, and murder at historic homestead on South Pearl St.

O Albany! Improbable City of Political Wizards, Fearless Ethnics, Spectacular Aristocrats, Splendid Nobodies, and Underrated Scoundrels
William Kennedy. Viking and Washington Park Press, 1983. Dubbed by an editor "An Urban Tapestry," this collection shows the author's deep knowledge and unwavering love for his city, with all its glory, folly, grace, and shame.

Old Albany, Volumes I-V
Compiled by Morris Gerber. Valuable collections of photographs and reprints of newspaper articles and columns. Includes many superb historic photographs by Stephen Schreiber.

Ornamental Ironwork:
Two Centuries of Craftsmanship in Albany and Troy, New York
Diana S. Waite. Mount Ida Press Ltd., 1990. Handsomely illustrated analysis of ironwork which embellishes interiors and exteriors in the two cities.

The People's Choice
Allison Bennett. Albany County Historical Society, 1980. Well illustrated, carefully documented history of Albany County from 1630 to the turn of the century.

Provisions: 109 Great Places to Shop for Food in the Capital District
Peter Zaas, Sue Jones, Gary Jones, and Lindy Guttman. Washington Park Press Ltd., 1987. Comprehensive guide to the best ingredients and prepared foods in the region.

Saving Union Station: An Inside Look at Historic Preservation
Thomas Finnegan. Washington Park Press Ltd., 1988. Beautifully illustrated chronicle of the salvaging of Albany's Union Station in the 80s.

Seventeenth Century Albany: A Dutch Profile
Charlotte Wilcoxen. Albany Institute of History and Art, 1981. Insightful study of life in the city's first century.

Source Materials for Black History, Albany, NY
Edited by Adele Jackel. New York State Library, 1972. Helpful compilation of background sources for uncovering information about African American community in Albany.

The Texture of a Neighborhood: Albany's South End, 1880-1940
Virginia Bowers, 1991. Interesting blend of personal recollections and well-researched facts by a loving resident of this old neighborhood.

Times Remembered
Allison Bennett. Collection of articles originally published in the **Spotlight** about the towns of Bethlehem and New Scotland.

Rensselaer County
The City of Troy and Its Vicinity
Arthur James Weise. Edward Green, 1986. Classified history of Troy's businesses and industries.

Down from Troy—A Doctor Comes of Age
Richard Selzer M.D., William Morrow and Co 1992. Having grown up in Troy during the depression, the author describes the rich and varied life in Troy during the 1930's and 40's.

Guide to Historical Resources in Rensselaer County, New York Repositories
Cornell University, 1983. Helpful guide to finding manuscripts, archival materials, and other unpublished records throughout the county.

History of Rensselaer County New York
Nathaniel Bartlett Sylvester. Everts and Peck, 1880. Rensselaer County town histories, church histories, and biographies of pioneer citizens.

The Hudson Mohawk Gateway: An Illustrated History
Thomas Phelan. Windsor Publications, 1985. Well written, handsomely illustrated depiction of Troy.

Landmarks of Rensselaer County, New York
George Baker Anderson. D. Mason and Company Publishers, 1987. Detailed account of the county's early history, its towns and leading citizens.

Looking Back: A History of Troy and Rensselaer County, 1925-1980
Joseph A. Parker, 1982. A chronology of recent events.

Ornamental Ironwork:
Two Centuries of Craftsmanship in Albany and Troy
(See Albany).

A Resourceful People: A Pictorial History of Rensselaer County, New York
Rensselaer County Historical Society, 1987.

Troy and Rensselaer County New York: A History
Rutherford Hayner. Lewis Historical Publishing Company, 1925. The social, fraternal and cultural history of the city.

Schenectady County
Door to the Mohawk Valley: A History of Schenectady for Young People
Millicent W. Veeder, 1947. A general history aimed at a youthful audience, but highly useful to adults in its factual information.

Enclave of Elegance: The General Electric Realty Plot
Bruce Maston, 1984. Handsomely illustrated overview of the evolution of a unique neighborhood, with commentary on architectural details.

The General Electric Story: A Photo History
The Elfun Society—Hall of History, 1976-80. Vol. 1: **The Edison Era, 1876-1892** (1976); Vol. 2: **The Steinmetz Era, 1892-1923** (1977); Vol. 3: **On the Shoulders of Giants, 1924-1946** (1979); Vol. 4: **Pathways of Progress, 1947-1978** (1980).

Guide to Historical Resources in Schenectady, New York Repositories
Cornell University, 1983. List of unpublished sources of information, including manuscripts and archival materials.

A History of Schenectady During the Revolution
Willis T. Hanson, Jr, 1916, rpt, 1974. An invaluable account of Schenectady during the Revolution, including a list of individual war records of many Schenectadians.

Illustrated Treasury of the American Locomotive Company
O. M. Kerr. Norton, 1990.

The Markers Speak: An Informal History of the Schenectady Area
John Birch. Schenectady County Historical Society, 1962. History of Schenectady told through the historic markers in the Stockade area.

The Mohawk
Codman Hislop, 1948. Wealth of historical information on Schenectady, written by a retired Union College professor.

Schenectady, A Pictorial History:
Schenectady's First Complete Story—Presettlement to Present
Larry Hart. Old Dorp Books, 1984.

Schenectady County, New York:
Its History to the Close of the 19th Century
Austin A. Yates, 1902. Includes over 240 pages of biographical sketches.

The Schenectady Scene
Compiled by the Newcomers and Wives Club, G.E. Corporated Research and Development, 1981. A pamphlet designed to acquaint newcomers with community facilities and activities.

Schenectady's Golden Era (Between 1880 and 1930)
Larry Hart. Old Dorp Books, 1974. Required reading on the history of Schenectady. Includes appended chronology of historic events in the area.

Tales of Old Schenectady
Larry Hart. Old Dorp Books, 1975-77. Vol. 1: **The Formative Years** (1975); Vol. 2: **The Changing Scene** (1977). Depiction of early Schenectady by the **Schenectady Gazette** columnist and historian for city and county of Schenectady.

FICTION AND BIOGRAPHIES

A number of gifted novelists and biographers have published superior books in recent years. In their work they tell of notable denizens of area cities and towns— fictional and real. Their stories have contributed significantly to the region's sense of itself and enhanced the stature of all who people its streets.

Billy Phelan's Greatest Game
William Kennedy. Viking, 1978. Fictional depiction of dazzling and dangerous mix of nightlife and politics in downtown Albany in 1938.

Dexterity
Douglas Bauer. Simon and Schuster, 1989. Fictional portrayal of a young woman's search for herself in the years after her first child is born. Set in a small town in northern Columbia County.

Fire Along the Sky
Robert Moss. St Martin's Press, 1991. First book of a trilogy set in the region, this centers on the pre-Revolutionary period and the always fascinating Sir William Johnson.

The Ink Truck
William Kennedy. Viking, 1969. Novel revolving around newspaper strike in Albany in the 1960s.

Legs
William Kennedy. Viking, 1975. Fictional portrait of the vortex in and around the legendary Legs Diamond, underworld figure and man-about-town—Albany, that is.

The Imperial Rockefeller
Joseph Persico, Insightful look at the man who changed the face of Albany's South End, Nelson A. Rockefeller.

Ironweed
William Kennedy. Viking, 1983. Fictional portrayal of one Francis Phelan's return to Albany to seek forgiveness for having harmed and abandoned his family. Set at Halloween, 1938. Awarded National Book Critic Circle's Award and Pulitzer Prize, 1983.

The Jameses: A Family Narrative
R.W.B. Lewis. Farrar Straus Giroux, 1991. Acclaimed biography which includes an opening chapter on James family in Albany.

Mohawk
Richard Russo. Random House, 1986. Fictional portrayal of a boy growing up in the limiting life of a small Mohawk Valley town centered around a tannery.

Quinn's Book
William Kennedy. Viking, 1988. Acclaimed bildungsroman featuring Billy Quinn in search of himself in Albany in 1849 and thereafter.

Risk Pool
Richard Russo. Random House, 1988. Family life in a small town in the Mohawk Valley.

Through the Darkest Hour
Larry Hart. Old Dorp Books, 1990. Fictional portrayal of a Union College man's adventures during the Civil War, written by Schenectady County historian.

Very Old Bones
William Kennedy. Viking, 1992. The Phelan family saga—begun in **Billy Phelan's Greatest Game** and **Ironweed**—continues into the 50s.

World's End
T. Coraghessan Boyle. Viking, 1987. Fact and fantasy intertwine across the generations in the lower Hudson Valley.

INDEX

Index

. . . .

Notes

Book and Cover Design: Media Logic/Peggy Robertson
Typography: Word Management
Printing: Thomson-Shore, Inc.
Principal Photographer: Timothy Raab, Northern Photo
Additional Photo credits: Michael Fredericks, Jr., pages 28, 48, 57, 167, 169, 195, 302, 321

The following institutions are thanked for the use of their photographs:
Adirondack Museum, page 256
Albany Institute of History and Art, Nicole Keys photographer, page 192
Ellis Hospital, page 306
National Baseball Hall of Fame and Museum, page 250
National Park Service, Roosevelt-Vanderbilt National Historic Sites, page 264
Sterling and Francine Clark Art Institute, page 271

The Authors

Anne Older was born in Montreal and graduated from the New England Deaconess Hospital School of Nursing in Boston. She has been actively involved in the Albany community for over twenty years. Currently she serves as Vice-President of the Albany Institute of History and Art, Treasurer of Westminster Church and is on the board of Key Trust, Maria College, St. Catherine's Center for Children and the Preservation League of New York State. She is President of Washington Park Press Ltd. which was founded in 1980.

Peggy DiConza, a native of Lenox Massachusetts, is a graduate of Union University School of Nursing and retired as the Operating Room Supervisor at Albany Medical Center Hospital. She was a member of the Board of Directors of Historic Albany Foundation in its formative years and is interested in health, environmental and historic preservation issues.

Susanne Dumbleton received her Ph.D in English from the University at Albany, State University of New York, and is presently Dean of Liberal Arts Programs at Regents College of the University of the State of New York. She has served for fifteen years on the board of St. Margaret's Center for Children and is a non-attorney member of the Committee on Professional Standards of the Third Judicial Department. She serves as Editor of Washington Park Press Ltd.